THE EDUCATIONAL SIGNIFICANCE OF SIXTEENTH CENTURY ARITHMETIC

FROM THE POINT OF VIEW OF THE PRESENT TIME

AMS PRESS
NEW YORK

TEACHERS COLLEGE, COLUMBIA UNIVERSITY
CONTRIBUTIONS TO EDUCATION
No. 8

THE EDUCATIONAL SIGNIFICANCE OF SIXTEENTH CENTURY ARITHMETIC

FROM THE POINT OF VIEW OF THE PRESENT TIME

BY

LAMBERT LINCOLN JACKSON, Ph.D.
*Head of the Department of Mathematics
State Normal School, Brockport, N. Y.*

PUBLISHED BY
Teachers College, Columbia University
NEW YORK

Library of Congress Cataloging in Publication Data

Jackson, Lambert Lincoln, 1870-1952.
  The educational significance of sixteenth century arithmetic.

  Reprint of the 1906 ed., which was issued as no. 8 of Teachers College, Columbia University. Contributions to education.
  Originally presented as the author's thesis, Columbia.
  Bibliography: p.
  1. Arithmetic--History. 2. Arithmetic--Study and teaching. I. Title. II. Series: Columbia University. Teachers College. Contributions to education, v. 8.
QA142.J14   1972   513'.07   75-176900
ISBN 0-404-55008-8

ISBN 0-404-55000-2 (set)

Reprinted by Special Arrangement with Teachers College Press, Columbia University, New York

From the edition of 1906: New York
First AMS edition published in 1972
Manufactured in the United States

AMS PRESS, INC.
NEW YORK, N.Y. 10003

PREFACE

ALTHOUGH there is much material on the history of sixteenth century arithmetic, comparatively little has been written on the teaching of the subject at that time, and less upon the educational significance of that teaching from the point of view of the present.

This dissertation is the result of a research into the arithmetic of the fifteenth and sixteenth centuries for the purpose of showing its bearing upon the present teaching of the subject. The exact period chosen is that from 1478, the date of the first printed arithmetic, to 1600, because between these dates arithmetic took on the form which it retained for three centuries, besides setting forth for the first time its educational functions. So little was written at that time on the educational values of studies that it is necessary to examine with unusual care the treatises and text-books on arithmetic in order to determine the principles and aims which guided their authors in creating them.

No general history of mathematics can be of use in a research of this kind, unless it contains extensive extracts from the original sources, and there is only one such work, namely, that of Cantor.[1] But, if one were to depend upon Cantor for a treatment of sixteenth century arithmetic, he would obtain an exhaustive knowledge of the leading writers only, whereas the great mass of minor works is necessary to supply a large portion of the data needed to determine the educational significance of the subject. No one has expressed more clearly than DeMorgan[2] the relative value of major and minor works for the purpose of interpreting history. "Unfortunately, history must of necessity be written mostly upon those works

---

[1] Cantor, M., "Vorlesungen über Geschichte der Mathematik," 3 vol. (Leipsic, 3d ed., 1900).

[2] DeMorgan, A., "Arithmetical Books," p. vi (London, 1847).

which, by being in advance of their age, have therefore become well known. It ought to be otherwise, but it cannot be, without better preservation and classification of the minor works which people actually use, and from which the great mass of those who study take their habits and opinions;—or—until the historian has at his command a readier access to second and third rate works in large numbers; so that he may write upon the effects as well as the causes." Other general histories of mathematics like those of Kästner,[1] Suter,[2] Hankel,[3] Günther,[4] and Gerhardt[5] contain very brief expositions of the arithmetic of the Renaissance, and all having been written before Cantor's work furnish little, if anything, of importance not covered by him.

Among those histories devoted entirely to arithmetic and drawn from original sources, only two discuss to any considerable extent the works which form the basis of this dissertation. These are Unger's,[6] chiefly on the arithmetic of the Germans, and Peacock's[7] on the history of arithmetic in general. Unger's treatise, because of its accuracy and its systematic form, has become the standard work on the history of arithmetic and its teaching in Germany. Its foundation, however, is limited, for, although thirty-two original works of the period in question are mentioned, only twenty are drawn upon, three being Italian, one French, one Flemish, and fifteen German. Thus, Unger's work, excellent as it is, does not furnish the historical material necessary for a study of sixteenth century arithmetic from an international point of view. Peacock's article is the most extensive exposition of the sub-

[1] Kästner, "Geschichte der Mathematik" (1796-1800).
[2] Suter, "Geschichte der math. Wissenschaften" (1873-75).
[3] Hankel, "Zur Geschichte d. Math. in Alterthum u. Mittelalter" (1874).
[4] Günther, "Vermischte Untersuchungen z. Geschichte d. math. Wissenschaften" (1876).
[5] Gerhardt, "Geschichte der Mathematik in Deutschland" (1877).
[6] Unger, "Die Methodik der praktischen Arithmetik in historischer Entwickelung vom Ausgange des Mittelalters bis auf die Gegenwart" (1888).
[7] Peacock, "History of Arithmetic" in Encyclopedia Metropolitana, vol. I, pp. 369-476 (London, 1829).

PREFACE 5

ject, but, besides emphasizing the Italian works in undue proportion, it omits an important link in the French contribution and ignores the Dutch arithmetic altogether. Had Peacock been able to supply these important departments, and had he, like Unger, added a history of the teaching of the subject, the historical research on which the present dissertation is based would have been unnecessary. Besides the histories of Unger and Peacock there are several important works which contain matter germane to this subject, but they deal either with a small portion of the history of the period in question or with some particular phase of it. Thus: Günther,[1] who probably is second only to Cantor as an authority on the early history of arithmetic, closed his work with the critical date, 1525. Sterner[2] covers practically the same ground as Unger, but draws the bulk of his illustrative material from the arithmetics of Köbel,[3] Böschenstein, and Riese only, and gives a much inferior treatment of the teaching of the subject. Heinrich Stoy[4] gives very little concerning sixteenth century arithmetic and confines his investigation to the development of the number concept and to the various modes of its expression. Grosse,[5] as indicated by the title of his book, discusses those arithmetics which apply the rules and processes to quantitative data which have a historical setting; for example, the periods of reigning dynasties or the size of armies that participated in the great battles of the past. There were only a half-dozen such arithmetics of which Suevus's and Meichsner's are the best types. Treutlein,[6] Villicus,[7] and

[1] Günther, "Geschichte des math. Unterrichts im deutschen Mittelalter bis 1525 (in Monumenta Germaniae Paedagogica, 1887).
bis 1525 (in Monumenta Germaniae Paedagogica, 1887).

[3] See bibliographical list, page 1 of Sterner's work.

[4] Stoy, H., "Zur Geschichte des Rechenunterrichts" (Diss., 1876).

[5] Grosse, "Historische Rechenbücher des 16 und 17 Jahrhunderts (1901).

[6] Treutlein, "Das Rechnen im 16. Jahrhundert" (1877).

[7] Villicus, "Das Zahlenwesen der Völker im Alterthum u. die Entwickelung d. Zifferrechnens" (1880).

"Geschichte der Rechenkunst" (a slight revision of the former work) (1897).

Kuckuck[1] are other German writers who touch this period, but their works are earlier and briefer than that of Unger. Treutlein's work is a standard, but it treats of a limited number of authors, mostly German, emphasizes a few special subjects, and neglects close comparative study. Leslie[2] deals with the theory of calculation in its historical development. For example, he pays much attention to the reasons for the origin of the various scales of notation, and to the systems of objective representation of numbers, called Palpable arithmetic. The subject-matter of sixteenth century arithmetic found in this work is very limited. It is unnecessary to mention more recent philosophical treatises, like Brooks's,[5] because they contain no history of value, with which this article is concerned, not found in Peacock or Leslie.

Thus, in order to accomplish the purpose of this dissertation, it was necessary to make a more extended and systematic research into the arithmetic of the fifteenth and sixteenth centuries than has hitherto been made. It was imperative first of all to supply those departments of French and Dutch arithmetic missing from the best historical treatises. Then, it was necessary to consult the original sources already examined by others in order to find matter of educational significance, much of which had not been noted by other investigators, as well as to obtain a broader basis for detailed comparisons.

The dissertation is divided into two chapters. Chapter I contains the result of the research into the subject-matter and teaching of arithmetic in the fifteenth and sixteenth centuries. Chapter II contains an exposition of the bearing of the arithmetic of that period upon the present teaching of the subject.

It is a great satisfaction to the author to acknowledge his indebtedness to Professor David Eugene Smith of Teachers

---

[1] Kuckuck, "Die Rechenkunst im 16. Jahrhundert" (1874).

[2] Leslie, "Philosophy of Arithmetic," Edinburgh (1820).

[3] Brooks, "Philosophy of Arithmetic" (1901).

College, Columbia University, for directing the research, to George A. Plimpton, Esq., of New York City, for access to his extensive collection of rare mathematical works, a privilege which alone made this research unique, and to Professor Frank M. McMurry of Teachers College, Columbia University, for his help in making the article of practical value.

L. L. JACKSON.

BROCKPORT, NEW YORK, 1905.

BIBLIOGRAPHY

Original Sources on Which This Research is Based

Anonymous, "Thaŭmatŭrgŭs Mathematicus, Id est Admirabilium effectorum e mathematicarum disciplinarum Fontibus Profluentium Sylloge."
Munich, 1651.

Anonymous. Treviso Book. (So called from the place of printing. This is the earliest printed Arithmetic known to exist.) "Incommincio vna practica molto bona et vtile a ciafchaduno chi vuole vxare larte dela merchadantia chiamata vulgarmente larte de labbacho."
Colophon: "A Triuifo :: A di. 10. Decēb 4 :: .1478."
It contains 123 pages, not numbered. Size of page, 14.5x20.6 cm. 32 lines to the page.

Baker, Humphrey, "The Well spring of sciences which teacheth the perfect worke and practife of Arithmeticke, both in whole Numbers and Fractions: set forthe by Humphrey Baker, Londoner, 1562. And now once agayne perused augmented and amended in all the three parts, by the sayde Aucthour: whereunto he hath also added certain tables of the agreement of measures and waightes of divers places in Europe, the one with the other, as by the table following it may appeare."
London, 1580; 1st ed., 1562.

"In spite of the date 1562 on the title page, I find no edition before 1568. Indeed in the 1580 edition Baker says: 'Having fometime now twelve yeres fithence (gentle reader) publifhed in print one Englifhe boke of Arithmetick . . . I have been . . . requefted . . . to adde fomething more thereunto.'" D. E. Smith.

Belli, Silvio, "Qvattro Libri Geometrici Di Silvio Belli Vicentino. Il Primo del Mifurare con la vifta. Nel Qvale S'Insegna, Senza Travagliar con numeri, à mifurar faciliffimamente le diftantie, l'altezza, e le profondità con il Quadrato Geometrico, e con altri ftromenti, de' quali facilmente fi può prouedere con le Figure. Si mostra ancora vna belliffima via di retrouare la profondità di qual fi voglia mare, & vn modo induftriofo di mifurar il circuito di tutta la Terra. Gli Altri Tre Sono Della Proportione & Proportionalità communi paffioni de Quanta.
"Vtili, & necellarij alla vera, & facile intelligentia dell' Arithmetica, della Geometria, & di tutte le fcientie & arti."
Venice, 1595.

Belli, Silvio, "Silvio Belli Vicentino Della Proportione, et Proportionalita communi Paffioni del quanto Libri Tre."
Venice, 1573.

Boetius, Anicius Manlius Torquatus Seuerinus, "Opera." Venice, 1491.

Boetius, "Boetii Arithmetica." Augustae, E. Rotdolt, 1488.

Borgi, Piero, "Qui comēza la nobel opera de arithmeticha ne laquel se tracta tute cosse amercantia pertinente facta τ compilata per Piero borgi da Venesia."
Venice, 1488; 1st ed., 1484.

Brucaeus, Henricus, "Henrici Brucaei Belgae Mathematicarum exercitationum Libri Duo."
Rostock, 1575.

Buteo, Joan., "Logistica. Quae & Arithmetica vulgò dicitur in libros quinque digesta: quorum index summatim habetur in tergo."
Leyden, 1559.

Calanderi, Philipi, "Philippi Calandri ad nobilem et studiosum Julianum Laurentii Medicem de Arithmethrica opusculum."
Florence, 1491.

Cardanus, Hieronymus, "Hieronimi C. Cardani Medici Mediolanensis, Practica Arithmetice, & Mensurandi singularis. In quaque preter alias cōtinentur, versa pagina demonstrabit."
Milan, 1539.

Cataneo, Girolamo, "Dell' Arte Del Misvrare Libri Dve, Nel Primo De' Qvale S'Insegna a mifurare, & partir i Campi.
"Nel Secondo A' Misvrar le Muraglie imbottar Grani, Vini, Fieni, & Strami; col linellar dell' Acque, & altre cose necessarie à gli Agrimenfori."
Brescia (no date).

Cataneo, Pietro, "Le Pratiche Delle Dve Prime Matematiche Di Pietro Cataneo Senese."
Venice, 1567; 1st ed., Venice, 1546.

Champenois, Jacques Chavvet, "Les Institvtions De L'Arithmetique De Jacques Chavvet Champenois, Professeur és Mathematiques en quatre parties: auec vn petit Traicté des fractions Astronomiques."
Paris, 1578. There is no evidence of an edition earlier than 1578.

Chiarini, Giorgio, "Qvesta e ellibro che tracta de Mercatantie et vsanze de paesi." Florence, 1481.
Colophon: "Finito ellibro di tvcti ichostvmi: cambi: monete: ... Per

me Francifco di Dina di Iacopo Kartolaio Fiorētino adi x di Decembre MCCCCXXXI."
"I Firenze Apreffo almuniftero di Fuligno."

Ciacchi, Givseppe, "Regole Genarali D'Abbaco Con Le Sve Dichiarazioni, E Prove Secondo L'Vso praticato da' più periti Arimmetici; Con Vn Breve Trattato Di Geometris, E Modi del mifurare le superficie de' terreni, e corpi solidi. Descritte Da P. Givseppe Ciacchi Fiorentino."
Florence, 1675.

Cirvelo, Petro Sanchez, "Tractatus Arithmeticae practice qui dicitur algorifmus. Venundantur Parrhifijs a johāne Lâberto eiufdem ciuitatis bibliopola in stēmate diui claudij manente iuxta gymnafium coquereti."
Paris, 1513; 1st ed., 1495 (Treutlein).

Clavius, Christopher, "Christophori Clavii Bambergensis E Societate IESV Epitome Arithmeticae practicae."
1621; 1st ed., Rome, 1583.

Clichtoveus, "Introductio Jacobi fabri Stapulēfis in Arithmeticam Diui seuerini Boetii pariter Jordani.
"Ars fupputāditam per calculos ꝗ p notas arithmeticas fuis quidem regulis elegāter expreffa Iudoci Clichtouei Neoportuenfis.
"Queftio haud indigna de numerorū - - -, Aurelio Augustino.
"Epitome rerum geometricarum ex Geometrico introductorio Carolio Bouilli, De quadratura circuli Demonstratio ex Campano."
Paris, c. 1506; 1st ed., Paris, 1503.

de Muris, John, "Arithmeticae Speculativae Libri duo Joannis de Muris ab innumeris erroribus quibus hactenus corrupti, & vetustate per me perierant diligenter emendati.
"Pulcherrimis quoque exemplis. Formisꝗ nouis declarati & in usum studiosae iuuentutis Moguntinae iam recens excusi."
Moguntiae, 1538.

di Pasi, Bartholomeo, "Tariffa de i Pesi e Misure corrispondenti dal Levante al Ponente e da una Terra a Luogo all' altro, quasi per tutte le Parti del Mondo. Qvi comicia la utilissima opera chiamata tariphà laq val tracta de ogni sorte de pexi e misure conrispondenti per tuto il mondo fata e composta per lo excelente et eximo Miser Bartholomeo di Paxi da Venetia."
Venice, 1557; 1st ed., 1503.

Finaeus, Orontius, "De Arithmetica Practica libri quatuor: Ab ipsa authore vigilanter recogniti multisque accessionibus recēns locupletati."
Paris, 1555; the 1st ed. was probably printed under the title "Arithmetica Practica libris quatuor absoluta" in 1525.

Gemma Frisius, "Arithmeticae Practicae Methodus Facilis, per Gemmam Frisium Medicum ac Mathematicum, in quatuor partes divisa."
Leipsic, 1558; Leipsic, 1575; 1st ed., Antwerp, 1540.

Ghaligai, Francesco, " Pratica D'Arithmetica."
Florence, 1552.
"This is a reprint of his Suma De Arithmetica. Firēze M.CCCCC.XXI." DeMorgan, (n.) p. 102.
The title of the 1521 edition is given in the Boncompagni Bulletino, 13: 249.

Gio, Padre, " Elementi Arithmetici Nelle scvole Pie."
Rome, 1689.

Grammateus, H., " Ein neu künstlich Rechenbüchlein uff alle kauffmannschafft nach gemeinen Regeln de tre, Welschenpractic."
Frankfort, 1535.

Heer, Johann, "Compendium Arithmeticae das ist: Ein neues kurtzes vñ wolgegrůndtes Schul Rechenbůchlein/ von allerley Hauss: vnnd Kauffmansrechnung/ wie die tåglich fůrfallen mōgen/ so per Regulam Detri vnd Practicam lieblich zu Resolvirn vnd auff zulõsen sein?
"Meinen lieben Discipulis, bene=ben allen anfahenden Rechenschulern/ auch sonsten Manniglich zu nutz/ also auffs fleissigste (So wol fůr Jungfråulein als Knaben) auss rechtem grund gestellet vnd inn Druck gegeben/ Durch Johann Heern Seniorem, Rechenmeistern vnd verordneten Visitatorn der Teutschen Schreib vnd Rechenschulen inn Nürmberg."
Nuremberg, 1617.

Huswirt, Johannes, " Enchiridion Novus Algorismi."
Cologne, 1501.

Jacob, Simon, " Rechenbuch auf den Linien und mit Ziffern/ sampt allerley vortheilen/ fragweise/ Jetzt von neuem und zum neuntenmal mit vielen grůndtlichen anweisungen/ oder Demonstration/ sampt derselben Vnderrichtung gemehret."
Frankfort-on-the-Main, 1599; 1st ed., Frankfurt, 1560.

Jean, Alexander, "Arithmetique Av Miroir Par lequelle on peut (en quatre vacations de demie heure chacune) pratiquer les plus belles regles d'icelle. Mise en lumiere, Par Alexandre Iean, Arithmeticien."
Paris, 1637.

Jordanus Nemorarius, " Jordani Nemorarii Arithmetica cum Demonstrationibus Jacobi Fabri Stapulensis - - - episdem epitome in Libros Arithmeticos D. Seuerini Boetii, Rithminachia (edidit David Lauxius Brytannus Edinburgensis)."
Paris, 1496.

Köbel, Jacob, " Zwey rechenbůchlin, uff der Linien vnd Zipher/ Mit eym

angehenckten Visirbûch/ so verstendlich für geben/ das iedem hieraus on eiñ lerer wol zulernen.
"¶ Durch den Achtbaren und wol erfarnen H. Jacoben Kôbel Statschreiber zu Oppenheym."
Oppenheim, 1537; 1st ed., 1514.

Masterson, Thomas, " His first book of Arithmeticke."
London, 1592.

Masterson, Thomas, " His second book of Arithmeticke."
London, 1594.

Masterson, Thomas, " His Thirde booke of Arithmeticke."
London, 1595.

Maurolycus, Franciscus, " D. Francisci Mavrolyci Abbatis Messanensis, Mathematici celeberrimi, Arithmeticorum Libri Duo, Nunc Primum In Lucem Editi, Cum rerum omnium notabilium. Indice copiosissimo."
Venice, 1575.

Noviomagus, Joan, " De Numeris Libri II. Quorum prior Logisticen, & veterum numerandi consuetudinem: posterior Theoremata numerorum complectitur, ad doctissimum virum Andream Eggerdem professorem Rostochiensem."
Cologne, 1544; 1st ed., Cologne, 1539.

Pugliesi, "Arithmetica di Onofrio Pvgliesi Sbernia Palermitano."
Palermo, 1670; 1st ed., 1654.

Paciuolo, Lucas, " Sũma de Arithmetica, Geometria, Proportioni et Proportionalita - - -."
Tusculano, 1523; 1st ed., Venice, 1494.

Peurbach, Georg von, " Elementa Arithmetices."
Wittenberg, 1536.

Perez de Moya, Jvan, "Arithmetica practica."
Barcelona, 1703; 1st ed., Madrid, 1562.

Raets, Willem, " Arithmetica Oft Een niew Cijfferboeck/ van Willem Raets/ Maesterichter. VVaer in die Fondamenten feer grondelijck verclaert eñ met veel schoone queftien gheilluftreert vvorden, tot mit ende oorbaer van alle Coopliede ende leefhebbers der feluer Consten.
" Met noch een Tractaet van de VViffelroede, met Annotatien verciert, door Michiel Coignet."
Antwerp, 1580 (probably 1st ed.). (Original privilege dated May 22, 1576.)

Ramus, Peter, " Petri Rami Professoris Regii, Arithmeticae Libri Duo."
Paris, 1577; 1st ed., Paris, 1555.

Recorde, Robert, "The Ground of Artes: Teaching the woorke and practiſe of Arithmetike, both in whole numbres and Fractions, after a more easyer and exaoter ſorte, than anye lyke hath hytherto beene set forth: with divers new additions. Made by M. Roberte Recorde, Doctor of Physike."
London, 1558; 1st ed., c. 1540 (DeMorgan, p. 22).

Riese, Adam, "Rechnung auff der Linien und Federn/ auff allerley Handtierung/ Gemacht durch Adam Risen (auffs newe durchlesen/ und zu recht bracht)."
Leipsic, 1571; 1st ed., Erfurt, 1522.

Rudolff, Christopher, "Kunstliche rechnung mit der Ziffer und mit den zal pfennigẽ/ sampt der Wellischen Practica/ und allerley vorteil auf die Regel de Tri. Item vergleighũg mancherley Land uñ Stet/ gewicht/ Elnmas/ Muntz ec. Alles durch Christoffen Rudolff zu Wien verfertiget."
Wien, 1534; 1st ed., 1526.

Sacrobosco, Johann von, "Algorismus."
Venice, 1523; 1st ed., 1488.

Schonerus, Ioannes (Editor), "Algorithmus Demonstratus."
Nuremberg, 1534.

Stevinus, Simon, "Les Oeuvres Mathematiques de Simon Stevin de Bruges, Ou ſont inſerées les memoires mathematiques. Le tout, corregé & augmenté Par Albert Girard Samielois, Mathematicien."
Leyden, 1634.

Scheubel, Johann, "De numeris et diversis rationibus."
Argent., 1540.

Suevus, Sigismund, "Arithmetica Historica. Die Lôbliche Rechenkunst. Durch alle Species vnd furnembste Regeln/ mit schônen gedenckwirdigen Historien vnd Exempeln/ Auch mit Hebraischer/ Grichischer/ vnd Rômischer Mûntze/ Gewicht vnd Mass/ deren in Heiliger Schrifft vnd gutten Geschichte = Bûchern gedacht wird/ Der lieben Jugend zu gutte erkleret. Auch denen die nicht rechnen kônnen/ wegen vieler schônen Historien vnd derselbigen bedeutungen lustig vnd lieblich zu lesen.

"Aus viel gutten Buchern vnd Schrifften mit fleis zusammen getragen. Durch Sigismundum Sueuum Freystadiensem, Diener der H. Gôttlichen Worts der Kirchen Christi zu Breslaw/ Probst zum H. Geiste/ vnd Pfarrherr zu S. Bernardin in der Newstadt."
Breslau, 1593.

Tagliente, Giovanni Antonio and Girolamo, "LiBro DABACO Che in Segna a fare ogni ragione mercadantile, & pertegare le terre cõ l'arte dj la Geometris, & altre nobiliſsime ragione ſtra ordinarie cõ la Tariffa come

respondeno li pefi & monede de molte terre del mondo con la inclita citta di Venegia. El qual Libro fe chiama Thefavro vniuersale."
Venice, 1515.

Tartaglia, Nicolo, " La Prima Parte del General Trattato di Numeri, et Misure, di Nicolo Tartaglia, Nellaquale in Diecisette Libri si Dichiara Tutti Gli Atti Operativi, Pratiche, et Regole Necessarie non Solamente in tutta l'arte negotiaria & mercantile, ma anchor in ogni altra arte, scientia, ouer disciplina, doue interuenghi il calculo."
Venice, 1556.

Tartaglia, Nicolo, " La Seconda Parte del General Trattato Di Numeri, et Misure --- Nella quale in Vndici Libri Si Notifica La piv Ellevata, et Specvlativa Parte Della Pratica Arithmetica, la qual è tutte regole, & operationi praticali delle progressioni, radici, proportioni, & quantita irrationali."
Venice, 1556.

Tartaglia, Nicolo, " Tvtte L'Opera D'Arithmetica del famosissimo Nicolò Tartaglia."
Venice, 1592; 1st ed., Venice, 1556-1560.

Therfeldern, Caspar, "Arithmetica Oder Rechenbuch Auff den Linien vnd Ziffern/ mit Vortheyl vnd Behendigkeit/ auf allerley gebraûchliche Hauss/ vnd Kauffmans Rechnung/ Mûntzschlag/ Beschickung des 3 Thigels/ Kunstrechnung/ grûndlich beschrieben/ inn Frag und Antwort gestellet. Durch Caspar Thierfeldern Schul und Rechenmeyster zu Steyer."
Nuremberg, 1587.

Tonstall, Cuthbert, " De Arte Supputandi. Libri Quattuor Cutheberti Tonstalli."
London, 1522.

Trenchant, Jan, " L'Arithmetique de Ian Trenchant, Departie en trois liures. Ensemble un petit discours des Changes. Avec L'Art de calculer aux Getons. Reueiie & augmentée pour la quatrième edition, de plusiers regles & articles, par L'Autheur."
Lyons, 1578; 1st ed., Lyons, 1566.

Unicorn, Giuseppe, " De L'Arithmetica vniuersale, del Sig. Ioseppo Unicorno, mathematico excellentissimo. Trattata, & amplificata con somma eruditione, e connoui, & isquisiti modi di chiarezza."
Venice, 1598.

Van Ceulen, Ludolf, " De Arithmetische en Geometrische fondamenten, van Mr. Ludolf Van Ceulen, Met het ghebruyck van dien In veele verscheydene constighe questien, soo Geometricé door linien, als Arithmeticè door irrationale ghetallen, oock door den regel Coss, ende de tafeln sinuum ghesolveert."
Leyden, 1615.

Van der Schuere, Jaques, "Arithmetica, Oft Reken=const/ Verchiert met veel schoone Exempelen/ seer mit voor alle Cooplieden/ Facteurs/ Cassiers/ Ontfanghers/ etc. Gehmaeckt/ Door Jaques van der Schvere Van Meenen. Nu ter tijdt Françoysche School-meester tot Haerlem."
Haarlem, 1600.

In the voor-Reden of the 1625 edition written by his son, Denys van der Schuere, it is stated that the book was published by the father "eerſt in't Iaer 1600. Ende dit is al de vierde mael dat het gedrukt is."

Wencelaus, Martin, T'Fondament Van Arithmetica: mette Italiaensch Practijck/ midtsgaders d'aller nootwendichste stucken van den Reghel van Interest.

"Beydes in Nederduyts ende in Franchois/ met redelicke ouereenstemminghe ofte Concordantien. Alles Door Martinvm VVenceslaum."
Middelburg, 1599.

Signs preface in Dutch, Marthin Wentſel; in French, Marthin Wentſle.

Widman, Johann, "Behend und hupsch Rechnung uff allen Kauffmanschafften. Johannes Widman von Eger."

Pforzheim, 1508; 1st ed., Leipsic, 1489 (Unger, p. 40).

Although there was a 1500 edition, the 1508 edition was set up anew.

CONTENTS

CHAPTER I

ESSENTIAL FEATURES OF SIXTEENTH CENTURY ARITHMETIC

	PAGE
I. *Productive activity of writers of that period*	23
1. Number of works and editions	23
2. Causes of this awakening	23
a. Revival of scientific interest	23
b. Commercial activity	23
c. Invention of printing	23
II. *Transitions through which the subject passed*	24
1. From the use of Roman symbols and methods to the use of Hindu symbols and methods	24
2. From arithmetic in Latin to arithmetic in the vernacular	24
3. From arithmetic in Mss. to arithmetic in printed books	24
4. From arithmetic for the learned to arithmetic for the people	24
5. From arithmetic theoretic to arithmetic practical	24
6. From the use of counters to the use of figures	24–29
III. *Nature of the subject matter of sixteenth century arithmetic*	29–168
1. Definitions	29–36
a. Of numbers, unity, and zero	29–32
b. Of classes of numbers	32–35
c. Of processes	35–36
2. Processes with integers	36–77
a. Notation and numeration	37–41
b. Addition	41–49
c. Subtraction	49–57
d. Multiplication	57–69
e. Division	69–76
f. Doubling and Halving	76–77
3. Denominate numbers	77–85
4. Fractions	85–110
a. Definitions	85–93
b. Order of processes	93–95
c. Reduction	95–98
d. Addition	98–102
e. Subtraction	102–104
f. Multiplication	104–107
g. Division	107–110

CONTENTS

	PAGE
5. Progressions	110–117
6. Ratio and Proportion	117–121
7. Involution and Evolution	121–127
8. Applied arithmetic	127–168
a. Number of writers of practical arithmetic compared with the number of writers of theoretic arithmetic	127–128
b. Examples of exceptional writers—Champenois, Suevus.	128–131
c. List of business rules	131–132
Rule of Three (Two and Five)	132–135
Welsch Practice	135–138
Inverse Rule of Three	138–139
Partnership (with and without time)	139–141
Factor Reckoning	142
Profit and Loss	142–143
Interest, Simple and Compound	143–145
Equation of Payments	145–146
Exchange and Banking	146–148
Chain Rule	148–150
Barter	150–151
Alligation	151–152
Regula Fusti	152–153
Virgin's Rule	153
Rule of False Assumption, or False Position	153–156
Voyage	156
Mintage	156–157
Salaries of Servants	157
Rents	157
Assize of Bread	157
Overland Reckoning	157–158
d. Puzzles	159–163
e. Mensuration	163–168
IV. *Summary*	168–170
1. This was an important period in perfecting the processes of arithmetic	168
a. The four fundamental processes with integers perfected.	168
b. The four fundamental processes with fractions perfected.	168
c. Arithmetic, geometric, and harmonic series (finite) fully treated	168
d. Involution and evolution practically complete	168
e. Tables for shortening computation were not unknown.	168
f. Decimal fractions and logarithms were the only subjects not matured	168
2. Constructive period for applied arithmetic	168–169
a. Subject matter of applied arithmetic	169
(1) Extent	169
(2) Rich in types	169
b. Methods of solution of applied problems	169

CONTENTS 19

	PAGE
(1) Unitary analysis	169
(2) Rule of Three	169
3. A comparison of the status of arithmetic at the beginning of this period with that at the close	169–170
V. *The place of arithmetic in the schools of that period*	170–184
A. In the Latin Schools	170–178
1. The function of the Latin Schools	170
a. To teach the Latin language	170
b. To contribute to general culture	170
2. Courses of study in the Latin schools	170–172
a. Language—Latin	170–171
b. Music	172
c. Arithmetic	172
d. Astronomy	172
e. Geometry	172
3. Writers of Latin School Arithmetics	172–174
a. Profession—vocation	174
b. Scholarship	174
4. Character of the contents of Latin School Arithmetics	174–177
a. Prominence of pure arithmetic	174–175
(1) Definitions	174–175
(2) Classifications	175
(3) Plans of organization	175
b. Applications—chiefly artificial or traditional problems	176
c. Absence of commercial arithmetic	176
5. Reasons for teaching arithmetic in the Latin Schools	176–178
a. It was part of the classical inheritance	178
b. It was supposed to contribute to general culture or to mental efficiency	178
B. In the Reckoning Schools	178–184
1. The rise of the Reckoning Master	178–179
a. General duties	179
b. Relation to schools and education	179
2. The function of the Reckoning Schools	180
a. To teach business methods	180
b. To teach commercial arithmetic	180
3. Courses of study in the Reckoning Schools	180
a. Practice in reading and writing the mother tongue	180
b. Business customs and forms	180
c. Arithmetic	180
4. Writers of Reckoning School Arithmetics	180–183
a. Profession—vocation	183
b. Scholarship	183
5. Character of the contents of the Reckoning School Arithmetic	183–184
a. Meagre treatment of pure arithmetic	183
(1) Little emphasis on definitions	183

		PAGE
(2) Little emphasis on classifications		183
(3) Processes confined to comparatively small numbers—those used in practical applications		184
b. Prominence of applied arithmetic		184
(1) Applications followed closely upon the presentation of processes		184
(2) Concrete problems often proposed before the required process had been developed		184
(3) Commercial problems and problems in mensuration were the chief applications		184
6. Reasons for teaching arithmetic in the Reckoning Schools		184
a. Because of its use to artisans		184
b. Because of its use in commercial pursuits		184

CHAPTER II
EDUCATIONAL SIGNIFICANCE OF SIXTEENTH CENTURY ARITHMETIC

I. Introduction		185
II. Subject Matter		186–201
A. Kinds		186
1. Reckoning with counters and figures		186
2. Properties of numbers		186
3. Denominate numbers		186
4. Business problems		186
5. Amenity and puzzle problems		186
B. Bases of selection		186–199
1. Needs of the trader		186–190
a. Commercial development tends to vitalize arithmetic		187
b. Modern conditions will not revive the Reckoning Book		188
c. The needs of the trader lead to improved methods of calculation		189
d. Business needs condition the selection of denominate number tables		190
2. Needs of the scholar		190–196
a. The modern disciplinary ideal demands concrete subject matter		191–193
b. The culture ideal encourages the selection of subject matter with a many-sided interest		194–196
c. The propaedeutics of arithmetic demand the retention of certain theoretic matter		196
3. Tradition		196–199
This tends to perpetuate obsolete material		197–199
C. Plans of arrangement		199–201
1. By kinds of numbers		199
2. By kinds of processes		199
3. Modern needs are met by a combination of (1) and (2)		200–201

CONTENTS

	PAGE
III. *Method*	201–222
A. Meaning	201
B. Suggestiveness of sixteenth century arithmetic	201
C. General principles of treatment of subject matter	201–202
1. The synthetic method not adapted to elementary arithmetic	202
2. The analytic method may improve books, but cannot supplant the teacher	203
3. The psychological method produces the best books in all particulars	203–204
D. Details of development	204–222
1. Definitions	204–205
2. Notation	205–206
a. The use of improved notations may be hastened	205
b. Roman notation to thousands should be retained	205
c. Notation for large numbers is necessary and belongs to grammar school arithmetic	206
3. Processes with integers	207–211
a. In general, there is no best method for performing processes	207–208
b. Artificial means for making number work interesting should not be abandoned	208
c. Incorrect language not an inheritance from sixteenth century arithmetic	208
d. Methods of testing work are derived from the early arithmetics	208–209
e. Number combinations are not all equally important	209–210
f. Explanations of processes should not be neglected	210
g. Books should explain mathematical conventions	210
h. Unabridged processes should precede abridged ones	211
4. Processes with fractions	211–214
a. Common fractions are still necessary	211
b. There are three ideas necessary to the concept of fractions	211–212
c. Formal multiplication should precede formal addition and subtraction	212
d. The use of the word "times" in multiplication	212–213
e. The two customary methods of division of fractions are related	213
f. Fractions should be correlated with denominate numbers	213–214
5. Denominate numbers	214–215
a. Operations with compound numbers should be limited to two or three denominations	214
b. There is no good reason for continuing the practice of reduction from one table of denominate numbers to another	214–215
c. Denominate numbers should be presented under each process with integers and with fractions	215

		PAGE
6. Applications		216-222
a. Applications may be proposed as incentives for learning the processes		216-218
b. Applications should be appropriate to the different school years		218-219
c. Mensuration work should be graded		219
d. Factitious problems have no place in elementary arithmetic		219-220
e. Unitary Analysis, Rule of Three, and the Equation are related processes of solution		220-221
f. The simple equation will become the leading method of solution		221
g. Arithmetic has an interpretative function		221-222
IV. *Mode*		223-225
A. The heuristic mode suggests that oral work should develop new ideas		223
B. The individual mode is apt to result in dogmatic teaching.		224
C. The recitation mode finds no precedent in sixteenth century arithmetic		224
D. The lecture mode has no place in elementary arithmetic		224-225
E. The spirit of the laboratory mode may be helpful in teaching arithmetic		225
V. *Summary*		226-228

CHAPTER I

THE ESSENTIAL FEATURES OF SIXTEENTH CENTURY ARITHMETIC

THE arithmetic of the last quarter of the fifteenth century and that of the sixteenth century show that great productive activity possessed the arithmeticians of that period.[1] Approximately three hundred works were printed on this subject, some of which ran through many editions.[2] This awakening was part of the great Renaissance and was due to the same causes; those influencing arithmetic most directly were the revival of scientific interest, commercial activity, and the invention of printing. The first cause was the incentive which led scholars to develop the science of figure reckoning; the second made a knowledge of casting accounts and of reckon-

---

[1] De Morgan (Arithmetical Books, pp. v-vi) says that from 1500 to 1750 probably three thousand works on arithmetic were printed in all languages. He mentions fifteen hundred of them, but only seventy of the number printed before 1600 had been seen by him. It is probable, according to De Morgan, and by reference to Peacock's article in the Encyclopedia Metropolitana, that Peacock was familiar with a still smaller number.

According to Kuckuck (Die Rechenkunst im sechzehnten Jahrhundert, p. 16) over two hundred works on arithmetic were published in this period. He quotes Michel Stifel (1544) as saying that a new one came out every day.

Riccardi (Bibliotica Mathematica Italiana, Vol. II, pp. 20-22), the great authority on the bibliography of Italian mathematics, gives one hundred and twelve Italian works under the title: "Trattati e Compendi di Arimmetica." Of the extant works the number in German is about equal to the number in Italian. There are one-fourth as many Dutch, one-fourth as many French, one-fifth as many English, and one-tenth as many Spanish. Assuming that Riccardi's list is complete, and that the books lost bear a constant ratio to the number extant in all languages, one may conclude that there were approximately three hundred arithmetics printed before 1600.

[2] Professor Smith has found that Gemma Frisius's "Arithmeticae Practicae Methodus Facilis" saw fifty-six editions before 1600, although Treutlein (Abhandlungen, 1: 18) found only twenty-five.

Adam Riese's books in various combinations saw at least twelve editions before 1600. Unger, pp. 49-51.

Recorde's and Baker's works in England enjoyed a similar popularity.

ing exchange indispensable; and the third made the dissemination of this knowledge possible. Another circumstance which encouraged both the development and the use of arithmetic was the expression of the subject in the vernacular, for hitherto a knowledge of theoretical arithmetic had been possible to scholars only. In the sixteenth century arithmetics appeared in nearly all European languages, especially in Italian, French, German, Dutch, and English.

Thus, the first century of printed arithmetics marks several important transitions: The transition from the use of the Roman symbols and methods to the use of the Hindu symbols and methods;[1] from arithmetic expressed in Latin to arithmetic expressed in the language of the reader;[2] from arithmetic in manuscript to arithmetic in the printed book;[3] from arithmetic for the learned to arithmetic for the people;[4] from arithmetic theoretic to arithmetic practical;[5] and from the use of counters to the use of figures.[6] Although the Hindu numerals had been generally known to European mathematicians after the twelfth century,[7] the devotion to classical

[1] E. g., compare Jacob Köbel, Zwey rechenbüchlin uff der Linien und Zipher/ - - - (1537) with Robert Recorde, The Ground of Artes - - - (c. 1540).

[2] E. g., compare Gemma Frisius, Arithmeticae Practicae Methodus Facilis (1558) with Ian Trenchant, L'Arithmetique, Departie en trois livres - - - (1578).

[3] The Treviso Arithmetic (1478), so called from the place of printing, is the earliest printed arithmetic known to exist.

[4] E. g., compare Hieronimus Cardanus, Practica Arithmetice & Mensurandi singularis - - - (1539) with Willem Raets, Ein niew Cijfferboeck - - - (1580).

[5] E. g., compare Joannis de Muris, Arithmeticae Speculativae Libri duo (1538) with Adam Riese, Rechnung auff der Linien und Federn/ - - - (1571).

[6] Adam Riese (1522) and Robert Recorde (1557) show this transition by treating both systems of reckoning in their books.

[7] M. F. Woepcke, Propogation des chiffres indiens, Journal Asiatique, 6 sér, t. 1, pp. 27, 234, 442.

Ch. Henry, Sur les deux plus anciens traités Français d'Algorisme et de' Géométrie, Bonc. Bull., 15:49.

Freidlein, on John of Seville and Leonardo of Pisa, Zeitschrift der Mathematik und Physik, Band 12, 1867.

A. Kuckuck, Die Rechenkunst im sechzehnten Jahrhundert (1874). "In

study and the neglect of science tended to perpetuate the Roman numerals. Not until the introduction of printing did a full comparison of the Roman and Hindu arithmetics find expression, and a working knowledge of the latter sift down to the common people.

Owing to the Romans' lack of appreciation of pure science and to the awkwardness of their system of notation, their contribution to arithmetic was small. Arithmetic, in the form of the ancient Logistic, was of use to them chiefly in making monetary calculation, for which they used some form of the abacus. The nations of Europe received as a legacy from the Romans the Roman numerals and the art of reckoning with counters. This art, also called line reckoning, was widespread in the fifteenth century, excepting in Italy. The calculations were effected by means of parallel lines drawn on a board or table, and by movable counters or disks placed upon them. The lines taken in order from the bottom upward represented units, tens, hundreds, thousands and so on. The spaces taken in the same order represented fives, fifties, five hundreds, and so on, the space below units being used for halves. The table on the next page shows Riese's explanation of the lines and spaces: [1]

einer Regensburger Chronik von 1167 befinden sich die Zahlen von 1-68, aber nur wie zur Uebung geschreiben. In Schlesien kommen sie erst im Jahre 1340 vor. In einem Notatenbuch des Dithmar von Meckelbach aus der Zeit Kaiser Carls IV stehen die Ziffern 1-10." Pp. 4-5.
    See also the following general references:
    Treutlein, Geschichte unserer Zahlzeichen (1875—Program Gymn. Karlsruhe), Bd. 12, 1867
    Gerhardt, Geschichte der Math. in Deutschland (1877).
    Freidlein, Die Zahlzeichen und das elementare Rechnen der Griechen, Römer u. des christl. Abendlandes vom 7. bis 13. Jahrhundert, 1869.
    Wildermuth, Rechnen, in Schmids Encyklopädie, Bd. 6.
    [1] Adam Riese, Rechnung auff der Linien und Federn/ - - - (1571 ed.), fol. Aiij recto.

SIXTEENTH CENTURY ARITHMETIC

```
100000 ——— 6 ——— Hundert tausent.
 50000             Funfftzig tausent.
 10000 ——— 5 ——— Zehen tausent.
  5000             Fûnf tausent.
  1000 ——— 4 ——— Tausent.
   500             Fûnf hundert.
   100 ——— 3 ——— Hundert.
    50             Fünfftzig.
    10 ——— 2 ——— Zehen.
     5             Fûnff.
     1 ——— 1 ——— Eins.
    ji             Ein halbs.
```

Cross lines were drawn dividing the board into sections, which could be used for different denominations of numbers, for the addends in a problem of addition, for the minuend and the subtrahend in subtraction, or for any other sets of numbers.

The illustration[1] shows four compound numbers arranged for addition and the result expressed in floren, groschen, and denarii.

Addition and subtraction with counters are evidently quite easy. In fact, line reckoning was often recommended as preferable to the processes with Hindu numerals.[2] All that is necessary, after

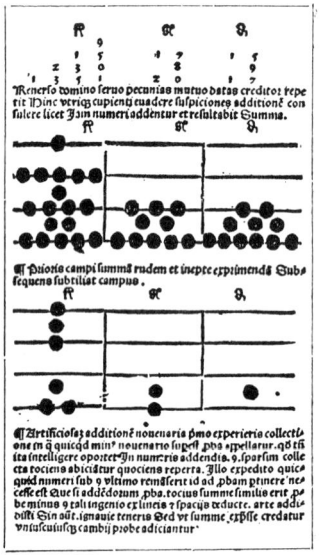

---

[1] From Balthazar Licht's Algorismus Linealis (1501 ed.).

[2] Rudolff, Kunstliche rechnung mit der Ziffer und mit den zal pfennigê/ - - - (1526), "Das die vier spezies/ auff den linien durch viel ringere ybung auff der Ziffer gelernt werde/ mag ein yeder aus obenanzeigter vnterweisung bey jm selbst ermessen. - - - Warlich was Fürsten vnd Herrn Rentkamer/ vrbarbücher/ register/ aussgab/ empfang/ vnd ander gemeine hausrechnung belangt/ dahin ist sie am bequemisten/ zu subtilen rechnungen zum dickermal seumlich."

See also:

Sterner, Geschichte der Rechenkunst, I Teil, pp. 218, 219.

Kästner, Geschichte der Mathematik, Bd. I, p. 42.

Knott, C. G., The Abacus in its Historic and Scientific Aspects, Trans-

having expressed the numbers, is to shift or set them so as to express the sum or difference of the numbers found on each line. The processes of multiplication and division are more complex; so much so, that, when the multiplier or divisor contains more than one figure, the Hindu algorisms are far superior. Several modern authorities give detailed explanations of these processes.[1]

The transition from line reckoning to reckoning with the Hindu numerals, or pen reckoning, as it was often called, was slow. So difficult was it to abandon the old line and space idea and the Roman symbols, that writers mixed the old and the new symbols in calculation. This is plainly shown in Tollet reckoning [2] (tabular calculation), a process used in a few early works, as in the Bamberg Arithmetic and in the arithmetics of Widman and Apianus. For example, the problem: " What is the cost of 4,367 ℔. 29 lot 3 quintl of ginger at 16 shillings a pound?" is solved thus by Widman: [3]

---

actions of the Asiatic Society of Japan, vol. xiv, part i, pp. 19, 34 (Yokohama, 1886).

[1] Knott, C. G., The Abacus in its Historic and Scientific Aspects, pp. 18, 45-67. See preceding note.

Kuckuck, A., Die Rechenkunst im sechzehnten Jahrhundert, pp. 10-13 (Berlin, 1874).

Villicus, Geschichte der Rechenkunst, pp. 68-76 (Wien, 1897).

Leslie, Philosophy of Arithmetic, under "Palpable Arithmetic" (Edinburgh, 1820).

A more accessible work to many is:

Brooks, Philosophy of Arithmetic, pp. 115, 160 (Lancaster, Pa., 1901).

For the historical development of the abacus see:

Cantor, M., Vorlesungen über Geschichte der Mathematik, Vol. I (Leipsic, 2d ed., 1894).

Also articles by Boncompagni in Atti dell' Accademia pontificia de nuovi Lincei.

[2] P. Treutlein, Abhandlungen Zur Geschichte Der Mathematik, vol. 1, p. 98 (Leipsic, 1877).

[3] Johann Widman, Behend und hüpsch Rechnung (1508 ed.). "Es hat einer kaufft 4367 lb' Ingwer 29 lot 3 quintl/ ye 1 lb' für 16 p in goldsetz also." Fol. Fi verso, Fii recto.

(A mistake was evidently made in this edition, since the problem reads " 13 shillings a pound " in the early editions.)

SIXTEENTH CENTURY ARITHMETIC

4 M	13000 p	4 M	52000		2600
3 C	1300 p	3 C	3900		195
6 X	130 p	6 X	780		39 floren
7 lb'	13 p	7 lb'	91 p	facit	4 fl 11 p
2 X	130/32 p	2 X	260/32		8 4/32
9 lot	13/32 p	9 lot	117/32		3 21/52
3 quintñ	13/128 p	3 quitl	39/128		39/128

The first column at the left is the multiplicand, 4 thousand, 3 hundred, 6 tens and 7 ℔.; 20 lot and 9 lot and 3 quintl. The lot and the quintl are first expressed as fractional parts of a pound. The Roman symbols, M, C, X, at the right of this column are superfluous, since the figures, 4, 3, 6, placed above one another designate by their positions the orders for which they stand. The columns beginning 13000 p form the multiplier, 13, set down for each order. In modern work the 4000 would be multiplied by 13, but here 4 is multiplied by 13,000. The fourth group represents the results of the multiplications. The numbers in the last column at the right express these results in florins and shillings. More than half a century after Widman, Robert Recorde, in the later editions of his "Ground of Artes," says that before studying arithmetic proper the Roman numerals must be learned.[1]

A method of calculating, or a mnemonic to assist in abacus work, called Finger Reckoning, was explained by a few writers of this period.[2] But as the method was then obsolete in

---

[1] Robert Recorde, The Ground of Artes (1594 ed.). "Before the introduction of Arithmeticke, it were very good to have ſome vnderſtanding and knowledge of theſe figures and notes:"
This is followed by a table of Roman numerals with the corresponding Hindu numerals and the corresponding words, as:

i	1	one
ii	2	two
iii	3	three

Fol. Bviii verso.

[2] Noviomagus, De Numeris Libri II, Cap. XIII.
Paciuolo, Sūma de Arithmetica Geometria Proportioni et Proportionalita (1494 ed.), fol. 36 verso, or Eiiij verso. (He does not explain, but gives a page of pictures.)
Andres, Sumario breve de la practica de la arithmetica, Valencia (1515).
Tagliente, Libro de Abaco, Venetia, M. D. XV (1541 ed.), fol. Aiii verso.
Apianus, Ein newe vnd wolgegründte vnderweysung aller Kauffmansrechnung, Ingolstadt (1527).
Aventinus, Abacvs at qve vetvstissima, vetervm latinorum per digitos

THE ESSENTIAL FEATURES

Western Europe, it has no significance here. Accounts of this method are given in standard authorities.[1]

In order to exhibit the essentials of the arithmetic of this period briefly and systematically, it is best to treat it by topics, as was the common practice of its authors.

DEFINITIONS

It was the common practice among Latin School writers, especially among those who were influenced by the works of the Greeks on theoretic arithmetic, to begin with a formidable list of definitions.

Definitions of Number, Unity, and Zero

Number was generally defined thus: "Number is a collection of units." The following is Paciuolo's definition:[2] "Number is a multitude composed of units. Aristotle says, if anything is infinite, number is, and Euclid in the third postulate of the seventh book says that its series can proceed to infinity, and that it can be made greater than any given number by adding one."

The meaning of unity caused writers much concern and was variously defined, as appears from the following:

1. Unity is the beginning of all number and measure, for as we measure things by number, we measure number by unity.[3]

manusqʒ numerandi (quin etiam loquendi) cōfuetudo, Ex beda cū picturis et imaginibus - - - Ratispone - - - (1532).

Moya, Tratado de Matemáticas, Alcabà, 1573 (1703 ed., chap. ix). "Trata dela orden que los antiquos timierō en cōtar con los dedos de las manos, y otras partes del cuerpo."

[1] Leslie, Philosophy of Arithmetic (Edinburgh, 1820), p. 101.

Villicus, Geschichte der Rechenkunst (1897), pp. 10-14.

Stoy, H., Zur Geschichte des Rechenunterrichts, I. Teil, § 9, p. 47. See plates at end of volume.

Sterner, Geschichte der Rechenkunst, I. Teil, p. 77.

Cantor, Vorlesungen über Geschichte der Mathematik (1900 ed.), Bd. I, see index.

[2] Paciuolo, Suma de Arithmetica Geometria Proportioni et Proportionalita (1523 ed.) "Numero: è (fecondo çiafchuno philofophante) vna moltitudine de vnita cōpofta: - - - Ariftotile dice: cioe. Si quid infinitum eft: numerus eft. E per la terza petitione del feptimo de Euclide: la fua ferie in infinito potere procedere: ʒ quocūqʒ numero dato: dari poteft maior: vnitatem addendo." Fol. A i recto.

[3] Joan Noviomagus, De Numeris Libri II (1544).

2. Unity is not a number, but the source of number.[1]

3. Unity is the basis of all number, constituting the first in itself.[2]

4. Unity is the origin of everything.[3]

This difference of opinion as to the nature of unity was not new in the sixteenth century. The definition had puzzled the wise men of antiquity.[4] Many Greek, Arabian, and Hindu writers had excluded unity from the list of numbers. But, perhaps, the chief reason for the general rejection of unity as a number by the arithmeticians of the Renaissance was the misinterpretation of Boethius's arithmetic. Nicomachus (c. 100 A. D.) in his $Ἀριθμητικῆς βιβλία δύο$ had said that unity was not a *polygonal number* and Boethius's translation was supposed to say that unity was not a number.[5] Even as late as 1634 Stevinus found it necessary to correct this popular error and explained it thus: $3 - 1 = 2$, hence 1 is a number.[6]

---

[1] Gemma Frisius, Arithmeticae Practicae Methodus Facilis (1575 ed.). "Numerum autem vocant multitudinem ex unitatibus conflatam. Itaque unitas ipsa numerus non erit, sed numerorum omnium principium." Fol. A$_5$ verso.

Jacques Chavvet Champenois, Institvtions De L'Arithmetique (1578 ed.). "Vn, qui n'est pas nombre, mais comencement de nombre, & origine de toutes chofes, - - -." Page 3.

Humphrey Baker, The Well Spring of Sciences (1580 ed.). "And therfore an vnitie is no number, but the begining and originall of number, as if you doe multiplie or deuide a vnite by it felfe, it is refolued into itfelfe without any increafe. But it is in number otherwife, for there can be no number, how great foeuer it bee, but that it may continually bee encreafed by adding euermore one vnitie vnto the fame." Fol. Bi recto.

[2] Franciscus Mavrolycus, Arithmeticorum Libri Duo (1575). "Unitas est principium & constitutrix omnium numerorum, constituens autem imprimis seipsam." Page 2.

[3] See definition by Champenois in note 1 above.

[4] In Plato's Republic we find: "To which class do unity and number belong?" Monroe's Source Book, p. 203.

[5] Weissenborn, H., Gerbert, Beiträge zur Kenntniss der Mathematik des Mittelalters, p. 219 (Berlin, 1888).

[6] After reviewing the various arguments which history has handed down, Stevinus says: "Que l'unitie est nombre. Il est notoire que l'on dict vulgairement que l'unite ne soit point nombre, ains seulement son principe, ou

Zero was referred to merely as a symbol used in connection with the digits to express number. When taken alone it was said to have no meaning. The prevalence of *nulla, nulle* and *rein* in the terms used to express it is suggestive of this meaning.[1]

So far were the mathematicians of that period from the conception of number as a continuum that they emphasized the difference between continuous and discrete quantity and limited arithmetic to the latter domain.[2] So long as they

commencement & tel en nombre come le point en la ligne; ce que nous nions, & en pouvons argumenter enter en cefte forte:
La partie eft de mefme matiere qu'eft fon entier,
Vnité eft partie de multitude d'unitez;
Ergo l'unitié eft de mefme matiere qu'eft la multitude d'unitez;
Mais la matiere des multitude d'unitez est nombre,
Doncques la matiere d'unité eft nombre.
Et qui le nie, faict comme celuy, qui nie qu' une piece de pain foit du pain. Nous pourrions auffi dire ainfi:
Si du nombre donné l'on ne foubftraict nul nombre, le nombre donné demeure,
Soit trois le nombre donné, & du mefme foubftrayons un, qui n'est point nombre comme tu veux.
Doncques le nombre donné demeure, c'eft à dire qu'il y reftera encore trois, ce qui eft abfurd. Fol. A recto.

[1] The various names for the symbol o in this period were: Zefiro and nulla, Piero Borgi (1488 ed.); çero and nulla by Paciuolo (1523 ed.); nulla, Rudolff (1534 ed.); cyphar, Recorde (1540); circolo, cifra, zerro, nulla, Tartaglia (1556); cyphram, Gemma Frisius (1558 ed.); circulus, Ramus (1577 ed.); nulle or zero, Trenchant (1578 ed.); nul and rein, Champenois (1578); ciphar, Baker (1580 ed.); and nullo, Raets (1580). Buteo (1559) says that the zero could be called omicron because of its form.

The oldest manuscript actually known to have the zero bears the date 738 A. D., by Jalka Rashtrakúta.

[2] Unicorn, De L'Arithmetica vniuersale (1598 ed,), "Quantity is divided into two classes: continua and discreta. La quantità continua is formally defined to be that of which the terminus of every part joins the terminus of another part. a c b As, for example, in the line ab, the point c is the terminus of the part ac, and this is also a terminus of the part bc, and a common terminus. Or in the surface abcd, the line ef is the common terminus which divides it into two parts. Of this division of quantity there are five kinds: lines, surfaces, solids, place and time. The treatment of these belong to geometry.

Quantità discreta is defined to be such that no part is joined to another

held to this limitation, they could never think of the one-to-one correspondence of numbers to points on a line.[1] The Greek method of representing surds by lines was well known, and it would have been easy to arrive at the conception of filling in the points of a line with numbers, had not continuity been excluded.

Definitions of Classifications

The definition of number was followed by definitions of the various classifications of numbers. The following taken from Paciuolo will illustrate:[2]

A number is *prime* when it is not divisible by any other integral number but one and the number itself. Otherwise it is *composite*. Examples of primes: 3, 7, 11, 13, 17, etc. Examples of composites: 4, 8, which is 2×4, 12, 14, 18, etc.

Lateral or linear numbers. Different numbers which may be multiplied together, as 3 and 4, 6 and 8, compared to the sides of a rectangle.

common part of another quantity, as a number. For example, in numbers with periods containing three orders (the usual method of numeration), the last number is the last of that group, and is not the beginning of the next group.

Another difference between quantità discreta and quantità continua is that the continua is divisible ad infinitum and the discreta is increasable ad infinitum.

The quantità continua is divided into *mobile* and *immobile*, and by *immobile* is meant the earth, and by *mobile* the heavens. Under the immobile is included geometry, and under mobile, astrology.

Two other kinds of quantity: that which has position, as the solid, continuous thing; the other which has not position, as time, which is constantly passing, and water and other liquids, which have not position but which are limited by other things, as by the vessel containing the water.

Quantità { 1. Continua { mobile—cielo. / immobile—terra.   3. Hauēte positiōe.
         { 2. Discreta { numero. / oratione.   4. Nō hauēte positione.

Fol. A$_2$ recto.

[1] Dedekind, R., Essays on the Theory of Numbers (Beman's translation, Chicago, 1901).

[2] Paciuolo, Summa (1523 ed.), fol. Ai recto, Aij verso *et seq.*

THE ESSENTIAL FEATURES 33

Superficial (plane) number. The product of two linear numbers, as 12 from 3 × 4, 48 from 6 × 8.

Square number. The product of two similar numbers, as 9 from 3 × 3, 16 from 4 × 4, 25 from 5 × 5, etc.

Solid number. The product of three linear numbers, as 12 from 2 × 3 × 2.

Cubic number. The product of three equal numbers, as 8 from 2 × 2 × 2, 27 from 3 × 3 × 3, 64 from 4 × 4 × 4, etc.

Triangular numbers. Those which commence with unity, and which increase upward in the form of a triangle by adding a unit, always keeping the sides equal.[1]

Besides this there are *pentagonal numbers*, etc.

Circular numbers, as 5 and 6; so called because each multiplied by itself to infinity always gives a product ending in itself, as 5 × 5 = 25 × 5 = 125 × 5 = 625 - - -; 6 × 6 = 36 × 6 = 216 × 6 = 1296 - - -.

Defective numbers are those the sum of whose factors is less than the number itself, as 8 and 10. 8 = 4 × 2 × 1; 4 + 2 + 1 = 7; 10 = 5 × 2 × 1; 5 + 2 + 1 = 8.

Superfluous numbers. Those the sum of whose factors is more than the number itself, as 12, 24, etc. The factors of 12 are 6, 4, 3, 2, 1; 6 + 4 + 3 + 2 + 1 = 16: factors of 24 are 12, 8, 6, 4, 3, 2, 1; the sum of these is 36.

Perfect numbers are those the sum of whose factors equals the number itself; *e. g.*, the factors of 6 are 3, 2, 1, and their sum is 6; the factors of 28 are 14, 7, 4, 2, 1, and their sum is 28.

The manner of designating various ratios was also peculiar and elaborate. For example, the relation of any two numbers whose ratio is 1½ to 1 was called *sesquialteral*, meaning that the antecedent contains the consequent once and one-half more.[2]

---

[1] See marginal illustrations in Paciuolo

[2] The sesquialtera stop of an organ which furnishes the perfect fifth interval, 1 : 1½, is named from this old Greek ratio.

Similarly the ratio

1⅓ : 1, or 4 : 3 was called *sesquitertial*.

1¼ : 1, or 5 : 4 was called *sesquiquartal*, and so on.

Of all the pairs of numbers that can result in *sesqui* ratios, the antecedents were called *superparticularis* and the consequents *subsuperparticularis*.[1]

When the integral part of the ratio is greater than 1 the above ratios were preceded by the corresponding adjectives, thus the ratio

2½ : 1 was called duplex sesquialteral.

2⅓ : 1 was called duplex sesquitertial.

3¼ : 1 was called triplex sesquiquartal, and so on.

When the fraction in the ratio exceeds a unit fraction, the ratio was named according to the numerator, thus the ratio

1⅔ : 1 was called superbipartiens.

1¾ : 1 was called supertripartiens, and so on, meaning excess by two parts, by three parts, and so on.

The prefix *sub* was used to designate the inverse of the above ratios, thus the ratio

1 : 1⅔ was called subsuperbipartiens.

1 : 1¾ was called subsupertripartiens.[2]

The reason for emphasizing these peculiar classifications of number is not manifest. Legendre[3] explained the prominence given to the subject on the ground that its study becomes a sort of passion with those who take it up. This phase of

---

[1] A discussion of the classifications of Nicomachus may be found in Gow, History of Greek Mathematics (Cambridge, 1884), page 90.

[2] After so much of explanation, a characteristic remark of DeMorgan will be appreciated: "For some specimens of the laborious manner by which the Pythagorean Greeks, in the first instance, and afterwards Boethius in Latin, had endeavored to systematize the expression of numerical ratios, I may refer the reader to the article *Numbers, old appelations of*, in the Supplement to the Penny Cyclopedia (London, 1833-43). If I were to give any account of the whole system, on a scale commensurate with the magnitude of the works written on it, the reader's patience would not be *subquatuor decupla subsuperbipartiens septimas*, or, as we should now say, *seven per cent* of what he would find wanted for the occasion." DeMorgan, Arithmetical Books, p. xx.

[3] Legendre, Théories des Nombres (1798), preface.

arithmetic had its origin in the products of the Pythagorean School, was expounded by Nicomachus,[1] and was communicated to the scholars of the Renaissance by Boethius's translation [2] of Nicomachus. Among the works of the sixteenth century which treated this subject, that of Maurolycus [3] is noteworthy both for its exposition of the Greek classifications [4] and for its doctrine of incommensurables.

Writers on commercial arithmetic in the sixteenth century introduced their works by definitions of arithmetic, quantity, and number, but discarded the fanciful theory of numbers so attractive to theoretic writers.

Definitions of Processes

Each process was defined when first introduced, which was in connection with integers, since most of the writers treated the four fundamental processes with integers before doing so with fractions and denominate numbers. These definitions related to integers only, and often failed to have meaning when applied to fractions. Addition was generally defined as *the collection of several numbers into one sum*,[5] and subtraction as *taking a smaller number from a larger one*.[6] Certain writers [7] improved on this, and even recognized subtraction to be the inverse of addition.[8] Multiplication was generally defined

---

[1] See page 34, note 1.   [2] See page 34, note 2.

[3] Mavrolycus, Franciscus, Arithmeticorum Libri Duo (1575), p. 3.

[4] Jordanus (1496 ed.) also is noted for its extensive treatment of the Greek properties of numbers.

[5] E. g., Trenchant, L'Arithmetique (1578), "Aiouter, eſt aſſembler pluſieur nombres en une ſomme," fol. B_4 recto; and Clichtoveus, Ars ſupputâdi - - - (Paris, c 1507) "Additio eſt multorum numeroɜ ſigillatim ſumptorum in una𝑚 ſummam collectio." Fol. b iiij recto.

[6] E. g., Tartaglia, General Trattato di Numeri (1556). "Sottare non è altro, che duoi propoſti numeri, inequali saper trouare la loro differentia, cioe quanto che il maggiore eccede il menore." Fol. Bvi verso.

[7] E. g., Tonstall, De Arte Supputandi (1522). "Subducto numerorvm est minoris numeri a maiore; uel aequalis ab equale ſubtractio." Fol. E_2 recto.

[8] Clichtoveus, Ars ſupputâdi (c. 1507). "Subſtractio est numeri minoris a majori subductio. Et additioni ex opposito respondet." Fol. biiii verso.

as *repeating one number as an addend as many times as there are units in another*,[1] a definition not directly applicable to fractions without modification. Division was generally defined as *finding how many times one number is contained in another*,[2] the partitive phrase being often included. Its relation to subtraction was also recognized.[3]

PROCESSES WITH INTEGERS

The writers of that period did mathematics a service in reducing the number of processes in arithmetic. The processes were commonly called Species,[4] due to the influence of the Latin manuscripts. In 1370 Magistro Jacoba de Florentia gave 9 Species, the number common in mediæval times, viz.: numeratio, additio, subtratio, duplatio, mediatio, multiplicatio, divisio, progressio, et radicum extractio. The Hindus, according to the Lilavati,[5] had eight processes, which were increased to ten by the Arabs, who added Mediatio and Duplatio. These latter are found in El Hassar (c. 1200), and probably, according to Suter, are of Egyptian origin. Their presence in mediæval Latin manuscripts is due to the influence of Al Khowarazmi.[6] In the sixteenth century the number ranged

[1] Gemma Frisius, Arithmeticae Practicae Methodus Facilis (1575 ed.). "Multiplicare est ex ductu vnius numeri in alterum numerum producere, qui toties habeat in se vnum multiplicantium, quoties alter vnitatem, Hoc est, Multiplicare est numerum quemcumqɜ aliquoties aut mul-toties, exaggerare." Fol. B_2 verso.

[2] Trenchant, L'Arithmetique (1578). "Partir, eſt chercher quantes foys vn nombre, contient l'autre." Fol. D_2 recto.

[3] Ramus, Arithmeticae Libri Duo (1577 ed.). "Divisio est, qua divisor subducitur á dividendo quoties in eo continetur & habetur quotus." Fol. A vii verso.

An interesting comparison of definitions current in the seventeenth century is found in DeMorgan, Arithmetical Books, pp. 59-61.

[4] The origin of the word "species" has been traced to the Greek word εἶδος, meaning member of an equation. This word appeared in rules for adding to and subtracting from the members of an equation, and was translated into Latin as species, which later came to be used to designate all of the fundamental processes of arithmetic. Cantor, Vorlesungen über Geschichte der Mathematik (3d ed., 1900), Bd. I, p. 442.

[5] The work of Bhaskara, a Hindu writer (c. 1200 A. D.).

[6] An Arabian mathematician (c. 800 A. D.).

from nine to five. Some writers excluded extraction of roots, others progressions also. Piero di Borgi argued that the number should be reduced to seven in order that it might correspond to the number of gifts of the Holy Spirit.[1] Later in the century duplatio (multiplying by 2) and mediatio (dividing by 2) were excluded, reducing the processes to numeration and the four fundamental operations recognized to-day.[2] It is probable that numeration was not always included, in which case the number would be four. "The lack of agreement with reference to the number of Species finds its explanation in the circumstance that they fail to define the idea of Species. Gemma Frisius is the only one who attempted a definition: 'Moreover, we call certain kinds of operations with numbers Species.'"[3] But this is too indefinite to give any basis of selection.[4]

Notation and Numeration

The object of numeration was to teach the reading of numbers written in the Hindu notation. For a hundred years after the first printed arithmetic many writers began their works with the line-reckoning and the Roman numerals, and followed these by the Hindu arithmetic.[5] The teaching of

[1] Cardan, Practica Arithmetice (1539), Chapter II, gives seven: numeration, addition, subtraction, multiplication, division, progression, and the extraction of roots.

[2] Sigismund Suevus, Arithmetice Historica (1593), fol. aii recto.
Gemma Frisius, Arithmeticae Practicae Methodus Facilis (1575 ed.). "Solent nonnulli Duplationem & Mediationem assignare species distinctas à Multiplicatione & Divisione. Quid vero mouerit stupidos illos nescio, cū & finitio & operatio eadem sit." Fol. B$_5$ verso.

[3] Unger, Die Methodik, page 72, § 41.

[4] A few writers included the Rule of Three—Riese for example.

[5] Köbel, Zwey rechenbüchlin (1537 ed.). After teaching the Roman symbols, I, V, X, L, C, D, M, and the digits, 1, 2, 3, - - - 9, Köbel gives a comparative table entitled: "Tafel zu erkennen vnd vergleichen die zal der Büchstabn auß dem A. b. c. genömen/ vnd der Figuren/ die man ziferen nennet/ Underrichtung." Fol. B 6 recto and verso, or 14 recto and verso.

In the table Köbel uses small letters for all numbers except ten and multiples of ten, as i, ij, iij, iiij, v, - - X, xj, xij, - - XX - - -. For 500 he uses D^c; for 1000, j^M; 2000, ij^M; for 100 he gives both C and j^c;

numeration was a formidable task, since the new notation was so unfamiliar to the people generally. The feeling was prevalent that one must learn the Roman system and then graft on the new system.

Numbers in the Hindu system were divided into three classes: (1) digits (digiti), 1, 2, —, 9; (2) articles (articuli), ten and multiples of ten, 10, 20, 30, —; (3) composites (compositi), combinations of digits and articles, as 25, 37. Most writers stated the idea of place-value simply and directly, but some, owing to its novelty, gave it an elaborate treatment.[1]

The names of the orders and the device used as a separatrix varied extensively. The names to hundred thousands were the same as now used, but the period now called millions was usually called thousand thousand.[2] The word *million* dates

200, cc and ij^c; 1100, MC, also Mj^c; 1200, Mcc, also Mij^c; for 1300, Mccc, also Miij^c.

[1] Widman, Behend und hüpsch Rechnung (1508 ed.), fol. 6 recto.

Robert Recorde, The Ground of Artes (1594 ed.). Recorde, whose book is in dialogue form, thus quaintly develops the idea of place value:

"But here must you marke that everie figure hath two values: One alwayes certaine that it fignifieth properly, which it hath of his forme: and the other vncertaine, which he taketh of his place." Fol. Cvi verso.

- - - - - - - - -

"M. (Master). Now then take heede, thefe certaine values euery figure reprefenteth, when it is alone written without other figures joyned to him. And alfo when it is in the firfte place, though manie other do follow; as for example: This figure 9 is ix. standing now alone.

"Sc. (Scholar). How: is he alone and ftandeth in the middle of fo many letters?

"M. The letters are none of his felowes. For if you were in France in the middle of a M. Frenchman, if there were none Englifh man with you, you would reckon your felfe to bee alone.

- - - - - - - - -

"Sc. I perceiue that. And doeth not 7 that standeth in the second place betoken vii? and 6 in the third place betoken vi? And so 3 in the fourth place betoken three?

"M. Their places be as you haue faid, but their values are not fo. For, as in the first place, euery figure betokeneth his owne value certaine onely, fo in the second place euerie figure betokeneth his owne value a hundreth times, fo that 6 in that place betoken vi. C. - - -." Fol. Cvii verso.

[2] Raets, Een niew Cijfferboeck/ (1580). "Duyfentich duyfent - - - - 1000000." Fol. Aiij recto.

THE ESSENTIAL FEATURES 39

back to the thirteenth century;[1] but the sixteenth century records the struggle of the word for its place in numeration. Borgi[2] (1484) has it in "Million de million de million," Chuquet (1484) used it in reading numbers on the six-figure basis.[3] Paciuolo[4] (1494) used "milione." Cirvelo[5] (1495) used million for 1,000,000,000,000. La Roche (1520), like Chuquet, used it on the six-figure plan. After 1540 the word appeared in many standard works.[6] The present names for higher periods, though much slower to come into use, were known to fifteenth century scholars. Chuquet (1484) gave the remarkable list: "byllion, tryllion, quadrillion, quyllion, sixlion, septyllion, ottyllion, nonyllion," using them on the six-figure basis. La Roche (1520) gave billion and trillion.

Tonstall, De Arte Supputandi (1522). Tonstall reads in Latin the number 3210987654321 as Ter millies millena millia millies, ducenties decies millies millena millia, noningenties octvagies septies millena millia, sexcenta quinquinta quattuor millia, trecenta viginti unum. Fol. C₂ verso.

[1] The word "million" is first found in Marco Polo (1254-1324).

[2] The 1540 edition of Borgi's work gives the following names of high periods: "Miar de million, million de million, miar de millio de million, million de million de million." Fol. 5 verso.

The word is also used in the Treviso arithmetic (1478).

[3] By the six-figure basis is meant the use of millions to cover six orders beyond hundred thousands, billions to cover the next six orders, and so on. Thus, 18,432,750,198,246,115 would be read eighteen thousand four hundred thirty-two billion, seven hundred fifty thousand one hundred ninety-eight million, two hundred forty-six thousand one hundred fifteen; instead of eighteen quadrillion, four hundred thirty-two trillion, seven hundred fifty billion, and so on, on the three-figure plan. The six-figure grouping of Chuquet and La Roche entered Germany in 1681, according to Unger (Die Methodik ---, p. 71) and came into general use there in the eighteenth century. France early adopted the three-figure system. England used the old terminology at the opening of the sixteenth century, for Tonstall (1522) says that *millena millia* (thousand thousand) is commonly called "million" by foreigners. But before the middle of the century we find Recorde using million.

[4] Paciuolo, Sūma (1494 ed.), fol. 9 verso.

[5] Cirvelo, Tractatus Arithmetice practice (1505), uses the same notation.

[6] Recorde, The Ground of Artes (1540); Gemma Frisius (1552, Antwerp ed.); Cataldi (1602 ed.).

Van der Schuere (1600) gave a very large number field. He used millioen for million, duysêt mill. (thousand million) for billion, bimillioen for trillion, duysêt bimill. for quadrillion, and so on up to duysêt quadrimill. for octillion. Trenchant (1578) gave millions for million, miliar for billion, and milier de miliars for trillion.

The following devices were used for separating the periods:

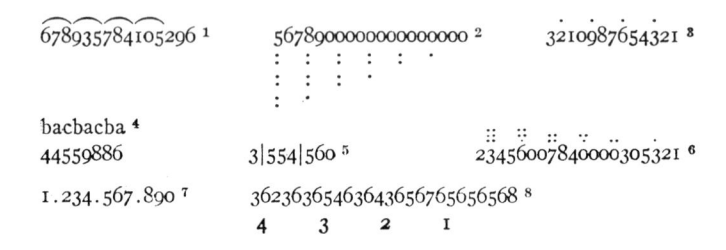

$\overbrace{678}\overbrace{935}\overbrace{784}105296$ [1]   567890000000000000 [2]   3210987654321 [3]

bacbacba [4]
44559886   3|554|560 [5]   23456007840000305321 [6]

1.234.567.890 [7]   3623636546364365676565
6568 [8]
                          4   3   2   1

Recorde (1540) called the numbers in each period ternaries and the periods denominations to assist in reading. Thus, as in 222 pounds, pounds is the denomination, so in every period (620,000) the last place (thousand) is the denomination.

[1] Leonardo of Pisa, Liber Abaci (1202, or 1228), p. 1.

[2] Borgi, Qui coměza la nobel opera (1540 ed.), fol. Av verso; Paciuolo, Sūma (1523 ed.), fol. 19 verso, ciii verso.

[3] Tonstall, De Arte Supputandi (1522), fol. C_2 verso; Köbel, Zwey Rechenbüchlin (1537 ed.), fol. B_4 verso; Rudolff, Kunstliche rechnung (1534 ed.), Aiij recto; Riese, Rechnung auff der Linien und Federn/ (1571 ed.), fol. Aij verso; Baker, The Well Spring of Sciences (1580 ed.), fol. Biiii recto.

[4] Köbel, Zwey Rechenbüchlin (1537 ed.), fol. B_5 recto.

[5] Gemma Frisius, Arithmeticae Practicae Methodus (1581 ed.), fol. Aiv.

[6] Tartaglia, La Prima Parte (1556).

[7] Ramus, Arithmeticae Libri Duo (1577 ed.), fol. Aii verso.

[8] Unicorn, De L'Arithmetica vniversale (1598), reads this number thus: 36. millioni quatro volte, & ducento trenta sei millia, & trecentosessanta cinque millioni tre volte, et quatro cento e sessanta tre millia & sei cento e quaranta tre millioni due volte, & sei cento cinquanta sei millia e settecento sessanta cinque millioni vna volta, & sei cento e cinquata sei millia, e cinquecento sessanta otto. Fol. A_4 recto.

THE ESSENTIAL FEATURES 41

The number in the period he called the numerator. Thus, in 203,000,000, 203 is the numerator.[1]

Addition

The treatment of addition presents much diversity, but the general characteristics are the absence of tables of sums, full explanations of column-adding, and tests of the work.

It would seem that the sums corresponding to the modern addition table would necessarily have received first attention at a time when the Hindu numerals were so unfamiliar. But the writers who used these were the exception.[2]

The explanation of the processes of column-adding usually

---

[1] Recorde, The Ground of Artes (1540).
Scholer. What call you Denominations?
Master. It is the laste value or name added to any summe. As when I say: CCxxii. poundes: poundes is the Denomination. And likewise in saying: 25 men, men is the Denomination, and so of other. But in this place (that I spake of before) the last number of euery Ternarie, is the Denomination of it. As of the first Ternarie, the Denomination is Unites, and of the seconde Ternarie, the Denomination is thousandes: and of the third Ternaries, thousande thousandes, or Millions: of the iiii, thousande thousande, thousandes, or thousande Millions: and so foorth.
Scholer. And what shall I call the value of the three figures that may be pronounced before the Denominators: as in saying 203000000, that is CCiii. millions. I perceyue by your wordes, that millions is the denomination: but what shal I call the CCiii joyned before the millions.
Master. That is called the Numerator or valuer, and the whole summe that resulteth of them both, is called the summe, value or number. Fol. Dii recto (1594 ed.).

[2] Tartaglia, La Prima Parte Del General Trattato (1556). Tartaglia gives the addition tables as follows:

0. e 0. fa 0 (0+0=0)	1. e 1. fa 2	
0. e 1. fa 1 (0+1=1)	....	
0. e 2. fa 2 (0+2=2)	1. e 10. fa 11	and so on with all the tables to
....		
0. e 10. fa 10	2. e 2. fa 4	10. e 10. fa 20
	....	
	2. e 10. fa 12	Fol. B i verso.

That these tables were regarded as fundamental to further progress is shown by the following remark from the same folio: "Imparate adunque li soprascritti sumari necessarij di saper a menti." (Therefore to learn to add, it is necessary to commit the tables written above to memory.)

received first attention. Two abstract numbers were proposed for addition, such that the sum of one column of figures, at least, would equal or exceed ten. The first example in Een niew Cijfferboeck, by Willem Raets (1580) is:

$$\begin{array}{r} 354 \\ 898 \\ \hline 1252 \end{array}$$

Cardan's (1539) first example is:

$$\begin{array}{r} 73942 \\ 4068 \\ 273 \\ 52759 \\ \hline 131042 \end{array}$$

Noviomagus (1539) first shows the arrangement by columns, as in (1); then adds without carrying, as in (2); then adds with carrying, as in (3):

(1)		(2)	(3)
321, not 321		321	2354
124	124	421 [1]	620
530	530	530	76
		975	3050

Tonstall (1522) gives:

(1)	(2)	(3)	(4)
4	309	59	389
3	204	34	204
7	513	93	93

He points out in example (2) that the ten in the sum of the first column falls under the second column, because the second column is composed of zeros. Examples (3) and (4) are explained in order, although it would seem that (4) should precede (3). The student is advised by Tonstall to learn the ele-

---

[1] Typographical error in the original for 124.

THE ESSENTIAL FEATURES 43

mentary sums, and is encouraged by the remark that it will require only an hour.

It was usual in addition to arrange the addends in order of size, placing the largest at the top. It is easy to state a reason for this, although none is given; for by this plan the columns were more easily preserved—a real difficulty for beginners, especially for those to whom the Hindu system was unfamiliar. It also prepared for subtraction, but this was probably not the reason for using it, as is shown by by the following examples:[1] The first is the only one that corresponds to an example in subtraction, since it has only two addends, but here the smaller is written at the top. In the other examples, which do not correspond to those of subtraction, the numbers are in the order of their size from the top down. The illustration at the left shows how arrangement according to size was occasionally disregarded.[2]

```
  234
  345
  438
  564
  763
  832
 3450
  100
   63
   13
    8
   13
 1000
 ----
 7825
```

```
3456      4602     56789
9054      3405     23458
          2300     12345
-----              6789
10307              3239
                   2848
                   1327
                    456
                    349
                    228
                    327
                    129
                     38
                   -----
                   10832 [5]
```

The sums of the several columns in a problem of addition were commonly added as at present, by writing the first right-hand figure of the sum of any column and adding the rest to the next column. When the columns are long, however, this is not the easiest way, and occasionally a writer of that period wrote the partial sums and added them to obtain the result.[3] A slight modification of this was the placing of the numbers to be added to the next column below that column to be added to its sum.[4]

```
 3963
 2651
 9786
-----
14290
  211
-----
  16 [5]
```

A feature that is written large in arithmetic of the six-

---

[1] Rudolff, Kunstliche rechnung (1534 ed.), fol. Aiiij recto.

[2] Tagliente, Libro Dabaco (1541 ed.), fol. Ci recto.

[3] Gemma Frisius, Arithmeticae Practicae Methodus facilis (1575 ed.), fol. Aviii verso.

[4] Buteo, Logistica (1559), fol. a$_7$ verso.   [5] Error in the original.

44   SIXTEENTH CENTURY ARITHMETIC

teenth century is the matter of the so-called proofs of operations. These were generally not proofs, but tests more or less reliable. The most common form was that of casting out nines. Thus, in the annexed case of addition, the remainder arising from dividing 354 by 9 is 3, and from dividing 898 by 9 is 7. The excess of nines in $7 + 3$ is 1; this is the 1 above the line in $\frac{1}{1}$. The excess of nines in 1252 is 1; this is the 1 below the line. $\frac{1}{1}$ shows that the excesses agree and that the work checks, or proves, as it was called. It was customary to give a long explanation of the proof, and a few writers gave a table of remainders arising from dividing numbers from 0 to 90 by 9, and showed how to find the remainders for large numbers.[2]

$$\begin{array}{r} 354\,{}^{1} \\ 898 \\ \hline 1252 \end{array} \quad \begin{array}{r} 1 \\ - \\ \hline 1 \end{array}$$

That tests were given exaggerated importance is shown by the fact that several writers extended them to the case of adding denominate numbers. The excess of nines was found for the highest denomination; this was expressed in terms of the next lower denomination and combined with it. Then the process of finding the excess was repeated. Each addend and the result were similarly treated, the work of testing becoming more difficult and complicated than the solution of the problem.

The test by casting out sevens was also common, but being

[1] Raets, Een niew Cijfferboeck (1580), fol. Aiiij recto.
[2] Tartaglia, La Prima Parte (1556), fol. Bij verso and fol. Biij recto.

Li termini della proua del. 9.

De 0. la proua è —— 0	De 10. la proua è —— 1
De 9. la proua è —— 0	De 11. la proua è —— 2
De 18. la proua è —— 0	De 12. la proua è —— 3
....	....
De 90. la proua è —— 0	De 19. la proua è —— 1

De 0. la proua è —— 0   De 21. la proua è —— 3
De 1. la proua è —— 1   De 22. la proua è —— 4
De 2. la proua è —— 2   ....
   ....   De 30. la proua è —— 3
De 9. la proua è —— 0, and so on to:
           De 81. la proua è 0
           ....
           De 90. la proua è 0.

more difficult, it was placed second. Several authors mention the fact that it is more accurate than that by casting out nines.[1] The proof by elevens was sometimes used. In addition, an author occasionally used the method of adding the columns of figures both upward and downward.[2] A few used subtraction,[3] in the case of two addends taking one addend from the sum to see if the result is the other. The use of subtraction in the case of more than two addends was rare.[4] The reason

[1] Unicorn, De L'Arithmetica vniuersale (1598), "Che la proua del 7. sia men fallace, che la proua del 9," fol. B$_2$ verso.

[2] Paciuolo, Sūma (1523 ed.), fol. 20 recto, or Ciiij recto.

[3] Tartaglia, La Prima Parte (1556), gives this example:

```
    8756
a    678  b
   ─────
    9434
```

and says: "Perche inuero il sommare è proprio in atto contrario al sottare, & similmente il sottrare è in atto contrario al sommare," fol. Bij recto (because, indeed, addition is properly the inverse of subtraction, and similarly subtraction is properly the inverse of addition).

[4] Champenois, Les Institvtions De L'Arithmetique (1578).

```
            4325    Preuue.
             132    4878 fóme de l'Addition.
             421    4325 premiere fomme.
Addition    4878    0553 premier refte.
                     132 feconde fomme.       Page 15, or fol. Bviii recto.
                     421 fecond refte.
                     421 troifiefme fomme.
                     000
```

Also Simon Jacob, Rechenbuch auf den Linien und mit Ziffern/ (1599 ed.).

```
          597.a
          786.b
          978.c
         ─────
Summa    2361
          597.a
         ─────
          1764
          786.b
         ─────
           978        Fol. Cv recto.
          978.c
         ─────
           000
```

for the prominence of these tests is undoubtedly due to the use of the various forms of the abacus. When the beads were once shifted, or the counters displaced, or the symbols in the sand effaced, there was no record to retrace, no possibility of reviewing the work.[1] It was, therefore, very advantageous to have means of testing the result by some comparison with the original numbers. These means were supplied by the proofs of nines and sevens. It was natural, then, that these tests should appear with due emphasis in most of the first printed books.

Besides the general characteristics of sixteenth century addition there were a few special features that have educational significance; namely, the order of adding, certain short methods, and the use of concrete problems to introduce the process.

We have noted that Paciuolo added upward and then added downward as a test of the work, but only one writer among those examined confined his addition to the downward process.[2] Thus, whatever virtue there may be in precedent is in favor of adding upward instead of downward.

[1] For some time after arithmeticians formed the habit of writing numbers in the Hindu notation, they used line-reckoning to perform the processes, and to watch their progress they crossed the figures as they were used. The influence of this is seen in the following example from Köbel (Zwey Rechenbüchlin (1537 ed.), fol. 111 verso, 112 recto), in which he crossed the figures of the addends, although using the Hindu algorism:

Zum erſten wil ich zuſammen thûn 103 zu 966. - - - Ich ſprich/ 6. vnd 3. ist 9. vnd ſetz die 9 vnder das ſtrichlin vff die erſt ſtat/ vnd durchſtreich die 6. vnd 3. ſo ſteht es alſo. - - - 6 ſtetz ich vnd den ſtrich/ vff die zweyte ſtat neben die 9. zu der lincke̊ hand vnder die 6. vnnd durchstreichs o. vnd 6.

```
1̶0̶3̶
9̶6̶6̶
   9
1̶0̶3̶
9̶6̶6̶
  69
```

[2] Trenchant, L'Arithmetique (1578 ed.).

"Je veux aiouter ces nombres, 581, 192, & 264. - - - Commençant à main droite, i'aioute toutes les figures du denier reng enſemble, diſtant, 1 & 2 font 3, & 4 font 7. ie poſe 7 ſous celuy reng an deſſous du tret, & vien ſemblablement cueillir e precedent reng, diſtant 8 & 9 font 17, & 6 font 23, ie poſe le digite 3 ſous ce reng, & retien le nombre des dizeines qui eſt 2, que i'adioute auec l'autre reng, diſtant, 2 que te tien & 5 font 7, & 1 font 8, & 2 font 10, ie poſe o & retien 1, que ie poſe deuant o, & c'eſt fét. Ainſi ces troys nombres aioutez montent 1037. Fol. Biv verso.

|581
|192
|264
|1037

THE ESSENTIAL FEATURES

Another feature of sixteenth century calculation that one would not expect so early in the history of European figure-reckoning was the use of short methods. They were not commonly used, but there is a fair sprinkling of them through the various operations. A few writers showed how equal numbers are combined while adding a column.[1] A few cases occur in which the associative law is used to break up a long problem into shorter ones.[2]

[1] Recorde, The Ground of Artes (1594 ed.): "I would adde thefe xiii fumes into one, which I fet after this manner: then doe I begin and gather the fumme of the firft rowe of figures which commeth to 107, for I take 9 there x. times and that is 90, then 9 and 8 is 17, that is in all 107, of which fumme I write the 7 under the firft rowe of figures, and then for that 100 is x. tens, I keepe x. in mind: which ten I muft adde vnto the nexte rowe of figures when they are added together with the x. that I had in my minde, make in all 125, of which fumme, I write the digit 5 vnder the fecond rowe, τ. Then for that 120 conteineth xii tens. Fol. Cii recto.

Cirvelo, Tractatus Arithmetice practice (1513 ed.).

"Et nota q̃ ad iftam fpeciem reducitur alia fpecies minus principalis que dicitur duplatio aut triplatio nam fi eundem numerum bis fcripferis et addideris in vnam fummam habebis duplum illius: vnde pro re tam facili nõ oportebat dare fpeciale capitulum. Exemplum." Fol. aiiij verso.

```
 496   2              496   3
 496   2   Exemplũ    496
 ---                  496   3
 992       duplum     ---
                     1488  triplũ
```

An application of doubling and tripling to addition.

[2] E. g., Clavius, Arithmetica Prattica (1626 ed.), fol. a$_4$ recto.

6008	308	108	3009	6008
5009	239	309	209	5009
4009	108	4128	308	4009
----	---	----	----	308
15026	655	4545	3526	239
				108
				108
15026				309
655	The top row furnishes partial sums			4128
4545	of the column at the right.			3009
3526				209
----				308
23752				----
				23752

```
4889
4599
2299
3699
2399
4090
1099
3198
 299
 699
 899
 499
 389
-----
29057
```

The plan of proposing a concrete problem in addition as a motive for explaining the process occurs in several works. The following will serve to illustrate:

"As if there were due to any man 223 pounds by some one body, and 334 pounds by another, and 431 by another, and you would know how many pounds is due to the same man in all." [1]

"A merchant has three purses in which there is a certain number of ecus. There are known to be 3,231 ecus in the first, 2,312 in the second, and 1,213 in the third. The merchant put the contents of these purses into one. It is required to know how many ecus there are in this purse." [2]

"For example, if it is asked how long ago Homer lived, and Gellius replies: 160 years before the founding of Rome, which was founded 752 years before the birth of Christ. Christ was born, however, 1,567 years ago. These three numbers are added. The sum showing that Homer flourished 2,479 years ago will be as follows ": [3]

```
 160
 752
1567
————
2479
```

It is somewhat remarkable that the idea of introducing a process through concrete examples should have taken root in so many countries within a period of fifty years at a time when communication of ideas was so slow. Köbel in Ger-

---

[1] Baker, The Well Spring of Sciences (1580 ed.), fol. Bvi recto.

[2] Champenois, Institvtions De L'Arithmetique (1578).

"Vn marchant a trois bourſes où il y a certaines ſommes d'eſcus, ſçauoir en la premiere 3231 eſcus, en la ſeconde 2312 eſcus, & en la troiſieſme 1213 eſcus.

Ce marchāt vuide ſes trois bourses en vne. Lon demande combien il y a d'eſcus en ceſte bourſe." Fol. Biiij recto, or page 7.

[3] Ramus, Arithmeticae Libri Duo (1577 ed.).

"Ut ſi quaeratur quampridem vixerit Homerus, & respondeatur é Gellio, 160 annis ante conditam Roman, quae condita ſit ante natum Chriſtum annis 752. Chriſtum vero natum anno abhinc 1567. addantur hi tres numeri: Summa inductionis indicans Homerum annos abhinc 2479 floruiſſe, erit hoc modo." Fol. Aiiij recto.

many (1531), Recorde (1540) and Baker (1562) in England, Ramus (1567), Trenchant (1571) and Champenois (1578) in France were the pioneers in their respective countries. Many who began with abstract numbers introduced denominate numbers after the first two or three problems.

Subtraction [1]

Another evidence that this was the formative period in elementary arithmetic is seen in the treatment of the subtraction of integers, for these writers were in possession of all the methods of subtraction that are taught or discussed at the present time.

There was little variation in their treatment where the figures of the minuend had greater value than the corresponding ones of the subtrahend. In fact, all the writers included in this investigation, with one exception, subtracted from right to left the figures of the subtrahend from the figures of the minuend written above, and placed the differences below the corresponding columns.

---

[1] A knowledge of the elementary differences required for this was presupposed, although the tables were given in the more elaborate works only. Ramus (1586 ed.) recommended learning the "alphabetum" both for addition and subtraction. By alphabetum he meant all the possible sums and differences of the digits, 1 - - - 9. "Subductionis mediatio in primis novem notis eadem hic effe debet, quae fuit in additione."
"Tolle 3 de 7 manent 4, tolle 4 de 9 manent 5, & fimiliter totū alphabetum 1, 2, 3, 4, 5, 6, 7, 8, 9. Omni genere verfandum est. Hic Pythagoreus fubductionis abacus eft." Fol. a$_4$ verso.

Tonstall (1522), after explaining how to subtract numbers of several figures, states in words the differences from 1 - - - 9 and recommends that they be learned.

"Quod fi quis ignorat: unius horae labor;
Modo intentus fit animus; fi suppeditabit."   Fol. F$_1$ recto.

50   SIXTEENTH CENTURY ARITHMETIC

Ramus began at the left and proceeded to the right.[1] This is his first example, where the influence of line-reckoning is again seen in the crossing of the figures. Ramus was not the first to subtract from left to right, for

111
345
234

The following is Tonstall's table:

[table of subtraction figures]

Folio F$_2$ recto.

The following is Tartaglia's (1556 ed.) table:

De 0. a cauarne 0. resta —— 0   De 2. a cauarne 2. resta —— 0
De 1. a cauarne 0. resta —— 1   De 3. a cauarne 2. resta —— 1
....
De 10. a cauarne 0. resta —— 10   De 10. a cauarne 2. resta —— 8

De 1. a cauarne 1. resta —— 0   De 3. a cauarne 3. resta —— 0
De 2. a cauarne 1. resta —— 1   De 4. a cauarne 3. resta —— 1
....
De 10. a cauarne 1. resta —— 9   De 10. a cauarne 3. resta —— 7,

and so on to the table 10 — 10 = 0, which contains this one fact only.
Fol. C$_1$ recto.

[1] Ramus, Arithmeticae Libri Duo (1586 ed.). "Si dati ſint plurium notarum ſubducendo infra alterum poſito, ſubductio ſit á ſiniſtra dextrorſum, reliquoq̧; ſupernotato delentur dati, ut ſi de ſumma aeris illius alieni 345 ſubducēda ſit 234: Diſpoſitis ordine numeris hoc modo: 345 ſubducendo infra, ſupra autem á quo ſubductio facienda, incipiam á   234
ſiniſtra dextrorſum, contra quā in additione, tollo 2 de 3 manet 1, & ſupernoto 1 deletis 3 & 2. Deinde ſubducam 3 de 4 manet 1, &
ſupernoto 1 deletis 4 & 3. Deniq̧ ſubductis 4 de 5 manet 1, &   111
ſupernotabo 1 deletis 5 & 4. Vnde inueniam reliquũ eſſe 111. cum   345
ſubduxero 234 á 345. Inductio tota ſic erit. Fol. A$_4$ verſo.   234

the same thing was done in the Lilivati, and possibly in older works.[1] Many calculators to-day recommend working from left to right in both addition and subtraction, usually confining the addition to two addends. But Ramus added from right to left in all cases and subtracted from left to right. He was unique in his century, also, in placing the difference above the minuend, as shown in the example.

The case of subtraction in which the subtrahend figure exceeds in value the minuend figure, received a diversity of treatment. The three distinct methods usually taught were: (1) Ten is added to the minuend figure before the subtrahend figure is subtracted; one is then added to the next subtrahend figure. (2) The arithmetic complement of the subtrahend figure is added to the minuend figure, and one is added to the next subtrahend figure. (3) Ten is added to the minuend figure, and the subtrahend figure is subtracted from this sum; one is then subtracted from the next minuend figure. The last is the form of solution most prevalent to-day. Lists of authors who used these respective methods are given below;[2] from these lists it will be noticed that the first and second methods were equally popular, while the third method was used very little. Ramus, subtracting from left to right, used the third method, for which he gave the following example

---

[1] See H. Suter, Bibliotheca mathematica, VII$_3$ 15. Gerhardt, "Etudes," page 5.

[2] Those who used the first kind were: Piero Borgi (1484), Tonstall (1522), Paciuolo (1494), Rudolff (1526), Cardan (1539), Noviomagus (1539), Tartaglia (1556), Van der Scheure (1600). Tonstall also gave this process in the following form:

$$\begin{array}{cccc} 2 & 9 & 10 & 10 \\ \not{3} & \not{0} & \not{1} & \not{0} \\ 1 & 1 & 1 & 1 \\ \hline 1 & 8 & 9 & 9 \end{array}$$

Those who used the second ford were: Widman (1489), Tonstall (1522), Paciuolo (1494), Tartaglia (1556), Gemma Frisius (1540), Riese (1522), Trenchant (1571), Baker (1562), Unicorn (1598), Huswirt (1501), and Finaeus (1525). This method goes back to the Hindu arithmeticians. Fink, Geschichte der Elementar-Math. (Beman and Smith's translation, Chicago, 1900), p. 98.

Those who used the third kind were: Paciuolo (1494), Köbel (1531), Tartaglia (1556), Champenois (1578), Buteo (1559), and Raets (1580).

and explanation: "When I take 3 from 4, I shall not write 1, because the following subtrahend figure, 4, is greater than the 3 placed above, but I shall keep this in mind and take the next figure below, which is 4, from 13. This leaves 9, which for the same reason I shall not write down, but shall take 1 from it and write 8 above, and keep 1 in mind, because the following figure to be subtracted is greater; then 5 from 12 leaves 7, which will be written above."[1]

    87
    432
    345

The proofs in subtraction, as in the case of all operations, were very prominent. The three standard methods were casting out nines, casting out sevens, and adding the subtrahend and difference.[2] About three times as many writers used the additive method as used either of the others, which was natural on account of its ease and effectiveness.[3] Tartaglia, who gave each of the proofs above, also subtracted the remainder

---

[1] Ramus, Arithmeticae Libri Duo (1586 ed.). "Vt ſi ſubducenda ſint 345 de 432, cúm ſubducam 3 de 4 non ſupernotabo 1, quia 4 ſequens ſubducenda nota major est ſuperapoſita 3, ſed illud mente reſervabo, 4 ſubductis á 13 manerēt 9, quae nequaquam propter eandem cauſam notabo, ſed uno minus 8 tantum ſupernotabo, & unum mente reſervabo, quia ſequens ſubducēda nota major est. Itaq; 5 ſubductis á 12 reliqua 7 ſupernotabo. Vnde inveniam ſubductis 345 de 432 relinqui 87. Tota inductio ſic erit: 87
               432
               345

"Trium ſociorum pecunia in unum acervum congeſta ſit 432: primiq; ſumma ſit incerta, conſtet tamen ſocios capere 345: ergo ſuam partem is per hac ſubductionem cognoſcet." Fol. A₅ recto.

[2] Piero Borgi, Arithmetica (1540 ed.), fol. C₆ verso. Example. Proof.
                                                                     456   333
                                                                     123   123
                                                                     333   456

[3] The proof by casting out nines was used by Rudolff (1526), Widman (1489), Cardan (1539), Tartaglia (1556), Gemma Frisius (1540), Suevus (1593).

The proof by casting out sevens was used by Widman (1489), Cardan (1539), Tartaglia (1556), Unicorn (1598).

The addition proof was used by Borgi (1484), Widman (1489), Cardan (1539), Tartaglia (1556), Riese (1522), Champenois (1578), Raets (1580), Unicorn (1598), Jacob (1599), Van der Scheure (1600).

from the minuend to find the subtrahend, as in addition he subtracted the sum of all the addends but one from the result to find the other addend.

The terminology and symbolism used have several points of interest. In those works which used the plan of supplying 10 from the next order of the minuend to make subtraction possible, one naturally seeks to find a trace of the modern vulgarism "to borrow," and recognizes it in the word "entlehen" used by Köbel.[1] This is suggestive, because Köbel was primarily an abacist, and he would probably employ the same word in the algorism that was employed to describe the actual borrowing process in abacus reckoning. In the tables and examples of subtraction there is suggested the word "rest" in the sense of difference, or remainder.[2] The book material of addition and subtraction presents

---

[1] Köbel, Zwey Rechenbüchlin (1537 ed.), fol. P$_4$ recto *et seq.*

For discussion see Brooks, Philosophy of Arithmetic (1901 ed.), pp. 45, 46; 219, 220. Unger, Die Methodik, pp. 73, 74.

[2] Tartaglia, La Prima Parte (1556). "Sottrare non è altro che duoi proposti numeri, inequali saper trouare la loro differentia, cioe quanto che il maggiore eccede il menore, come saria a sottrare .4. de .9. *restaria* .5." Fol. Bvi verso.

    79374
     5024
    ―――――
    74350 —— Il numero *restante.*

Unicorn, De L'Arithmetica vniversale (1598), calls the remainder *numero restante,* or *resta dare,* or *residue.*

Trenchant, L'Arithmetique (1578 ed.), calls the remainder *reste.* Fol. B$_8$ recto.

Baker, The Well Spring of Sciences (1580 ed.), does not use the terms minuend and subtrahend, but says, in taking 6 and 9, "there resteth 3." Fol. Ciii verso.

a much different appearance from that of the modern treatment, because of the lack of symbols of operation. Although the symbols + and — were in existence in the fifteenth century,[1] and appeared for the first time in print in Widman[2] (1489), as shown in the illustration (p. 53), they do not appear in the arithmetics as signs of operation until the latter part of the sixteenth century. In fact, they did not pass from algebra to general use in arithmetic until the nineteenth century. They were used in the sixteenth century to express excess and deficit in weight,[3] as shown in note 3, where the first column is *zentners* and the second *pounds*. These early printed examples substantiate the theory that the symbols +, —, originated

[1] Müller, Historisch-Etymologische Studien über mathematische Terminologie.

[2] Widman, Behend und hüpsch Rechnung uff allen Kauffmanschafften (1508 ed.), fol. h$_5$ recto.

[3] Wencelaus, T'Fondament Van Arithmetica (1599 ed.).

"Pijpen Olie van Oliven/ weghende alsoo hier naer volcht/ Tara op elcke pijpe/ 140. ℔.1. lauther 100. cost 50. fl. 6. d. Hoe veel beloopter in ghelde?"

WEECHT.

	cent. lb.		cent. lb.		cent. lb.
No. 1.	9 + 38.	No. 4.	9 + 50.	No. 7.	10 — 25.
No. 2.	9 + 44.	No. 5.	9 + 55.	No. 8.	9 + 68.
No. 3.	10 — 20.	No. 6.	9 + 56.	No. 9.	9 + 70.

"Dit + beteyckent Plus/ ende dit — Minus."

"Item 9. pipes, d'huyle d'Olives pesants comme s'ensuit tara pour chascune pipe 140. ℔. & couste 1. cent netto 50 fl. 6 d. Combien monte le tout en argent.

"Facit L. 186. fl. 4. d. 10^{14}/$_{25}$.

"Cecy + signifie plus, cecy — moins." Page 59.

The problem is the same in each case, the book being printed in two languages in parallel columns. The translation of the problem is:

"Nine casks of olive oil have the weights given below, the tare for each cask is 140 lb., and 1 centner net costs 50 florins 6 denarii. What is the entire cost?"

WEIGHT.

	cent. lb.		cent. lb.		cent. lb.
No. 1.	9 + 38.	No. 4.	9 + 50.	No. 7.	10 — 25.
No. 2.	9 + 44.	No. 5.	9 + 55.	No. 8.	9 + 68.
No. 3.	10 — 20.	No. 6.	9 + 56.	No. 9.	9 + 70.

Ans. L. 186, fl. 4, d. 10^{14}/$_{25}$.

+ means more, — means less.

THE ESSENTIAL FEATURES

from the marks placed on packages to designate excess and deficit with respect to listed weight.

Van der Scheure, in his Arithmetica (1600), fol. z_1 verso, defines the symbol + and — as signs of operation thus:

+ Plus Soubstraheert [1]
— Minus Addeert.

He lapses, however, into using ÷, an old form of the minus sign, in the solution of his problems.[2] The use of these signs is to indicate operation, and their algebraic meaning, when employed in equations, is seen in Thierfeldern.[3]

The lack of these symbols made tabulation in sentence form impossible without the use of words. Hence, the tabular facts of addition, subtraction, and also of multiplication were ex-

---

[1] This spelling for subtract is not an accident. The title of the chapter is Substractio, fol. B_2 verso. It was quite common in the Dutch books of that time to spell subtraction "substraction," a spelling not unheard of to-day and declared erroneous by lexicographers.

[2] Van der Scheure, Arithmetica (1600), fol. z_1 verso.
"+ Plus Soustraheert.
"— Minus Addeert.
"Soo 9. Eyers + 2. blancken soo veel weert zijn als 12. blancken ÷ 21. Eyers/ Hoe veel Eyers coopt men dan om een blancke."

If 9 eyers and 2 blancken are worth as much as 12 blancken minus 21 eyers, how many eyers are worth as much as one blancke?

```
    12 ÷ 21         9 + 2          1
     2              21
    ──             ──
    10             30              Facit 3 Eyers.
```

[3] Thierfeldern, Arithmetica (1587), page 110. "Item/ 18 fl. weniger 85 gr. machen gleich so vil als 25 fl. ÷ 232 gr. wie vil hat 1 fl. groschen? facit 21 gr."

18 florins minus 85 groschens are equal to 25 florins minus 232 groschens, how many groschens are there in 1 florin? Ans. 21 gr.

In disen beyden Exempeln (he has given another example)/ addir das Minus/ und subtrahir das Plus/ wie hie:

```
    18 fl. ÷ 85 gr. gleich 25 fl. ÷ 232 gr.
                         + 85
    ─────────────────────────────
    18 fl.    gleich     25 fl. ÷ 147 gr.
    18 fl.  |  147 gr. gleich 25 fl.
                         18
    ─────────────────────────────
          147 gr. gleich 7 fl.
    7 fl.       147 gr.       1 fl.  facit 21 gr.  Page 110.
```

pressed in words or in ruled tables according to a chosen device.[1] This condition of affairs in the formative period of arithmetic is responsible for the ruled tables still found in modern arithmetics, 300 years after the necessity for them has disappeared. Some of them should be retained, doubtless, because of their suggestiveness in showing number relations, but many of them might be omitted to advantage.

As in the case of addition, there are many instances of beginning with a concrete problem.[2] Some writers who began addition with abstract problems began subtraction with the concrete ones. The following will illustrate:[3] "A man owed 800,347 livres, of which he has paid 409,-653 livres: I wish to know how much he still owes." These problems are usually real situations, not concrete merely in the sense of being subtraction of denominate numbers. The problems given below from Champenois illustrate this tendency and also the care taken in grading the steps in the process:[4]

```
800347
409653
------
390694
```

[1] See page 50, of this article.
[2] See page 48, of this article.
[3] Trenchant, L'Arithmetique (1578 ed.). "Vn homme doit 800347 l'fur quoy il en payé 409653 liures: fi ie veux fçauoir combien il doit de refte." Fol. B₈ recto.

```
| Dette   800347
| Paye    409653
|        -------
| Refte   390694
```

[4] Champenois, "Les Institvtions De L'Arithmetique" (1578).

"Vn marchant a 58786 liures pefant de merchandife, & en vendu 35040 liures. On demande combien il a de refte." Page 17, or fol. C₁ recto.

"Le Commis general des viures a 478759 pains, & en diftribué 27000 pains. On demande combien il en de refte." Page 18, fol. C₁ verso.

"Vn Architect a marchandé faire vne muraille qui contiēt 876 toifes, en a faict 374 toifes. On demande combien il en a encor à faire." Page 19, fol. Cij recto.

"Le Commis des viures du camp du Roy a 548 muids de blé, defquels il en a diftribué 273 muids. On demande côbien il en a encor' de refte." Page 20, fol. Cij verso.

```
    4
  ⁄548
   273
   ---
   275
```

"A merchant had 58,786 livres weight of merchandise and sold 35,040 livres. It is required to find how much he had left."

"The commissary-general had 478,759 loaves of bread and distributed 27,000 loaves. It is required to find how much he had left."

"An architect had bargained to make a wall which should contain 876 toises, of which he had made 374 toises. It is required to know how much he had still to make."

"The steward of a royal camp had 548 measures of grain, of which he had distributed 273 measures. It is required to find how much still remains."

Multiplication

Two classes of writers may be distinguished easily by comparing their methods of treating multiplication. There were those who emphasized the formal processes themselves, and those who considered chiefly the applications of the processes. The former class of writers made much of tabular forms and devices, the latter made much of simple rules and commercial problems. Both gave the multiplication tables at the outset, which may be classified into three kinds: tabula per colonne,[1]

---

[1] Rudolff, "Kunstliche rechnung mit der Ziffer und mit den zal pfennige/" (1534 ed.), fol. Av verso.

```
        1    1
        2    2                2    4
        3    3                3    6            3     9
        4    4                4    8            4    12
1 mal   5 ist 5       2 mal   5 ist 10   3 mal  5 ist 15   and so on to 9
        6    6                6    12           6    18    mal 9 ist 81.
        7    7                7    14           7    21
        8    8                8    16           8    24
        9    9                9    18           9    27
```

Borgi, Arithmetica (1540 ed.), fol. A_6 verso.

```
1 via  1 sa   1      2 via  3 sa  6      3 via  4 sa 12     8 via  9 sa 72
2 via  2 sa   4      2 via  4 sa  8      3 via  5 sa 15     8 via 10 sa 80
3 via  3 sa   9      3 via  5 sa 10      3 via  6 sa 18
............        .............        ............      9 via 10 sa 90
10 via 10 sa 100    2 via 10 sa 20       3 via 10 sa 30
```

In the same way he gave tables of 16s, 20s, 24s, 32s, 36s.

or column tables; the tables ruled in squares,[1] or square tables; and the tables arranged in triangles,[2] or triangular tables.

Tartaglia gave the tables—

0. fia 0. fa 0   1. fia 0. fa 0
0. fia 1. fa 0   1. fia 1. fa 1   and so on to
0. fia 2. fa 0   1. fia 2. fa 2
....   10. fia 10. fa 100
0. fia. 10. fa 0   1. fia 10 fa 10

These tables were set apart to be learned. Then followed the tables of 11s, 12s, 13s, --- 40s for reference, and the first set of tables with the middle numbers ten times as large; that is, from 0. fia 0. fa 0 to 10. fia 100. fa 1000. These latter were next combined thus:

11. fia 20. fa 220   20. fia 10. fa 200
11. fia 30. fa 330   and so on to   20. fia 20. fa 400
....
11. fia 100. fa 1100   20. fia 100. fa 2000

Finally he completed the tables from 11. fia 11. fa 121 to 20. fia 20. fa 400. Thus,

11. fia 11. fa 121   12. fia 12. fa 144
11. fia 12. fa 132   12. fia 13. fa 156   and so on to
....
11. fia 20. fa 220   12. fia 20. fa 240   20. fia 20. fa 400

The tables of 12s, 20s, 24s, 25s, 32s, and 36s of this list he called "Per Venetia," because they were used in reckoning with Venetian money.

[1] Tonstall, De Arte Supputandi (1522), fol. G$_3$ recto.

1	2	3	4	5	6	7	8	9	10
2	4	6	8	10	12	14	16	18	20
3	6	9	12	15	18	21	24	27	30
4	8	12	16	20	24	28	32	36	40
5	10	15	20	25	30	35	40	45	50
6	12	18	24	30	36	42	48	54	60
7	14	21	28	35	42	49	56	63	70
8	16	24	32	40	48	56	64	72	80
9	18	27	36	45	54	63	72	81	90
10	20	30	40	50	60	70	80	90	100

[2] Cirvelo, Tractatus Arithmetice practice (1513 ed.), fol. Avi recto.

	0	9	8	7	6	5	4	3	2	1
	1	9	8	7	6	5	4	3	2	1
	2	18	16	14	12	10	8	6	4	
	3	27	24	21	*28	15	12	9		
	4	36	32	28	24	20	16			
	5	45	40	35	30	25				
	6	54	48	42	36					
	7	63	56	49						
	8	72	64							
*	6	81								

* Typographical errors in the original.

THE ESSENTIAL FEATURES

The column tables were used by the best commercial writers, and occasionally by the theoretic writers. The square arrangement, called the Pythagorean table, was used generally by authors of Latin School arithmetics. The triangular arrangement, constructed by some from left to right and by others from right to left, as shown in the notes, was the one in general favor. It will be noticed in the triangular table of p. 58, that the products 2 times 3 = 6, 3 times 4 = 12, and so on, appear, but that 3 times 2 = 6, 4 times 3 = 12, and so on, do not. Since any product, as 2 times 3, in one of these sets was deemed sufficient to represent itself and the corresponding product, as 3 times 2, in the other set, it is plain that writers recognized the commutative law of multiplication. The rows in the triangular table begin with square numbers. Gemma Frisius,[1] a famous Latin School writer, called attention to this, and Ramus[2] said that the pupil should first learn to multiply

[1] Gemma Frisius, Arithmeticae Practicae Methodus Facilis, fol. B$_1$ verso.

Quadratinumeri.

1	2	3	4	5	6	7	8	9	1
	4	6	8	10	12	14	16	18	2
		9	12	15	18	21	24	27	3
			16	20	24	28	32	36	4
				25	30	35	40	45	5
					36	42	48	54	6
						49	56	63	7
							64	72	8
								81	9

[2] Ramus, Arithmeticae Libri Duo (1586 ed.), fol. A$_7$ verso, says that the pupil should first learn to multiply single numbers by themselves, as twice 2 are 4, 3 times 3 are 9, 4 times 4 are 16, and so on, then the multiplication of each single number with other single numbers as twice 3 are 6, twice 4 are 8, twice 5 are 10, and so on, but more attention should be given to larger numbers, as 9 eights are 72, 9 sevens, sixes, fives are 63, 54, 45, - - -, 8 sevens, sixes, fives are 56, 48, 40.

"E notis autem multitudinis perdifcat primis fingulas per fe multiplicare:

Bis 2 funt 4   Ter 3 funt 9
Quater 4 funt 16   Quinquies quina funt 25
Sexies 6 funt 36   Septies 7 funt 49
Octies 8 funt 64   Novies 9 funt 81

Huiusmodo multiplicatio quadratura dividitur, & numero factus hoc modo quadratus, factor autem latus quadrati. Fitq; ut numerus fecundum fuas unitates pofituo & additus tantundem faciat, quantum per fe multiplicatur, ut 2 & 2 faciunt 4: & bis 2 faciunt item 4. Sic 3 & 3 & 3 faciunt 9. & ter 3 faciunt item 9. Analogia etiam in talibus est continua, ut 1 ad factorem five latus, fic latus ad quadratum, ut in primo exemplo, ut 1 ad

the single numbers by themselves, as twice 2 are 4, 3 times 3 are 9, and so on. This shows what the disciplinary teachers of that time regarded as important.

The utilitarian writers, like Riese, Rudolff, and Köbel limited the elementary products to 9 × 9 or 10 × 10, occasionally including the tables of twelves. It was more definitely stated that these facts should be learned [1] than in the case of the elementary sums. Tables given beyond 10 × 10, as the 12s, 15s, 20s, 24s, usually related to the reduction of denominate numbers.[2] Thus, there were 12 denarii in 1 soldus, 20

2, fic 2 ad 4. Tum fingularum notarum cum fingulis multiplicatione fciat quid efficiatur.

Bis 3 funt 6: & ter 2 funt item 6.
Bis 4 funt 8: & quater 2 tantundem.
....
Octies 9 funt 72; & novies 8 tantundem." Fol. A₇ verso.

[1] Riese, Rechnung auff der Linien und Federn/ (1571 ed.).
"Vnd du muft vor allen dingen das Ein mal eins wol wiffen/ und auswendig lernen/ wie hie." Fol. Avi verso.
Köbel, Zwey rechenbůchlin (1537 ed.).
"Lern auswendig das Ein mal ein
So wird dir alle Rechnung gmeyn." Fol. E verso.

[2] Cataneo, Le Pratiche Delle Due Prime Matematiche (1547 ed.).

DEL MULTIPLICARE LIRE, SOLDI ET DENARI.

```
           "Et fe ti fuffe detto multiplica L 36. β 12. & dena. 7 per
36.12.7    9. Segnato che harai le tue quantita come in margine, et tu
    9      multiplica 7. uia 9. che fa 63. dena. che per effere ogni 12.
---------  denari un foldo i detti denari 63. faranno foldi 5. & dena. 3.
329.13.3   di che fegnerai li. 3. denari & faluerai li 5. β. dipoi multiplica
```
9. uie 12. & aggiugneli il 5. faluato & fara β 113. che per effere ogni foldi 20 una L i dette β 113. fono L 5. & β 13. onde fegnerai li β 13. & faluerai le L 5. Dipoi - - - multiplica 6. uie 9. & aggiugneli il 5. faluato & fara 59. L dellequali fegnerai 9. faluerai 5. Poi multiplica 3. uie 9. & aggiugneli il 5. faluato & fara 32. ilquali fegna come da lato & harai L 329. β 13. et denari 3. per la detta multiplicatione.

DEL MULTIPLICARE, MOGGIA STAIA ET. QVARTI.

```
           "Et dicendofi multiplica moggia 35. ftaia 11. & quarti 3. per
           15. Segnato che harai le quantita come dal lato è tu multiplica
           3. uie 15. che fa 45. quarti, perche ogni 4. quarti fanno uno
35.11.3    ftaio, i detti quarti 45. feranno. ftaia 11. & un quarto, onde
   15      fegnerai un quarto & faluerai le 11. ftaia. Dipoi multiplica
---------  11. uie 15 & aggiugneli lo 11. faluato & fara ftaia 176. che per
532. 8.1   effere ftaia 24. il moggio, le dette ftaia 176. fono moggia 7.
```

soldi in 1 lire, 24 staia in 1 moggia, and so on. Tartaglia (1556) calls these tables "Per Venetia," because they were based on the system of Venetian measures. The theoretic writers often filled in other tables, which were not of use in denominate numbers, in accordance with their policy of emphasizing pure and formal arithmetic.

In the formal process of multiplication more care was taken to grade the presentation than in addition and subtraction. Easy-graded steps appear in some of the earliest printed arithmetics. For example, Piero Borgi (1484) began with multipliers of one figure; he next gave problems in which the multiplier was a small number of two figures; then one in which it was a number of two figures ending in zero; then some with multipliers of three figures, and so on. It will be noticed that the multiplication by multipliers of two figures, as shown in examples [1] 2, 3 and 4 in note 1, was often accomplished without partial products. This was done by referring to the corresponding tables. See notes, pp. 57, 58, under Borgi and Tartaglia. The following eight methods from Paciuolo (1494) show with what mastery the leading scholars of arithmetic handled the Hindu algorism in the fifteenth century: [2]

& ſtaia 8. di che ſegnerai le ſtaia 6. ſaluerai le moggia 7.

"Dipoi multiplica. 5. uie. 15. et aggiugneli il. 7. ſaluato & fara. 82. delquale ſegnerai. 2. et ſaluerai. 8. Poi multiplica .3. uie .15. et a quel che fa aggiugnelo .8. ſaluato et ſara .53. quale ſegna come in margine & harai moggia .532, ſtaia .8. et un quarto per lo detto multiplicamento per uia del quale & del antedetto ti ſera facile il multiplicamento de gli altri ancho che uariati peſi o miſure fuffero." Fol. Biiij verso.

[1] Piero Borgi, Arithmetica (1540 ed.), fol. B verso, B_2 recto and verso.

1st 25	54	795	2d 345	3d 3456	4th 3456
3	7	9	12	20	24
75	378	7155	4140	69120	82944

[2] Paciuolo, Sũma de Arithmetica Geometria Proportioni et Proportionalita (1523 ed.).

"Ora e da dire e moſtrare in quãti modi queſto acto del multiplicare per la practica operatiua ſe coſtumi fare. Per laqual coſa dico che ſimili acto de multiplicare ſi coſtuma fare principalmente in octo modi: di quali el primo e detto multiplicare per ſchachieri in vinegia ouer per altro nome per bericuocolo in Firenza. El ſecondo modo di multiplicare e detto caſtel-

1. Per schachieri, as called in Venice, meaning tesselated. In Florence it was called bericuocolo.
2. Castellucio.
3. A Taveletta, or Per Colonna (by tables).
4. Per crocetta (crosswise).
5. Per quadrilatero (in form of a rectangle).
6. Per gelosia,[1] or graticola (lattice-work).
7. Per repiego (breaking up = factoring multiplier).
8. A scapezza (distributing = separating multiplier into addends).

1. ⓒ Multiplicatio bricuocoli vel fchacherij.
   (Multiplication bricuocoli or schacherii. Tesselated form.)
   Fol. 26 recto, or Dij recto.

```
Multiplicandus      9 8 7 6
Producendus         6 7 8 . 9
Multiplicans      | 8 | 8 | 8 | 8 | 4 |
                  | 7 | 9 | 0 | 0 | 8 |
                | 6 | 9 | 1 | 3 | 2 |          fchachieri
              | 5 | 9 | 2 | 5 | 6 |            bericocolo
Sūma            6 7 0 4 8 1 6 4    ρ.1.
```

2. ⓒ De .2⁰. modo multiplicandi dicto caftellucio.
   (The second method of multiplication called castelluccio.)
   Fol. 27 recto, or Diij recto.

```
                9876      6     Per .7.
                          6
                6789      1     Proua
                ─────────────
                61101000
Castelluccio.    5431200         The proof in each case is that of
                  476230         casting out sevens.
                   40734
                ─────────────
Sūma.           67048164   .1.
```

The chief feature consists in running the partial products to the right and filling the vacant places with zeros.

lucio. El terzo e detto multiplicare per colona ouer a tauoletta. El quarto modo de lo multiplicare e detto per crocetta: e altramente per casfelle. El quinto modo e detto per quadrilatero. El fexto modo e detto per gelofia: ouer gratiola. El feptimo modo e detto per repiego. Loctauo modo e detto multiplicare a fcapezzo." Fol. Dij recto, or 26 recto.

[1] So called because Italian ladies were protected from public view by lattice-work over their windows.

3. ℂ De tertio modo multiplicandi ditto colōna.
   (The third method of multiplication called colonna. By tables.)
   Fol. 27 verso, or Diij verso.

```
        Per .7.
   4685         2
     13         6
   -----       ---
  60905         5
  Proua         5
```

No partial products were needed in this method, since a table of 13s was presupposed.

4. ℂ De quarto mõ multiplicandi ditto crocetta fiue cafella.
   (The fourth method of multiplication called crocetta or casella. Crosswise multiplication.) Fol. 27 verso, or Diij verso.

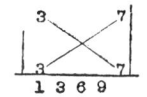

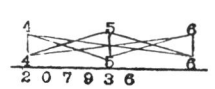

5. ℂ De quinto modo multiplicandi dicto quadrilatero.
   (The fifth method of multiplication called quadrilatero. In the form of a rectangle.) Fol. 28 recto, or Diiij recto.

29506624 Sũma

6. ℂ De fexto modo multiplicandi dicto gelofia: siue graticola.
   (The sixth method of multiplication called gelosia, or graticola. Lattice-work.) Fol. 28 verso, or Diiij verso.

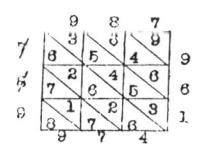

7. ℂ De feptimo modo multiplicandi ditto repiego.
   (The seventh method of multiplication called repiego. That is, multiplication by the factors of the multiplier separately.)

6[1] may be broken up into the factors 2 and 3. Since 2 times 3 make 6, the factors of 6 are 2 and 3. The factors of 10 are 2 and 5, since 2 times 5 make 10. It often happens that a number may be factored in different ways; for example, 12 has different groups of factors; it has the factors 2 and 6, since 2 times 6 are 12, also the factors 3 and 4, since 3 times 4 make 12. And thus 24 has several groups of factors, as 12 and 2, 3 and 8, and 4 and 6, which multiplied together make 24.

8. ⁌ De octauo modo multiplicandi dicto a ſchapezzo.
   (The eighth method of multiplication called a ſchapezzo, distributing.)

When[2] 42 is to be multiplied by 24, one of these numbers (it makes no difference which) may be resolved into several parts. As 24 may be resolved into four parts which added together make the whole number, as 4, 6, 5, 9, then commence with any one of these and multiply by 42. For instance, take 4, and 4 times 42 makes 168. Place this aside. Then 6 times

---

[1] Paciuolo, Sūma de Arithmetica Geometria Proportioni et Proportionalita (1523 ed.).
  "Si commo de .6. diremmo esfer el. 2. e. 3. Perche .2. via .3. fa .6. ſi che el repiego de .6. e .2. e .3. El repiego de .10. e .2. e .5. perche .2. via 5. fa 10. E acade molte volte vn numero hauer asfai repieghi varij e diuerfi: ſi como .12. ane piu repieghi: poche hane el repiego de .2. e .6. che .2. via .6. fa .12. Ane el repiego de .3. e .4. che .3. via .4. fa 12. E cosi .24. a piu repieghi/ cioe .2. e .12. e .3. e .8. e .4. e .6. che luno elaltro multiplicato fa .24. - - - : cioe per .6. e di .6. via .116. fa 696.
  Fol. 28 verso, 29 recto, or Diiij verso and Dv recto.

[2] Paciuolo, Sūma de Arithmetica Geometria Proportioni et Proportionalita (1523 ed.).
  "Si commo hauendo a multiplicare .42. via .24. dico che ne refolua vno de quefti numeri qual voli (che non fa cafo) in piu parti acio te ſia piu cō modo el multiplicare. Or ſia che tu refolua .24. in quatro parti che fieno luna .4. laltra .6. laltra .5. laltra .9. Dico che comenzi daqualuoli: e multiplicata via .42. Or fatte dal. 4. e di .4. via 42. fa .168. Qual metti da canto. E poi .6. via .42. fa .252. e poi falua fotto .168. de ritto luno e laitro: cioe numero fotto numero edicine fotto dicie ꝛc. E poi di .5. via .42. fa .210. e falua fotto le altre. E poi dirai .9. via .42. fa 378. Qual similmete falua fotto laltre e recogli mo tutte quefte .4. multiplicationi infieme cioe .168. 252. 210. e 378. fanno .1008. e tanto dirai che facia .24. via .42."
  Fol. 29 recto or Dv recto.

42 makes 252. Save this with the 168, etc. Then 5 times 42 makes 210. Place this with the others. Finally, 9 times 42 makes 378. Put this also under the others in the same manner, and then collect the four multiplications together, as 168, 252, 210 and 378 making 1008, which is the product of 24 and 42.

Tartaglia (1556) and Unicorn[1] (1598) each gave seven of the above methods, which shows not only Paciuolo's influence upon his countrymen, but also the tenacity with which theoretic writers held to disciplinary arithmetic.

Besides the above general processes, there are several particular ones of interest, such as complementary multiplication, arrangement of factors, and order of multiplying. The following is an example of complementary multiplication for finding the product of two digits, as given by Cirvelo (1513).[2] This was his plan of multiplying 6 by 8:

$$2 \text{ (the complement of 8)} \times 6 = 12 \qquad 6$$
$$\phantom{2 \text{ (the complement of 8)} \times 6 = 12 \qquad } 8$$
$$60 (= 10 \times 6) - 12 = 48 \qquad 48$$

A variation of this process was as follows: To multiply 7 by 8:

```
7.3    10 − 7 = 3     .Multiply the complements 3 and 2 (= 6).
8.2    10 − 8 = 2     Add the numbers 8 and 7, using only units'
___                   figure in the result.
56
```

Such multiplication was not commonly used. Riese justified its use because it was an available method for those who have not learned the tables.[3]

---

[1] Unicorn, De L'Arithmetica Universale (1598 ed.), often gives credit to Paciuolo.

[2] Cirvelo, Tractatus Arithmetice practice (1513 ed.). "Verbi gratia: octies ſex faciunt .48 nam octo diſtat a decez per duas vnitates: ergo ſubtrahitur .6. de ſexaginta q̄ ē ſua dena bis et remanebunt .48. Fol. a$_v$ recto.

According to Cantor, complementary multiplication was used by the Romans. It is possible that it antedates the invention of the abacus. Weissenborn, Gerbert, 171-2.

[3] Riese, Rechnung auff der Linien und Federn/ (1571 ed.). "Leret

Tonstall [1] said that, if the numbers are unequal, the larger should be placed above as the multiplicand. In the case of 185 times 13 bu., this arrangement would lead to a concrete multiplier, a form guarded against in modern teaching. But this was avoided by omitting all denominations from the numbers when used in calculation, as in example 2 above. The proper denomination was affixed to the result when obtained. Several examples of multiplication exist in which the higher orders of the multiplier are used first, the method da Fiorentini of Tartaglia being an example. The Castelluccio method of Paciuolo differs from these only in having the multiplier written above the multiplicand. There seems to have been no use at that time for beginning with the highest order of the multiplier. But, after the decimal fraction was introduced, this plan found a useful application in making approximations. For example, in the work in the margin the part at the right of the vertical line need not be calculated if the result is needed to tenths only.

```
    (1)        (2)
    185        185
   13 bu.       13
   ─────      ─────
```

```
   4567           3
   4326           0
   ─────────
   18268000
    1370100
     91340
     27402
   ─────────
   19756842
       0       0
```

```
    1.26
    2.35
   ──────
    2.5│2
     .3│08
     .0│630
   ──────
    2.9│610
```

Tests were prominent in multiplication, as in other operations, the proof by nines and the proof by seven being preferred. The example from Tartaglia at the top of p. 67 illustrates the proof by casting out sevens. Divi-

viel machen/ Muſt auch forne anheben/ Vnd fûr allen dingen das Ein mal eins/ auswendig lernen/ wie vorhin angezeiget/ oder mache es nach folgenden zweyen Regulen." Fol. Bv recto and verso.

| 8.2. | 7.3. | 6.4. | 6.4. |
9.1.	8.2.	8.2.	7.3.
7.2.	5.6.	4.8.	4.2.

The rule here suggested was known as the sluggard's rule.

Noviomagus (1544), Gemma Frisius (1540), Baker (1580), gave the second method.

[1] Tonstall, De Arte Supputandi (1522 ed.). "Et ſi numeri ſint inaequales: maior ſemper supra pro multiplicâdo ponatur: minor infra pro multiplicanti." Fol. G_8 verso.

sion was occasionally used to prove multiplication, although the explanation of division constituted a later chapter.[1]

$$\begin{array}{r} 5040 \\ 243 \\ 120960 \\ \hline 00 \end{array}$$

The short methods, although common, were confined to three classes: (*a*) the use of factors in the multiplier, (*b*) multiplication by multipliers ending in zero, and (*c*) cross-multiplication.

(*a*) Multiplication by using factors of the multiplier.

This plan has been illustrated already in Paciuolo's method, called repiego, number 7, page 63. The following occurs in Trenchant:[2] To multiply 87 by 9.

$$\begin{array}{r} 87 \\ 3 \\ \hline 261 \\ 3 \\ \hline 783 \end{array}$$

(*b*) Multiplication by numbers ending in zeros.

Piero Borgi, in multiplying 3456 by 20, gave the following explanation:[3] $6 \times 20 = 120$, then $5 \times 20 = 100$, $100 + 12 = 112$, of which the 2 belongs to tens' place; $4 \times 20 = 80$, $80 + 11 = 91$, of which the 1 belongs to hundreds' place; $3 \times 20 = 60$, $60 + 9 = 69$, the whole result is 69120. In his second method of multiplying by 20 he first multiplied by 2 and then by 10. Philip Calandri (1491) took up multiplication by 100 as a special case, giving problems about 100 oranges, 100 chickens, 100 calves, and various things. Tonstall directed placing at the right of the multiplicand as many zeros as there are in the multiplier.

$$\begin{array}{r} 3456 \\ 20 \\ \hline 69120 \end{array}$$

---

[1] Riese, Rechnung auff der Linien und Federn/ (1571 ed.), fol. Bvii recto.

[2] Trenchant, L'Arithmetique (1578 ed.), fol. C$_4$ recto.

[3] Borgi, Qui comēza la nobel opera de arithmeticha (1540 ed.).

"E fe hauefti a moltiplicar .3456. per .20. prima metterai le due figure in forma, poi cominciando dalle vnita dirai .6. via .20. fa .120. che fono apunto .12. defene fenza foprauanzo de vnita, & pero in luogo delle vnita metterai .0. e dirai nulla e tien .12. defene, poi alle defene .5. via .20. fa .100. e .12. che tenefti fa .112. che fono .11. centenara e .2. defene e metterai le defene a fuo luogo. e dirai .2. e tien .11. cētenara poi alli cētenara dirai .4. via .20. fa .80. e 11. che tenefti fa .91. che fono 9. miara e vn centenaro, e metterai il centenar a fuo luogo e dirai 1. e tiē 9. miara, poi alli miara dirai .3. via 20. fa .60. e .9 che tenefti fa .69. ilq̄l metterai a fuo luogo appreffo il. 1. fara 69120 adōque moltiplicato .3456. p. .20. fa 69120." Fol. B$_2$ recto.

$$\begin{array}{r} 3456 \\ 20 \\ \hline 69120 \end{array}$$

This method was also used by Rudolff and Cardan.[1] Gemma Frisius,[2] in multiplying two numbers, as 3600 by 7200, rejected the zeros, multiplied as usual, and then annexed the zeros to the result. This method was also used by Baker.[3]

(c) Cross-multiplication, known as per crocetta, or per crosetta.

The following example is taken from Tartaglia.[4] This method was also used by Paciuolo, Unicorn, Borgi, and several others who followed the Italian School.[5]

```
      36
      72
     ---
      72
     252
   2592|0000|

    4 5 6   1
    |×|×|
    4 5 6   3
1 4 8 2 0 0   3
        3    3
```

Cardan gave the following methods for aiding the memory in multiplication:

1. To multiply 27 by 33:
$27 + 33 = 60$ $60 \div 2 = 30$ $30^2 = 900$
$30 - 27 = 3$. $3^2 = 9$ $900 - 9 = 891 = 27 \times 33$.

2. To multiply 27 by 63:
$27 \times 6 = 162$ $27 \times 3 = 81$
$1620 + 81 = 1701 = 27 \times 63$.

3. To multiply 37 by 49:
$40 \times 50 = 2000$ $40 - 37 = 3$ $50 - 49 = 1$
$2000 + 3 = 2003$ $1 \times 40 = 40$
$3 \times 50 = 150 + 40 = 190$
$2003 - 190 = {*}2813 = 37 \times 49$.

4. To multiply multiples of 10:
$30 \times 70 = 21$ hundreds
$700 \times 800 = 56$ ten thousands $= 560000$
$17 \times 70 = 119$ tens $= 1190$.

Many writers of commercial arithmetic, and even some Latin School writers, as Gemma Frisius, proposed a concrete

[1] Cardan, Practica Arithmetice (1539 ed.), fol. Bvi verso.
[2] Gemma Frisius, Arithmeticae Practicae Methodus (1581 ed.), fol. B$_3$ recto.
[3] Baker, The Well Spring of Sciences (1580 ed.), fol. Dvi verso.
[4] Tartaglia, Tvtte L'Opere D'Arithmetica (1592 ed.), fol. E$_6$ recto.
[5] Cross multiplication is one of the six methods given by Bhaskara in the Lilivâti.

* Error in original.

example in multiplication before explaining the process. Calandri[1] gave as his first example: "Multiplica 9 vie 7389 ℈ 11 β 8 d. (Multiply 9 by 7389 ℈ 11 β 8 d.)" Gemma Frisius, for his first example with a multiplier of two figures, gave this example: "I wish to reduce 267 days to hours."[2] The following are from Champenois: "A squadron has 312 men in rank and 232 in file; how many men are there in the squadron?"

"A wall is 1212 toises in length and 4 toises high; how many toises are there in the wall?"[3]

Division

The methods of division used at that time have a peculiar interest. Most of the methods of adding, subtracting, and multiplying that were in general use in the sixteenth century are used to some extent at the present time, but the method of division most commonly used then is entirely obsolete now. This was known as the scratch, or galley method.[4]

A simple example from Baker will give the principles of the method:[5]

To divide 860 by 4.   The devidend.   860

Dividend 860   Deuisor.   4

Divisor 4 (2 quotient
         8 = (4 × 2) subtracting 8 from 8 leaves nothing to be placed above.

[1] Calandri, Arithmetica (1491 ed.), fol. 18 recto, or Cvi recto.

[2] Gemma Frisius, Arithmeticae Practicae Methodus Facilis (1581 ed.). "Exampli gratia, 267 dies valo redigere ad horas."

[3] Champenois, Les Institvtions De L'Arithmetique (1578 ed.). 'Vn efcadron contient en front 312 hommes, & en flanc 232. Lon demande combien il y a d'hommes en l'efcadron." Page 27, or fol. Cvi recto. "Vne muraille contient en longueur 1212 toifes, & en hauteur 4 toifes. On demande combien de toifes contiet la muraille." Page 29, or Cvii recto.

[4] The galley, or scratch, method of division is doubtless an inheritance, having its origin in the sand-table calculation of the Hindus. Treutlein, Abhandlungen, 1:55.
Maximus Planudes (c. 1330) also explains its origin in this way. Journal Asiatique, Series 6, vol. 1, p. 240.

[5] Baker, The Well Spring of Sciences (1580 ed.), fol. Dviii recto and verso, Ei recto.

SIXTEENTH CENTURY ARITHMETIC

In the next step the divisor is moved one place to the right.

$\not{8}\not{6}\not{0}(21$
$\overline{4}$

2 subtracting 4 (= 4 × 1) from 6)

4 is contained in 6 once, so 1 is written in the quotient.

2
$\not{8}\not{6}\not{0}(215$
4
$\not{2}\not{0}$

The 2 placed above is the remainder after having subtracted 4 from 6. This 2 in tens' place with the 0 still left in units' place forms 20. 20 divided by 4 leaves 5, the last figure of the quotient.

The following is an example of the scratch method from Tartaglia showing a remarkable form of galley:[1]

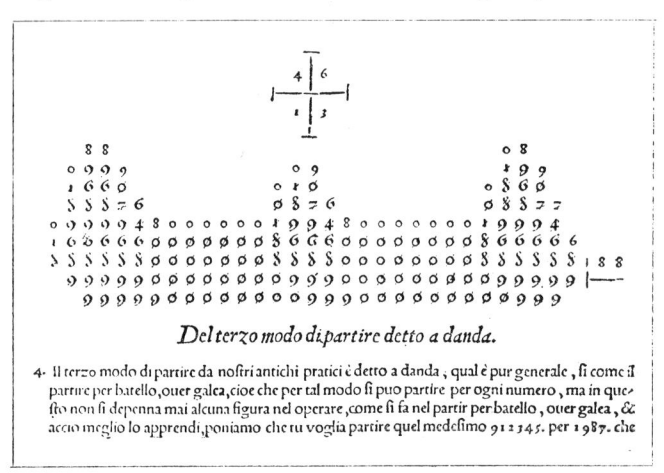

```
              4 | 6
           |--+--|
              1 | 3

    8 8                                              0 8
    0 9 9 9                    0 9                   1 9 9
    1 6 6 0                  0 1 6                 0 8 6 0
    5 5 5 7 6              0 8 5 6               0 8 5 7 7
  0 0 0 0 4 8 0 0 0 0   0 1 9 9 4 8 0 0 0 0   0 1 9 9 9 4
  1 6 6 6 6 6 0 0 0 0   0 0 8 6 6 6 0 0 0 0   0 0 8 6 6 6 6
  5 5 5 5 5 5 0 0 0 0   0 0 8 5 5 5 0 0 0 0   0 0 8 5 5 5 5 5 | 8 8
  9 9 9 9 9 0 0 0 0     0 0 9 9 9 0 0 0 0     0 0 9 9 9 9 9 9 |----
    9 9 9 9 9 0 0 0 0 0 0 0 9 9 9 0 0 0 0 0 0 0 9 9 9
```

Del terzo modo dipartire detto a danda.

4. Il terzo modo di partire da nostri antichi pratici è detto a danda, qual è pur generale, si come il partire per batello, ouer galea, cioè che per tal modo si può partire per ogni numero, ma in questo non si deponna mai alcuna figura nel operare, come si fa nel partir per batello, ouer galea, & accio meglio lo apprendi, poniamo che tu voglia partire quel medesimo 912345. per 1987. che

The downward method of the present day appeared among those used in the earliest printed arithmetics. This example is from Tartaglia:[2]

```
                      | auenimento (Quotient)
   partitore 1987     | 912345 | 459
   (Divisor)          --------
                        9123
                        7948
                        -----
                        11754
                         9935
                        -----
                        18195
                        17883
                        -----
   (Remainder) auanzo    312
```

[1] Tartaglia, La Prima Parte del general Trattato (1592 ed.), fol. Gv recto.

[2] Tartaglia, Tvtte L'Opere D'Arithmetica (1592 ed.), fol. G_6 verso.

THE ESSENTIAL FEATURES 71

Paciuolo also gave it as one of his methods, called division "a danda."

This illustration is from Calandri,[1] in whose book appears so far as known, the first downward division ever printed, although it is found occasionally in manuscripts of the fifteenth century.

The lists of writers given below show relatively the extent to which the galley method[2] and the downward method[3] were used. Nearly all who used the downward method also used the galley method, while many treated the galley method who did not explain the downward form.

Besides these general processes there were several other forms. The method a tavoletta, variously called per colona, di testa, per discorso, and per toletta, was used by Paciuolo

[1] Calandri, Arithmetica (1491 ed.), fol. 33 recto.

[2] Among those who used the galley methods were: Borgi (1484); Widman (1489); Cirvelo (1513); Tonstall (1522); Paciuolo (1494); Rudolff (1526); Köbel (1531); Cardan (1539); Noviomagus (1539); Tartaglia (1556); Gemma Frisius (1540); Riese (1522); Ramus (1567); Trenchant (1571), Champenois (1578); Baker (1568), Raets (1580); Unicorn (1598); Van der Scheure (1600).

[3] The downward method was used by Calandri (1491); Paciuolo (1523 ed.); Tartaglia (1556); Trenchant (1571); Unicorn (1598).

(1494), Tartaglia (1556), and Unicorn (1598). This is short division where the result of each part can be taken from the table. Tartaglia gave as examples:

Divisor 2)[1] 7953   Divisor 12)[2] 7630
Quotient   3976 Remainder 1. Quotient   635 Remainder 10.

The method a repiego (per repiego) was used by Paciuolo[3] (1494), Tartaglia, and Unicorn. In this method the divisor was separated into factors, as in the example:[4] To divide 5867 by 48. 5867 ÷ 6 = 733 with a remainder 3. 733 ÷ 6 = 122 with a remainder 1.

Wencelaus gave a form called by him Italian division, of which the following is an example:[5]

To divide 11664 by 48. He first divided the divisor, 48, into halves, fourths, eighths and sixteenths, the second group representing $1, \frac{1}{2}, \frac{1}{4}, \frac{1}{8}, \frac{1}{16}$. (The first zero evidently shows the lack of units, and the figures beginning at its right represent respectively tenths, hundredths,

Divisor		Quotient
48 ——	1	0125
24 ——	05	00625
12 ——	025	05
6 ——	0125	05
3 ——	00625	05

thousandths, and ten thousandths. It is a decimal system without the use of the decimal point, a device which did not appear until about 1600.) Beginning at the left of the dividend, 11,664, 11 is the first number that contains any one of the parts of the divisor as tabulated. The largest part which it contains is 6. The fraction which corresponds to it, 0125, is entered as part of the quotient, as tabulated at the right. 6 is then subtracted from 11 and the remainder, 5, is treated similarly. Since 5 contains

[1] Tartaglia, Tvtte L'Opere D'Arithmetica (1592 ed.), fol. F$_4$ recto.
a partir 2.//7953
ne vien — 3976 — e auanza 1
[2] Tartaglia, Tvtte L'Opere D'Arithmetica (1592 ed.), fol. F$_7$ verso.
a partir per 12// 7630
ne vien ——— 635 auanza 10
[3] Paciuolo gave four methods of division: first, a Regola, or a tavoletta (by table); second, per repiego (in parts); third, a danda (downward); fourth, a Galea or per galea (galley method).
[4] Tartaglia (1592 ed.), fol. G$_6$ verso.
[5] Wencelaus, T'Fondament Van Arithmetica (1599 ed.).

3, the next part of the quotient is the corresponding fraction, $\frac{1}{16}$, or 00625. 3 from 5 leaves 2, which is not in the list of parts of the divisor, hence the next figure of the dividend, 6, is annexed, making 26. This contains 24, so the corresponding 05 is written in the quotient, one place farther to the right, and so on. Whenever a new order of the dividend is used the partial quotient is set one place farther to the right. He gives as the complete form the example at the right.

```
    2
   522
 11664
  012 5
  0062 5
    05
     05
      0 5
  243
```

In the matter of detailed processes, Champenois was to French arithmeticians what Tonstall was to English writers, though less verbose. In his treatment of division Champenois gave twelve cases:[1]

1. To divide a digit by a digit.[2] (Exact division.)

[1] Champenois, Les Institvtions De L'Arithmetique (1578 ed.), Diij rector, or page 37 et seq.

[2] The division tables were not so common as the tables of multiplication. The inverse relation of division to multiplication was generally recognized, on which account one set of tables sufficed. A few writers who aimed at completeness gave tables of division.

E. g., Tartaglia, La Prima Parte (1556), fol. Eiiij recto.

1 in 0 intra 0 e auanza 0
(1 is contained in 0, 0 times with remainder 0.)
1 in 1 intra 1 e auanza 0
1 in 2 intra 2 e auanza 0
....
1 in 9 intra 9 e auanza 0

2 in 0 intra 0 e auanza 0   9 in 0 intra 0 e auanza 0
2 in 1 intra 0 e auanza 1   9 in 3 intra 0 e auanza 3
....
2 in 19 intra 9 e auanza 1   9 in 89 intra 9 e auanza 8

Tonstall, De Arte Supputandi (1522 ed.), used this inverted form of the Pythagorean table, fol. Y$_2$ recto.

100	90	80	70	60	50	40	30	20	10
90	81	72	63	54	45	36	27	18	9
80	72	64	56	48	40	32	24	16	8
70	63	56	49	42	35	28	21	14	7
60	54	48	42	36	30	24	18	12	6
50	45	40	35	30	25	20	15	10	5
40	36	32	28	24	20	16	12	8	4
30	27	24	21	18	15	12	9	6	3
20	18	16	14	12	10	8	6	4	2
10	9	8	7	6	5	4	3	2	1

2. To divide a digit by a digit with remainder.
3. To divide an article (a number ending in o) by a digit.
4. To divide a number whose first figure is smaller than the divisor.
5. To divide an article by an article.
6. To divide a composite number (a number formed by combining an article and a digit) by an article.
7. To divide a composite number by a composite number.
8. To divide a number when the number left after any subtraction is too small to be divided by the divisor, as $131328 \div 432 = 304$.
9. Inexact division.
10. When the remainder is greater than the divisor it proves that the division is incorrectly performed.
11. When the amount to be divided is less than the divisor, then fractions result.
12. To divide a number by 2.

Such development was not characteristic of the writers of that period. It was customary to begin with a dividend of several figures, but the methods of division were so radically different from our present ones that it is not safe to say that long division in the modern sense generally preceded short division. It is possible, however, to find indisputable cases of this plan.[1]

The proofs for division were casting out nines, casting out sevens, and the inverse operation. As has already been stated in this article, the prevalence of proofs was due to the influence of abacus reckoning, and not so much to a sense of the need for verification. Köbel in Germany and Baker in England seemed to realize the uselessness of appending several proofs to each operation, for they gave no proofs until all the operations with integers had been presented. Köbel then gave the proof of nines for all operations, and Baker gave the inverse operations. It would be a decided improvement on present teaching to introduce both the proofs by nines and by the inverse operations where practicable.

[1] Trenchant, L'Arithmetique (1578 ed.), fol. D$_3$ recto *et seq.*

A few short methods were used in division, the most common being those for dividing a number by 10, 100, and 1000. This example from Champenois will serve to illustrate:[1] "54736 livres are to be divided among 10 men." The quotient was formed by removing the last figure of the dividend and making it the remainder. Baker also explained in the same way the division by 100, 1000, and 10,000. Tagliente, after his explanation of division by 10, also explained division by 100 and 1000.[2] "And if you wish to divide 3497 by 100, do the same as above, taking off as many figures for a remainder as there are zeros in the divisor, as seen in the following division: 34|97." Similarly 749,745 by 1000, 749|745. A list of practical problems was given by Calandri in which the cost of 100 things was known and the cost of one required.[3]

A more general case is the division of numbers by multiples of 10. For example,[4] to divide 5,732 by 20, cut off the last figure of the dividend; divide the part at the left by 2. Change this remainder 1 to 10 and add the 2 cut off. Then 5732 divided by 20 gives 286 and the remainder, 12.

573|2
286 with
remainder 12

Finaeus[5] wrote down the multiples of the divisor before performing the division.

[1] Champenois, "Les Institvtions De L'Arithmetique (1578 ed.).
"Cōme f'il falloit diuifer 54736 liures à 10 hommes, fault trancher le dernier nombre de la fomme à diuifer 6. Le refte 5473. donnera le Quotient. Parquoy 54736. à partir à 10. hommes, c'eft à chacun 5473. liures, & 6. liures qui reftent à partir à 10 hommes." 5473(6
Fol. Eiij verso. 1(0

[2] Tagliente, Libro Dabaco (1515 ed.). "Et fe volefti partire 3497 per 100 tarai nel modo ditto dilopra taglia tante figuare quanti .o. li a el tuo parti doc come tu vedi qui fotto e fata partito. 34.|97." Similarly 749745 per 1000. 749|745. Note the bar used as a decimal point.

[3] Calandri, Arithmetica (1491 ed.). "Cento melarance choftorono 53 β 4 d. che uicne luna." 100 oranges cost 53 β 4 d., what is the cost of one? "Cento pollaftre (chickens) coftorono 26 y 10 β che uiene luna." "Cento capponi (capons) coftorono 97 y 1 β 8 d, che uiene luno." "Cēto uitelle (calves) coftorono 2354 y 10 β che uiene luna." Fol. 29 recto and verso, fol. (e) recto and verso.

[4] Tartaglia, Tvtte L'Opere D'Arithmetica (1592 ed.), fol. F$_7$ recto.

[5] Finaeus, De Arithmetica Practica (1555 ed.), fol. 9 recto.

Division, like the other processes, was occasionally introduced by concrete examples. Gemma Frisius follows his definitions of dividend, divisor, and the remainder with:[1] "433656 aurei are to be divided among 72 men, what will each receive?" and Köbel's first example is:[2] "There are 5 companions who must share equally 40 guldens. They would like to know what part each should have."

Doubling and Halving

A striking example of extreme subdivision and classification is the appearance of Duplatio (doubling) and Mediatio (halving) in the list of Species. To the student of the present there seems to be no reason why doubling and halving should have been treated independent of multiplication and division. That the reason was not apparent to scholars of that day is shown by this statement from Gemma Frisius:[3] "Some are wont to regard Duplatio and Mediatio as operations separate from multiplication and division. I do not understand what influences those stupid ones, since to double is to multiply by 2 and to halve is to divide by 2. If these operations are distinct, an indefinite number of operations will arise for consideration, as triplatio, quadruplatio, and so on." In discussing the contents of the Bamberg Arithmetic (1483), Cantor says:[4] "The treatment of doubling and halving as particular species or wholly unknown as such is the infallible sign of whether the writer belongs to the school of Jordanus or to that of Leonardo. The Bamberg Arithmetic treats of these

---

[1] Gemma Frisius, Arithmeticae Practicae Methodus Facilis (1581 ed.). "Ut fi diuidendi fint 433656 aurei 72 hominibus." Fol. B$_4$ recto.

[2] Köbel, Zwey rechenbüchlin (1537 ed.). "Es fein fünff Gefellen/ die haben zu theylen 40. gulden/ und wolten gern wiffen wie vil iedem zu seinem theyl werden solt." Fol. F verso.

[3] Gemma Frisius, Arithmeticae Practicae Methodus Facilis (1581 ed.). "Solent non nulli Duplationem & Mediationem a fignare species diftinctas à multiplicatione & divifione. Quid vero monuerit stupidos illos nefio, cùm & finitio & operatio eadem fit, Duplare enim, eft per duo multiplicare. Mediare vero, per duo partiri. Quod fi hae operationes fint diftincti, infinitae jam nobis exorientur fpecies, triplatio, quadruplatio &c. Sed fatis de illis." Fol. B$_3$ verso.

[4] Cantor, M., Geschichte der Mathematik (3d ed., 1900), Bd. II, page 227.

THE ESSENTIAL FEATURES 77

operations as special cases under the Species and knows nothing of them as separate species; thus it is an emanation of Italian teaching spreading to southern Germany." That these operations were accorded a high degree of independence is shown by the fact that Widman, Köbel, and Riese placed them before multiplication and division. The following may be taken as typical examples under these processes:

41232 [1]   1 1 1 [2]   15241578570190521½ [3]
─────   43672136(21836068   Divisor 2 Quo. 7620789285095260
 82464   22222222

The first is an example in duplatio from Riese and the second an example in mediatio from Gemma Frisius. Gemma Frisius, however, treats mediatio simply as a case under division.

DENOMINATE NUMBERS

Having now discussed the four operations with integers, the order of the remaining subjects must be taken arbitrarily, since there was no uniformity in this matter in sixteenth century works. By some writers fractions and denominate numbers [4] were both treated under operations with integers, and

[1] Riese, Rechnung auff der Linien und Federn/ (1571 ed.), fol. Biiij recto.

[2] Gemma Frisius, Arithmeticae Practicae Methodus Facilis (1581 ed.), fol. B$_6$ verso.

[3] Widman, Behend und hüpsch Rechnung (1508 ed.), fol. Ci verso.

[4] Among those who treated the operations with integers separately were: Riese (1522); Tartaglia (1556); Borgi (1484); Widman (1489); Tonstall (1522); Champenois (1578); Rudolff (1526); Gemma Frisius (1540); Noviomagus (1539).

Among those who treated operations with denominate numbers under the respective operations with integers were: Raets (1580); Unicorn (1598); Calandri (1491); Baker (1562); Van der Scheure (1600); Cataneo (1546); Cardan (1539).

Cardan treated under each operation all phases: e. g., under addition he treated addition of integers, denominate numbers, fractions, surds, powers, roots, similarly under the other operations.

The expression "denominate numbers" was used by Cardan to denote powers and roots of numbers. Thus,

cosa.   census.   cubus.   census census.   Relatum primum.
  2   4   8   16   32

or the first, second, third, fourth, fifth, powers of 2 are given under the last section of Chapter I on Arithmetic, fol. Avi recto.

seldom were fractions and denominate numbers wholly separated from each other.

A thorough treatment of denominate numbers was important, not only because of their relation to commercial arithmetic, but because the variety and complexity of the systems of weights and measures then in use laid a heavy burden on methods of calculation. This is well illustrated in a work by Cataneo.[1] In order to make his application of denominate numbers clear, it is necessary to explain a few tables:

Measures of Length.

12 momementi make one minuto
12 minuti make one atomo
12 atomi make one punto
12 punti make one oncia
12 oncie make one braccia
(6 braccie make one cauezza).
The braccia was equivalent to 31 inches.

Measures of Surface.

1 cauezza by 1 cauezza is an area of ¼ tauole, or 3 piedi
1 cauezza by 1 braccia is an area of ½ piede
1 cauezza by 1 oncia is an area of ½ oncia
1 cauezza by 1 punto is an area of ½ punto

1 braccia by 1 braccia is an area of 1 oncia
1 braccia by 1 oncia is an area of 1 punto
1 braccia by 1 punto is an area of 1 atomo

---

[1] Cataneo, Dell' arte Del Misvrare Libri Dve.
12, momementi fanno vn minuto.
12, minuti, fanno vn atomo.
12, atomi, fanno vn punto.
12, punti, fanno vn oncia.
12, oncie, fanno vn piede, in fuperficie, & vn braccia in linea.
                Fol. C₃ verso.
Cauezzi fia cauezzi, fanno quarti di tauole, ouero piede 3 fuperficiali.
Cauezzi fia braccie, fanno mezi piedi fuperficiali.
Cauezzi fia oncie, fanno meze oncie fuperficiali.
Cauezzi fia punti, fanno mezi punti fuperficiali.
Braccia fia braccia, fanno oncie fuperficiali.
Braccia fia oncie, fanno punti fuperficiali.
Braccia fia punti, fanno atomi fuperficiali.
Oncie fia oncie, fanno atomi fuperficiali.
Oncie fia punti, fanno minuti fuperficiali.
Punti fia punti, fanno momenti fuperficiali. Fol. C₃ recto and verso.

THE ESSENTIAL FEATURES

1 oncia by 1 oncia is an area of 1 atomo
1 oncia by 1 punto is an area of 1 minuto
1 punto by 1 punto is an area of 1 momento

The ratio between the consecutive square units is 12. That is, 12 mom. = 1 min., 12 min. = 1 atom, 12 at. = 1 punti, etc.

The following is Cataneo's method of computing the area of the trapezoid whose dimensions are given in the figure:

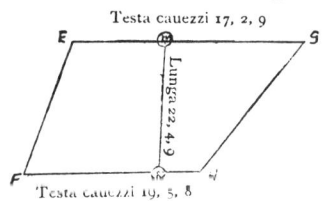

Testa cauezzi 17, 2, 9
Lunga 22, 4, 9
Testa cauezzi 19, 5, 8

	"Settima Ragione, Della quinta Figvra	(The seventh solution of the) (fifth figure = one above)
(Upper base)	Tefta cau. 17, bra. 2, on. 9.	(Lengths of bases as given
(Lower base)	Tefta cau. 19, bra. 5, on. 8.	in the figure.)
(Sum)	Somma cau. 37, bra. 2, on. 5.	(See linear table.)

[1] Larghezza cau. 18, bra. 4, on, 2, pun. 6. (Half sum of bases.)
Lunghezza cau. 22, bra. 4, on. 9. (Altitude.)

[2] Doppi cauezzi 9, bra. 4, on. 2, pun. 6.
Doppi cauezzi 11, bra. 4, on. 9.

Tauole 99.
Tauole 3, pie 8.
Tauole 0, pie 1, on. 10.
Tauole 0, pie 0, on. 5, pun. 6.
Tauole 3, pie 0.
Tauole 0, pie 1, on. 4.
Tauole 0, pie 0, on. 0, pun. 8.
Tauole 0, pie 0, on. 0, pun. 2.
Tauole 0, pie 6, on. 9.
Tauole 0, pie 0, on. 3.
Tauole 0, pie 0, on. 0, pun. 1, at. 6.
Tauole 0, pie 0, on. 0, pun. 0, at. 4, m. 6.

Tauole 106. pie 6. on. 8. pun. 5. at. 10. m. 6.
pun 2|6 min.
Proua   oncie 3|6 min.   Fol. G₄ recto.

[1] Larghezza is width and Lunghezza is length. The area of the trapezoid equals that of a rectangle whose dimensions are ½ the sum of the bases of the trapezoid and its altitude.

[2] Since 1 cau. × 1 cau. = ¼ Tauole (see tables), ½ of 18 and ½ of

The vigorous commercial activity of that time demanded a knowledge of weights and measures used in all the trading centers of Europe. A comparison of these reveals not only a great number of denominations, but also a lack of uniformity in each denomination. An idea of what a "hundred-weight" might mean in the fifteenth century may be obtained from this excerpt from Chiarini:[1] "The 100 lb. of Florence is 103 lb. in Siena, 102 to 104 in Perugia; in Lucca 102 lb. equals 105 lb. in Pisa, and at present is the same as Florentine weight."

A comparison of this list with corresponding data given by Raets a century later shows the persistency of a condition which finally led to the establishment of the International System. The following is a typical problem from Raets:[2] "If a centner of Nürnberg weighs as much as 108 lb. at Antwerp, how many centners do 11,682 lb. at Antwerp weigh?" In these problems the value of the centner of Genoa, Venice, and Antwerp is compared with that of Nuremberg, Aquila, Augsburg, England, Bruges, Lisbon, Sicily, and other cities and countries.

An idea of the field covered by the tables of denominate numbers required in the practical arithmetic of that time may be had from the following summary of Köbel's treatment:

1. A list of abbreviations of weight and money denominations.

2. Tables of money: Rhenish, Frankfurt, Nuremberg, Aus-

---

22 are written down before multiplying. Then the result is 99 whole tauole. The next step is to find 22 cau. × 4 bra. This is done by finding 11 cau. × 4 bra. = 3 tau. 8 pie. (See tables.) The result is placed as the second partial product. When all of the terms of the multiplicand have been multiplied by each term of the multiplier, all the results are added as shown.

[1] Giorgio Chiarini, Qvesta e ellibro che tracta de Mercatantie et vsanze de paesi (1481 ed.).
"I IBBRE cento Di Firenze fanna in Siena lib ō cēto tre i pugia lib. c.ii.I. c.iiij. In Lucca lib. c. ii. I Pifa lib. c.v. & hora e tucto uno conquel di Firenze - - -." Fol. 5.

[2] Raets, Een niew Cijfferboeck (1580 ed.), "So den Centner Nurenburghs weecht tot Antwerpen 108 lb. hoe veel Centners doē 11682 lb. Antwerps?" Fol. Hiiii recto.

THE ESSENTIAL FEATURES 81

trian, Hungarian, Meissen, Augsburg, Strassburg, Wirtenberg, Venetian, Parisian, with comparisons.[1]

3. Tables of common weight.[2]
4. The value of a centner in Venice, Nuremberg, Frankfurt, Genoa, Prussia.
5. Table of gold and silver weight. } Worms, Oppenheim,
6. Table of wine measure. } Mainz.
7. The number of Omen in a Fůder in Heidelberg, Speier, Wachenheim, Dürckeim.
8. Table of grain and fruit measure.
9. Table of time: minutes, hours, days, weeks, and years. He divided the minutes into 18 Puncten instead of into 60 seconds, and gave 364 days for a year.
10. Table of cloth measure.
11. Table of measure of Fustian.
12. Measure of salt fish.

Aliquot parts were commonly treated by commercial writers. Their importance has never waned, although they have often been neglected, and their character changed. Baker gave this definition of aliquot parts:[3] "An aliquot part

[1] Köbel, Zwey rechenbůchlin (1537 ed.). "Der Chůrfürften Müntz am Rhein, fol. B₇ verso; Müntz Franckfurter Wehrung, fol. B₈ recto; Müntz zu Nůrenbergk, fol. B₈ recto; Ofterreichifch Müntz, fol. B₈ verso; Vngerifch Müntz, fol. B₈ verso; Meißnifch Müntz, fol. B₈ verso; Müntz zu Augßburgk, fol. B₈ verso; Müntz zu Straßburgk, fol. B₈ verso; Müntz, in Wirtenberger land, fol. C recto; Der Venediger Müntz, fol. C recto; Müntz, zu Pariß." Fol. C verso.

[2] Köbel, Zwey rechenbůchlin (1537 ed.).

"Von gemeynen Gewichten.

	Centner	Cʒ		100. lb.
Ein	Pfundt	lb		32. lot.
	Lot	lt	hat	4. quintʒ/ad' ein halbe vntz.
	Quint	quĩ		4. ♃
	Mark	mar		*26. lot. "

*26 should be 16. Fol. C₂ verso.

One centner = 100 lb.
" pfund = 32 lot
" lot = 4 quintal, or ½ ounce
" Quintal = 4 pfennige
" Mark = 16 lot

[3] Baker, The Well Spring of Sciences (1580 ed.), fol. Mvii verso.

is an euê part of a shiling or of a pound or of any other thing, as ½, ⅓, ¼, ⅕, &c., are called aliquot parts." He then discussed the aliquot parts of a shilling so that in the reduction the fractions of a shilling may easily be replaced by pence.

Besides the tables of weights and measures there were tables to assist in the solution of problems containing denominate numbers. An excellent specimen is a work compiled by Jean,[1] in which the author showed how to work problems in multiplication, Rule of Three, Inverse Rule of Three, and interest. His first table composed of multiples of monetary units occupies forty-six octavo pages.

The numbers at the top of the column begin at 1 and proceed to 200,000. The numbers in the first column begin with 1 and proceed to 25. Under each of the column headings there are three divisions for the livre, sou, and denier respectively.

He gave a problem and explained its solution thus: " Suppose that 29 aunes of merchandise have been bought at 7 livres 11 sous 9 deniers an aune, to obtain the cost it is necessary to find column 29 and go down the column containing lira until you are opposite to the 7 of the small tree. Here you will

[1] Alexander Jean, Arithmetique Av Miroir (1637 ed.), fol. Aij verso.

find 203, the number of livres for the result." [1] He finds the other products in the same way and combines them to find the result.

If one were to pass from the field of arithmetical text-books and aim at completeness in describing the denominate number systems, the result would be voluminous. An excellent idea of the arithmetic of the custom-houses of that time is given by Bartholomeo di Pasi. His work [2] of 200 octavo pages is a compilation of tables mostly of this kind:

(The values of the lira in various cities.)

Melano	L 239	Bolzano	L 239
Firenza	227	Parma	140
Genoa	247	Nolimbergo	156
Bologna	216½	Geneura	164
Roma	217	Auignone	185
Napoli	244	Parife	179
Piafenza	239	Lione	182
Mantoa	239	Marfiglia	193
Ferrara	226	Valenza	215

Fol. D_8 verso.

The values of the lira, the pezza (measure of length) and others are given for over a hundred cities.

Writers of commercial arithmetic, on account of their tendency to emphasize the utility of the processes, generally placed denominate-number problems under each operation with integers instead of deferring the whole subject to a separate chapter. Baker, after having explained the addition of in-

[1] Jean, Arithmetique Av Miroir (1637 ed.). "Suppofez avoir achepte 29 aunes de marchandife à 7 liures 11 fols. 9 deniers l'aune, il faut trouuer la Colomne 29. & defcendre dans les liures d'icelle iufques vis à vis du 7 du petit arbre, vous y trouuerez 203. qui sont liures.

Pour les 11. fols, il faut defcendre dans les fols de la dite Colomne iufques vis à vis de 11. dudit petit arbre, où vous trouuerez 15 liures 19 fols.

Et pour les 9 denier, il faut defcendre dans les deniers d'icelle colomne iufques vis à vis du 9. du petit arbre, où vous trouuerez 21 fol 9 deniers.

Lefquelles trois fommes fcauoir pour les liures 203 liures, pour les fols 15 liures 19 fols, & pour les deniers 21 fols 9 deniers, il faut assembler & vous trouuerez que 29 aulnes à 7 liures 11 fols 9 deniers, vallent 220 liures 9 deniers." Fol. Aij verso.

[2] Bartholomeo Di Pasi da Vinetia (1557 ed.) Tariffa de i pesi, e misure corrispondenti dal Leuante al Ponente, e da una terra, e luogo all' altro, quafi per tutte le parti del mondo.

tegers, passed at once to the addition of pounds, shillings and pence. Adam Riese, by common consent the greatest reckoning master of his time, in his book on line-reckoning began addition and subtraction with examples of denominate numbers. Thus, in addition he used the annexed problem.[1] Even writers who were chiefly concerned with traditional arithmetic felt the demand for work in denominate numbers. For instance, under division Cirvelo says that division is used to reduce money of smaller denomination to larger, just as multiplication is used to reduce money of larger denomination to smaller.[2] Monetary systems generally took precedence over all others in order of treatment, as indicated by the examples above. In exceptional cases weight was placed first. The plan of introducing denominate numbers under addition of integers leads at once to a difficulty in sequence of processes. The reductions from one denomination to another in simplifying the result occasionally required a knowledge of division, as in these examples:

132	13	8
3456	16	5
789 fl.	17 gr.	7 d.
67	9	6
282	20	3
——	——	——
4729	14	5

340 flo.	7 p 25 d [3]		lib 7974	p 13	7 [4]
124	7 20		lib 879	p 12	6
98	6 27		lib 9400	p 5	7
49	0 12		lib 794	p 8	9
58	6 18	Sũma	lib 19049	p 0	5
672 flo.	5 12 d				

As to the general character of the exercises given under the subject of denominate numbers, it is worthy of note that they

[1] Riese, Rechnung auff der Linien und Federn/ (1571 ed.), fol. Aiiij recto.

[2] Cirvelo, Tractatus Arithmetice (1513 ed.).

"⁋ Finis diuifionis eft vt fciamus quo mõ pluribus debet diftribui aliqua pecunia fecundũ partes equales quantũ debet habere e quisqȝ eorum, et qñ habemus aliquã magnã copiã denariorum et voluerimus videre quot folidi vel quot aurei aut argentei fierent ex illis et ad plura alia valet. vnde ficut multiplicationem poffumus groffiorem reducere ad fubtiliorem: ita per diuifionem poffumus ex minore moneta conftituere maiorem." Fol. a$_{vii}$ recto.

[3] Rudolff, Kunstliche rechnung (1534 ed.), fol. Bvi verso.

[4] Cardan, Practica Arithmetice (1539 ed.), fol. Avi recto.

did not contain long lists of numbers to be manipulated merely for practice in figuring. Concrete applications were plentifully supplied, and ability on the part of the learner to solve these practical problems was evidently the goal of instruction.

FRACTIONS

Definitions

Two conceptions of the fraction were prevalent among the writers of that period: (1) A fraction is one or more of the equal parts of a unit. (2) A fraction is the indicated quotient of two integers. Among the examples of the former is the treatment by Köbel, which reminds us how long the worthy apple has done educational service.[1] He divides the apple into twenty parts, each part of which is called a twentieth. Ten of these parts make half the apple, and five of the twenty parts taken together make a quarter of the apple, and so on. Köbel is unique in opening the subject of fractions with a statement of their utility:[2] " Since it happens that commercial questions concerning measure, weight, and exchange are not always asked and reckoned with in whole numbers, I shall instruct you in the following pages, so that you may understand how to arrange, interpret, and reckon questions involving calculation with fractions occurring in measure and weight. I prom-

---

[1] Köbel, Zwey rechenbûchlin (1537 ed.). "So du ein gantzen apffel hast/ vnd zerſchneideſt oder theyleſt den ſelben/ in zwentzig teyl oder ſtuck/ ſo iſt der ſelben zwentzig theyl odder ſtuck/ ieglichs ein zwentzigſt theyl des gantzenn apffels genant/ vnnd wirt inn der rechenſchafft iedes ſtuck ein bruch geteutſcht/ der ſelben zwentzigtheyl/ zehen/ ſo man die widerumb zuſamen ſetzt/ zeygen ſie ein halben apffel an/ vnnd ſo du der zweintzigtheyl fünff zuſamen legſt/ ſiheſtu ein viertheil des apffels ꝛc. vnd alſo für vnd für zu rechnen ſein die theyl oder brüch zuuenſtehn." Fol. H$_3$ verso.

[2] Köbel, Zwey rechenbûchlin (1537 ed.). "Dieweil ſich nit allweg begibt/ das die hândel/ kåuff und fragen/ in gantzen zalen/ maſſen/ gewichten/ oder verwechßlungenn geſchehen/ gefragt vnnd gerechnet werden/ wil ich dich hernach leren/ ſo dir in fragenn/ oder rechnungen gebrochne zalen/ ungerade gelt/ maß oder gewicht fürkumpt/ wie du das ordnen/ verſtehn und rechnen ſolt/ ſo vil zu diſem gmeynem heußlichem gebrauch und Rechnen/ ich dir verheyſſen uñ einem angenden Rechner am erſten zu wiſſen not iſt offenbaren." Fol. H$_3$ recto.

ise to teach you as much as is evidently necessary for everyday use for a beginner in the art of calculation."

Another example of the first definition, and one in which the measured units of denominate numbers serve to define the fraction, is given by Champenois as follows:[1] "A fraction is part of an integral whole. As a livre is an integral whole, and its parts are 20 sous; and one sou is an integral whole whose parts are 12 deniers; an aune is an integral whole, and its parts are three tiers, four quarts, and other parts.

```
    a      c      d      e      b
    |──────|──────|──────|──────|
    |      |      |      |      |
```

"If the aune ab be divided into four equal parts at the points c, d, and e, $acde$ will be the three-fourths, which the purchaser took, and the other fourth, eb, will be kept by the merchant."[2] The graphical method of explaining fractions was very rare in that period.

The definition of Gemma Frisius is of the same kind and contains an explanation of the terms numerator and denominator.[3] "We call the numbers showing the parts of an integral thing fractions, or parts, as ½ signifies one-half; ¼, a

[1] Champenois, Les Institvtions De L'Arithmetique (1578 ed.). "Fraction eſt partie d'vn entier. Comme vne liure eſt vn entier, & ſes parties font 20. fols. & vn fols eſt vn entier, & ſes parties font 12 deniers, vne aulne eſt vn entier, & ſes parties fōt trois tiers, quatre quarts, & autres parties." Page 85, fol. Giij recto.

[2] Champenois, Les Institvtions De L'Arithmetique (1578 ed.). "Soit l'aulne .a.b. diuiſee en quatre parties egales, au poinct .c.d.e. les trois quarts feront a.c.d.e. que l'achepteur prēdra, & reſtera l'autre quart au marchant .e.b." Page 86, Giij verso.

[3] Gemma Frisius, Arithmeticae Practicae Methodus Facilis (1581 ed.). "Fractiones, minutias, aut partes, appellamus numeros integrae rei partes significantes, vt $\frac{1}{2}$ semissem significat, $\frac{1}{4}$ quadrantem siue quartam partem, $\frac{3}{4}$ dodrantem, aut tres quadrantes. Scribuntur duobus numeris, superiorem numeratorem, inferiorem denominatorem appellant: hunc quod denotet, quot in partes integrum secari oporteat: illum, quia quot huiusmodi sumendae sint particulae, numeret. Veluti $\frac{3}{7}$, hic inferior denotat integrum dividendum in 7, sumendas tamen tantū tres septimas innuit superior. Cum igitur duo hi fuerint aequales, semper integrum tantum denotatur, vt $\frac{12}{12}$. Cum superior maior est, plus integro: cum minor est, minus integro significat." Fol. C$_2$ verso.

fourth; and ¾, three-fourths. They are written with two numbers; the upper one is called the numerator, the lower one the denominator, the latter of which denotes into how many parts the integer must be divided, the former shows how many of these parts are to be taken. For example, in $\frac{3}{7}$ the lower number denotes that the integer is to be divided into seven parts; the upper one shows, however, that only three-sevenths are to be taken. Therefore, when these two numbers are equal, a whole number is designated, as $\frac{12}{12}$. When the upper number is greater, it signifies more than a whole number; when it is less, it signifies less than a whole number."

The second conception of the fraction is well illustrated trom Trenchant:[1] "The teaching of fractions, of which we have given the definition in Chapter 2, should follow division, so as to follow the proper source from which it originates. For this will happen most often when a smaller number is to be divided by a larger; or when it results from a division, as 24 divided by 60 makes $\frac{24}{60}$; or when it results from a division, as 24 resulting from a division by 60 makes $\frac{24}{60}$. The 24 is the numerator and 60 the denominator, and the fraction is called twenty-four sixtieths."

The second form of definition was used by Raets:[2] "Fractions arise (as has been explained) from division of a number by a greater number. For instance, when 2 is divided by 3, then $\frac{2}{3}$ results," and also by Tartaglia, who gave this illustration:[3] "To divide 15 by 2. It will be impossible to divide 15 into two equal parts. After dividing there will be one

[1] Trenchant, L'Arithmetique (1578 ed.). "La doctrine du nobre rompu, duquel auons donné la diffinition au 2 chap. doit fucceder à la diuifion, come fuyuant ea propre fouife dont il prent origine. Car iceluy auient le plus fouuent quand lon diuife vn moindre nombre, par vn maieur: comme 24 par 60, fét $\frac{24}{60}$: ou quand il refte d'vne partition: comme 24 reftant d'vne partition par 60 fét $\frac{24}{60}$: le 24 eft numerateur: & le 60, denominateur: & s'exprime vint & quatre foixantiemes." Fol. G₆ recto.

[2] Raets, Arithmetica Oft Een niew cijfferboeck/ (1580). "Die ghebroken ghetalen spruyten (als verclart is) wuter Diuision/ alsmen een ghetal divideert met een grooter. Ghrlijck alsmen divideert 2. met 3. foo comender $\frac{2}{3}$." Fol. Biiij verso.

[3] Tartaglia, La Prima Parte Del General Trattato (1556 ed.).

part left, which is still to be divided by the divisor. Then 1 is taken for the numerator and 2 for the denominator of the fraction."

Thus, the proper relation of the fraction to the process of division was recognized, and the fraction was taught as a necessary step in the growth of the number system.

The second method of approach to the fraction, though less common than the first, persisted for two centuries. It is interesting to compare Tartaglia's treatment quoted above with the following from Gio (1689) more than a century and a quarter later:[1] " When a divisor is greater than a dividend. When it is necessary to divide a smaller dividend by a divisor, place the divisor under the dividend, and, as no quotient is obtained, a fraction is formed. Thus, if the divisor is 40 and the dividend 20, place 40 below the 20, then the quotient $\frac{20}{40}$ results."

The degree to which these conceptions of the fraction were held to be incompatible by some is exemplified in the work of Unicorn,[2] who began with the first definition and ended a long treatment with these cases of division, the last and least of which is the second definition.

Division of fractions:
    A fraction by a fraction.
    An integer by a fraction.
    A mixed number by a fraction.
    A mixed number by a mixed number.
    A fraction by an integer.
    An integer by a mixed number.
    A fraction by a mixed number.
    A mixed number by an integer.

---

[1] Gio, Padre, Elementi Arithmetici (1689 ed.). Quando un Partitore foſſe moggiore de compoſto. Quanto s'haueſſe da partire vn Compoſto minore del Partitore; si mette il Partitore ſotto il compoſto, e ne viene di Quotiente quel rotto che ſi forma. Come se foſſe Partitore 40, Composto 20. Perche il 40. non può entrare in 20., percio neſſo 40. ſotto il 20, resta di Quotiente $\frac{20}{40}$. 40)$\frac{20}{40}$ Quotiente." Fol. Cviij verso.

[2] Unicorn, De L'Arithmetica universale (1598 ed.).

One integer by another; that is, in case the dividend is smaller than the divisor, as 48 by 64 gives $\frac{48}{64}$.

A curious mixture of the two definitions is found in Ramus:[1] "If 8 is divided by 3, the quotient is 2, and ⅔ are left. 2 is the number of parts, 3 the name.

If I wish to divide 11 asses by 3, this division $\frac{11}{3}$ (3⅔) will indicate 3 asses and ⅔ of 1 ass.

If the numerator and the denominator are equal, as $\frac{234}{234}$ the number is an integer; if larger, as $\frac{245}{234}$, it will be more than an integer."

Both were happily combined by Tonstall, whose definition is:[2] "Any integer may be divided into as many parts as one wishes from 1 to infinity." Although Tonstall often goes to extremes in details, his treatment of the relative size of fractions should have a mission. One of the chief reasons why children have difficulty in mastering fractions is that they do not make a sufficient number of comparisons. They do not observe the change in the fraction by varying its terms. Tonstall's comparisons are suggestive of good method:[3] "The greater the denominator and the fewer of these parts there are, the farther is the fraction removed from the integer; the smaller the denominator and the more of these parts there are,

[1] Ramus, Arithmeticae Libri duo (1586 ed.). "Ut efto 8. dividendus per 3. quotus integer est 2, & fuperfunt 2, que interpofita linea fupernotata divisori, tandem ipfa quoqȝ divifa funt, inventaqȝ fractio ⅔ quoto priori 2 ad dextram est affcribenda fic:

$$\begin{array}{c} 2 \\ 8\ (2\tfrac{2}{3} \\ 3" \end{array}$$
Fol. D₇ recto.

[2] Tonstall, De Arte Supputandi (1522 ed.). "Omne integrum in Partes, quotcūqȝ velis: folui per intellectū poteft et quemadmodum integrorum numeratio ab uno incipit: atqȝ in infinitum poteft extendi: fic integrorum fectio a fecūdis orditur partibus." Fol. O₄ recto.

[3] Tonstall, De Arte Supputandi (1522 ed.). "Semper autem in omnibus diffectorum minutijs, quo maior denominator fuerit: eo minores erunt partes, remotioresqȝ ab integris. et quo fuerit minor: eo partes maiores erunt. atqȝ ad integra propius accedēt. Nam duę partes fecundae maiores funt. q̄ duae tertię et duae tertiae maiores, q̄ duae quartae et duae quartę maiores, q̄ duae quintae. et fic in uniuerfum, quanto magis numerādo crefcit denominator: tanto magis quantitate partes diminuunter." Fol. P recto.

the more nearly a fraction approaches an integer. For 2 halves are greater than ⅔, ⅔ than 2/4, 2/4 than ⅖, and so on.

"In dealing with fractions these things should be noticed:

First. Whenever the numerator and denominator are equal, then the fraction equals an integer. Thus, ⅗, ⅝, 7/7 are equal to 1.

Second. Whenever the numerator is greater than the denominator, by as many units as the numerator exceeds the denominator, the value of the fraction exceeds an integer, as in 9/8, ⅞, 6/4, 9/8 is an integer and ⅛ over, and so on.

Third. By as many parts as the numerator is less than the denominator in units, by so much is the fraction less than an integer, ¾ is one-fourth less than an integer."

Classes of Fractions

Two classes of fractions were recognized:

Common fractions, variously called numeri rotti, fragmenta, nombres rouptz, fractiones,[1] minutiae vulgares seu mercatoriae.

Sexagesimal fractions, called fractiones astronomicae, or minutæ phisicæ.[2]

Cirvelo, in the third part of his Practica Arithmetica (1555 ed.), explained the operations with the sexagesimal fractions by reference to those with denominations of weight and value. The following shows his method of associating the addition of signs, degrees, minutes, etc., by reference to the addition of ducats, soldi, denarii, etc.

signa	gradus	minuta	secunda	tertia
5	47	39	53	15
3	26	54	18	34
2	17	23	45	45
—	—	—	—	—
11	31	57	57	45 ſūa

[1] The word "fractio" is as old as Hispalensis (c. 1150). Treutlein, Abhandlungen, 3 : 112.

[2] Planudes introduced sexagesimal fractions under the title "Zodiac" and showed how to use them in the four operations. According to Sayce and Bosanquet, the origin of these fractions is sometimes incorrectly attributed to the Assyrians. Publications of the Royal Asiatic Society, 1880, vol. xl, no. 3.

THE ESSENTIAL FEATURES

PRACTICA IN MONETIS.

Auri ducati	argenti solidi	denarii	oboli
12	23	9	4
8	16	7	3
23	14	11	5
—	—	—	—
53	25	4	0

fūa Fol. b$_{21j}$ recto.

6 oboli = 1 denarius. 12 denarii = 1 solidus. 30 solidi = 1 ducatum.

A double entry multiplication table is also given by Cirvelo, page 38, but it was not an invention of the sixteenth century, for the Arabs had used this means of calculation much earlier.

In German works that treated of line-reckoning, Roman notation was occasionally used to express fractions. An excellent illustration showing the struggle of the Hindu and Roman systems is the following from Köbel:[1]

" The numerator   I   This symbol is one-oneth,
  The separatrix   —   that is, the integer 1.
  The denominator I

" Then, whatever equal numbers are found in the numerator and denominator, they always mean in such a symbol the integer 1; for example, 4 fourths are 1 and written $\frac{IIII}{IIII}$ in the German numerals and $\frac{4}{4}$ in figures. Similarly, 6 sixths is also 1 and written $\frac{vi}{vi}$ or $\frac{6}{6}$." The illustration on the next page shows a part of a page from Köbel's arithmetic (1544).

[1] Köbel, Zwey rechenbüchlin (1537 ed.).
  " Der zeler   I   Diß figur ift vnd bedeut ein eintheyl/ das
    Das ftrichlin —   ift ein gantzs.
    Der Nenner   I
Dann in welcher zal du den Zeler vnd Neñer gleich findeft/ fo bedeutten die felbigen figuren alwegen ein gantze zal/ als vier vierthell/ die machen ein gantz/ vnd werden alfo mit teutfcher zal gefchriben $\frac{IIII}{IIII}$/ aber mit den ziffern alfo $\frac{4}{4}$ Dergleichen ift 6. fechfteil auch ein gantzs/ vñ fchreib es alfo $\frac{VI}{VI}$/ vnd mit den ziffern $\frac{6}{6}$." Fol. H$_4$ recto. For examples from other of Köbel's works see Unger, pp. 15-16.

> bedeüt diß figur der selben tayl ains.
>
> I Dieffe figur ist vn̄ bedeüt ain fiertel von aines
> IIII gantzen/also mag man auch ain fünfftail/ayn
> sechstail/ain sybentail oder zwai sechstail 2c. vnd alle
> ander brüch beschreiben/Als $\frac{I}{V}|\frac{I}{VI}|\frac{I}{VII}|\frac{II}{VI}$ 2c.
>
> VI Diß sein Sechs achtail/das sein sechstail der
> VIII acht ain gantz machen.
>
> IX Diß Figur betzaigt ann newn ayilfftail das seyn
> XI IX tail/der XI ain gantz machen.
>
> XX Diß Figur betzaichet/zwentzigk ainundrey=
> XXXI sigk tail /das sein zwentzigk tail .der ains=
> vndreissigk ain gantz machen.
>
> II^C Diß sein zwaihundert tail/der Fierhun=
> IIII^C.LX dert vnd sechtzigk ain gantz machen.

Many writers followed their definition of fractions by an explanation of numeration of fractions. This table from Van der Schuere was designed to teach numeration to $\frac{1}{10}$:[1]

$\frac{1}{1}$	$\frac{2}{2}$	$\frac{3}{3}$	$\frac{4}{4}$	$\frac{5}{5}$	$\frac{6}{6}$	$\frac{7}{7}$	$\frac{8}{8}$	$\frac{9}{9}$
	$\frac{1}{2}$	$\frac{2}{3}$	$\frac{3}{4}$	$\frac{4}{5}$	$\frac{5}{6}$	$\frac{6}{7}$	$\frac{7}{8}$	$\frac{8}{9}$
		$\frac{1}{3}$	$\frac{2}{4}$	$\frac{3}{5}$	$\frac{4}{6}$	$\frac{5}{7}$	$\frac{6}{8}$	$\frac{7}{9}$
			$\frac{1}{4}$	$\frac{2}{5}$	$\frac{3}{6}$	$\frac{4}{7}$	$\frac{5}{8}$	$\frac{6}{9}$
				$\frac{1}{5}$	$\frac{2}{6}$	$\frac{3}{7}$	$\frac{4}{8}$	$\frac{5}{9}$
					$\frac{1}{6}$	$\frac{2}{7}$	$\frac{3}{8}$	$\frac{4}{9}$
						$\frac{1}{7}$	$\frac{2}{8}$	$\frac{3}{9}$
							$\frac{1}{8}$	$\frac{2}{9}$
								$\frac{1}{9}$

[1] Van der Scheure, Arithmetica, Oft Reken=const (1600 ed.). Fol. D$_8$ verso.

Order of Processes

The order of the processes with integers seems to have impressed itself so generally upon writers that it was usually followed blindly in the case of fractions. The order of presentation in fractions now prevalent in formal arithmetic was the one commonly used in the sixteenth century, namely: 1. Definition. 2. Reduction to lower terms. 3. Reduction to the same denominator. 4. Addition. 5. Subtraction. 6. Multiplication. 7. Division.

The following outline from Tartaglia is typical as to the order of the main topics;[1] the order and number of minor topics differed with different authors:

Numeration, or representation of fractions.
Reduction of fractions to lower terms.
Changing mixed numbers to fractions.
Reduction to the same denominator.
Addition.
    Of fractions.
    Of fractions and mixed numbers.
    Of fractions, whole and mixed number.
Subtraction.
    Of fractions.
    Of fractions from mixed numbers.
    Of fractions from whole numbers.
    Of whole numbers from mixed numbers.
    Of mixed numbers from mixed numbers.
Multiplication.
    Of a fraction by a fraction.
    Of a mixed number by a fraction, and conversely.
    Of a fraction by a whole number.
    Of mixed numbers by mixed numbers.
    Of whole numbers by fractions.
    Of a fraction by a fraction by a fraction.
    Of a whole number by a mixed number by a mixed number.
Division.
    Of a fraction by a fraction of the same denominator.
    Of a fraction by a fraction of different denominator.
    Of a whole number by a fraction.
    Of a mixed number by a fraction.
    Of a mixed number by a mixed number.
    Of a whole number by a mixed number.
    Of a mixed number by a whole number.

[1] Tartaglia, La Prima Parte Del General Trattato di numeri, et misure (1556 ed.).

But should the order of processes with fractions in formal arithmetic necessarily be the same as that with integers? It is not followed in primary arithmetic, it does not conform readily to spiral treatment, and, furthermore, historical precedent is not unanimous in its favor. Calandri (1491), Borgi (1484), Paciuolo (1494), and Rudolff (1526) each gave the following order: multiplication, addition, subtraction, and division. Gemma Frisius introduced multiplication first and repeated it after subtraction. The subject was introduced by the definition of a fraction and its terms, and followed by the explanation of a fraction of a fraction.[1] "As $\frac{3}{4}$ of $\frac{2}{3}$ of $\frac{6}{7}$, that is, the integer is divided into 7 parts of which 6 are taken, this is again divided into 3 parts, of which 2 are taken, and the resulting fraction is divided into 4 parts, of which 3 are taken. The fractions are most easily multiplied by multiplying the numerators together for a new numerator and the denominators together for a new denominator." Francesco Ghaligai preceded addition and subtraction by both multiplication and division.[2] These presentations cannot be regarded as experiments of minor authors, for Paciuolo, Gemma Frisius, and Calandri were representatives of the highest scholarship and were leading spirits of both the Latin and the Commercial Schools. Neither can they be regarded as entirely arbitrary or accidental plans, for Paciuolo, who did more than any other writer (save possibly Borgi) to formulate the arithmetic of that period, actually expressed his purpose thus:[3] " In the ex-

[1] Gemma Frisius, Arithmeticae Practicae Methodus Facilis (1581 ed.). "Item $\frac{3}{4}$ | $\frac{2}{3}$ | $\frac{6}{7}$, hoc est, tres quare a duarum tertiarũ ex ſex ſeptimis: hoc eſt integri diuiſi in 7, cape ſex particulas: quas rurſus ſeca in tres: harum accipe duos: quas diuide in quatuor: tandem tres huiuſmodi ſignificatur particule." Fol. C₃ recto.

[2] Ghaligai, Practica D'Arithmetica (1552 ed.).

[3] Paciuolo, Sũma de Arithmetica Geometria Proportioni et Proportionalita - - - (1523 ed.).
" De multiplicatione fractorum inter se.
- - - Nelli ſani el ſummare: ſe ben notaſti fo piu facile che nullaltra a parte: el multiplicare fo piu difficile che lui. Qui nelli rotti asſai piu facile: e lo multiplicare che non e lo ſummare. E nelli ſani la piu difficile parte fo el partire. E qui nelli rotti e la piu facile: che quella intendi di

planation of reckoning with fractions, multiplication precedes addition, for fractions and whole numbers are so different that in whole numbers addition is more easily treated, while in fractions it is more difficult than multiplication and should follow."

Reduction

The reduction of fractions to lowest terms was effected in simple cases by inspection. In other cases it was necessary to apply tests of divisibility to find the common factors of the numerator and the denominator. Reduction to lowest terms was the only method of simplifying fractions, since the decimal fractions had not yet come into use; consequently, the tests of divisibility, and occasionally the Euclidean method of Greatest Common Divisor, were given by theoretic writers before fractions. For example, Ramus preceded his treatment of fractions by five chapters, as follows:[1]

Chapter VI.   Concerning odd and even numbers.
              From division arise different kinds of numbers: odd and even, prime and composite.
Chapter VII. Concerning prime and composite numbers, in which the sieve of Eratosthenes is used.
Chapter VIII. Concerning numbers prime to one another.
Chapter IX.   Concerning composite numbers and their Greatest Common Divisor.
Chapter X.   Concerning the Least Common Denominator.

iani. El fotrare in quelli ene asfai piu facile: che non e el fotrare in li rotti. E pero dal multiplicare me pare ben comenzare." Fol. 50 recto, Gij recto.

Recorde (1558 ed.) makes the same explanation. Fol. Riiij verso.

[1] Ramus, Arithmeticae Libri duo (1586 ed.).
"Caput VI De Numero Impari et Pari.
E divifione oritur numeri differentia duplex, imparis & paris, primis & compofiti. Fol. C$_5$ recto.
Caput VII.   De Numero Primo et Composito. Fol. C$_6$ recto.
Caput VIII. De Numeris Primis inter Se
Cap. IX.   De Numeris Inter Se compofitis, eorumq; communi divifore maximo. Fol. D$_3$ verso.
Cap. X.   De minimo Communi Dividuo." Fol. D$_4$ verso.

Stevinus under division of integers states the use to be made of the Greatest Common Divisor; namely, as an aid in the reduction of fractions.[1] It was more common, especially among commercial writers, to give the tests of divisibility under fractions or in connection with the actual problem solved. Thus, in Rudolff's second section in the treatment of fractions Reduction has this treatment:[2] The first example, solved by inspection, — both terms of $\frac{84}{294}$ divided by $2 = \frac{42}{147}$, which divided by $3 = \frac{14}{49}$, which divided by $7 = \frac{2}{7}$, — is followed by the rules of divisibility:

"In order to be divisible by 2 a number must be even;

"In order to be divisible by 3 it must have a remainder of 0, 3, or 6 after the nines have been cast out;

"A number is divisible by 5, when the number ends in 5 or 0;

"A number is divisible by 10, when the number ends in 0."

As an example of these tests he gives the one in the margin. Then follows the Euclidean method:

"How we may easily find whether a fraction may be made smaller or not.

"Divide the larger number by the smaller. If anything is left, divide the former divisor (the smaller number of the fraction) by this, and so on. Then divide the larger number of the fraction, and, if the division comes out even, the fraction is reducible. As,

$\frac{729}{2187}$
$\frac{243}{729}$
$\frac{81}{243}$
$\frac{27}{81}$
$\frac{9}{27}$
$\frac{3}{9}$
$\frac{1}{3}$

$\frac{286}{715}$

715 ÷ 286 = 2, remainder 143.
286 ÷ 143 = 2, no remainder.
715 ÷ 143 = 5."

---

[1] Stevin, Les Oeuvres Mathematiques (1634 ed.). "Eſtant doncques donnez nombres Arithmeticques entiers, nous avons trouvé leur plus grande commune meſure; ce qu'il falloit faire.

Problem VI.

Estant donné nombre Arithmetique rompu: Trouver ſon premier rompu. *Explication du donné.* Soit donné rompu $\frac{91}{117}$. *Explication du requis.* Il faut trouver ſon premier rompu. *Conſtruction.* On trouvera la plus grande commune meſure de 91 & 117." Fol. B$_5$ recto.

[2] Rudolff, Kunstliche rechnung mit der Ziffer und Zalpfennige/ (1534 ed.).

Another interesting example is found in Raets.[1]

The term, " reduction of fractions " meant several things: with some writers it meant reduction to lowest terms, with others it meant changing fractions to others having a common denominator, and with still others it meant expressing a fractional part of a denominate number unit in terms of lower orders. It is now customary for modern writers to precede the treatment of common denominators by that of reduction to lowest terms, but the influence of applied arithmetic, especially of denominate numbers, and the freedom accompanying dogmatic treatment sometimes led sixteenth century writers to reverse this order. Thus, Baker's second chapter is Reduction of Fractions to Common Denominator, and his third chapter is Reduction of Fractions to Lowest Terms. The influence of denominate numbers upon the treatment of fractions is apparent among both Commercial and Latin School writers. Thus, Adam Riese follows his definition of a fraction by:[2]

To reduce ¾ floren.
Solution. Multiply 3 by 21 and divide by 4, the result is 15 gr. and 9 d.

---

[1] Raets, Arithmetica Oft Een niew Cijfferboeck/ (1580 ed.).

" Abbreviatie int ghebroken.

" Leert/ hoemen die gebroken ghetalen reduceren sal in een minder proportie. Het welcke gheschiet nae der leeringhe Euclidis/ In der tweeder propohtien des feuenden boers der Elementen/ in deser voegen. Ten exemplel: Om habbbeuieren $\frac{108}{144}$ fubshaheert den Felder 108. vā den Kommer 144. ende daer fullen resteren 36. die subtrahert van 108

	144
	108
	36
	72
	36
	36
- - - - - - - - -	0

" Das voor $\frac{100}{144}$ unde plaet se van 108. fedt 3. ende voor 144. fedt 4. foo comender ¾ vor $\frac{108}{144}$ te meten/ die ¾ doen foo veel als $\frac{108}{144}$." Fol. Bv recto.

[2] Riese, Rechnung auff der Linien und Federn/ (1571 ed.).

" Wiltu wiffen/ wie viel ein jglicher Bruch in fich behelt/ fo refoluir den Zeler in fenien werdt/ vnd teil ab mit dem Nenner. Als ¾ floren/ multiplicir 3 mit 21 gr./ vnd theil ab mit dem Nenner/ als 4/ kommen 15 gr./ vnd 9 d. Alfo dergleichen von Gewichten vnd andern." Fol. D verso.

Gemma Frisius follows Reduction of Fractions to Lowest Terms by:

"$\frac{4}{9}$ Joachimi or Thaleri are worth how many grossi?"

124 grossi = 1 Thaler. $\frac{4 \times 24}{9} = 10\frac{2}{3}$ grossi.

$\frac{2 \times 12}{3} = 8$ numuli.

Ramus precedes his Chapter XIIII,[1] Operations with Fractions, by a chapter, Reduction of Integers and Fractions, in which examples of this type occur:

To reduce 12 asses to uncias $\frac{144}{12}$.
To reduce $\frac{144}{12}$ to an integer, divide 144 by 12.

Addition

The usual order in the addition of fractions was: (1) The addition of fractions with denominators alike, (2) Of those with denominators unlike. For example, the following problems are given by Noviomagus in this order:[2]

(1) $\frac{4}{3}$ and $\frac{4}{3}$ and $\frac{7}{3} = \frac{15}{3}$.
(2) $\frac{5}{7} \cdot \frac{3}{4}$. Multiply 7 by 3 = 21, 5 by 4 = 20.
The sum = 41 for numerator and $7 \times 4 = 28$ for denominator.
$\frac{5}{7} \cdot \frac{3}{4} = \frac{41}{28} = 1\frac{13}{28}$.

The second kind required reduction to a common denominator, which process was treated either in a section previous to addition or in connection with the actual problems to be added. The number of writers who followed each plan was about the same.

A typical case of reducing to a common denominator is the following from Trenchant:[3] To reduce $\frac{2}{3}, \frac{3}{4}, \frac{5}{6}, \frac{7}{8}$ to a common denominator:

16	18	20	21
$\frac{2}{3}$	$\frac{3}{4}$	$\frac{5}{6}$	$\frac{7}{8}$
	24		

The common denominator is written below, and the new numerators are written above the corresponding fractions.

[1] Ramus, Arithmeticae Libri duo (1577 ed.), fol. 4 recto; fol. D₈ recto.
[2] Noviomagus, De Numeris Libri II (1544 ed.).
[3] Trenchant, L'Arithmetique (1578 ed.), fol. G₇ verso.

THE ESSENTIAL FEATURES　　　99

The usual form of expressing the work of addition is shown in this example from Rudolff:[1]

$$\begin{array}{cc} 8 & 9 \\ 2 & 3 \\ 3 & 4 \\ \hline 12 & \end{array} \text{ makes } \frac{17}{12}$$

The fractions to be added, $\frac{2}{3}$ and $\frac{3}{4}$, appear in the center, the common denominator, 12, below, and the new numerators, 8 and 9, above.

A clever form of adding fractions, considering the fact that signs of operations were not in use, is illustrated by the following from Tartaglia:[2]

a summar $\frac{2}{3} \times \frac{3}{4} \begin{array}{c} \text{———} 9 \\ \text{———} 8 \end{array}$

fanno $\frac{17}{12}$ che saria $1\frac{5}{12}$

The cross indicates how the terms are multiplied, but it probably has no connection with the symbol of multiplication.

So rarely were reasons given for processes that the following explanation by Rudolff of why fractions must be reduced before adding is noteworthy:[3] "It is impossible to add 4 florins and 3 soldi to make either 7 florins or 7 soldi. It is also impossible to add $\frac{3}{8}$ and $\frac{1}{5}$ and to get either $\frac{4}{8}$ or $\frac{4}{5}$. The florins must be reduced to lower denomination, and the fractions must also be reduced to a common denominator. $\frac{3}{8} \frac{1}{5}$ or $\frac{15}{40} \frac{8}{40}$ make $\frac{23}{40}$."

The order,[4] or the method of grouping, used when several fractions were added was not uniform. The prevailing usage was to add the first fraction to the second, then to add this result to the third and this result to the fourth, and so on.[5]

[1] Rudolff, Kunstliche Rechnung (1534 ed.), fol. Cvii verso.

[2] Tartaglia, La Prima Parte Del General Trattato (1556 ed.), fol. Tiij verso.

[3] Rudolff, Kunstliche Rechnung, fol. Di recto.

[4] Baker, The Well Spring of Sciences (1580 ed.), adds $\frac{1}{2}$, $\frac{2}{3}$, $\frac{3}{4}$, $\frac{4}{5}$ by adding $\frac{1}{2}$ and $\frac{2}{3}$, then $\frac{3}{4}$ and $\frac{4}{5}$, combining the results. Fol. I$_v$ verso.

He also directs how to add a fraction of a fraction to a fraction of a fraction by making the multiplications first and then adding the results. This has significance in showing that Baker gave multiplication precedence over addition, as is done in the modern convention concerning a series of operations.

[5] Riese, Rechnung auff der Linien und Federn,' (1571 ed.), adds $\frac{2}{3}$, $\frac{3}{4}$, and $\frac{4}{5}$ thus: $\frac{2}{3}$ and $\frac{3}{4}$ are $\frac{17}{12}$ and $\frac{4}{5} = 2\frac{13}{16}$. "Summir die erfte zween brüche/ als nemlich/ $\frac{2}{3}$ vnd $\frac{3}{4}$/ werden $\frac{17}{12}$/ darzu $\frac{4}{5}$/ kommen $2\frac{13}{16}$ teil." Fol. Dij recto.

SIXTEENTH CENTURY ARITHMETIC

Some writers, as Cardan,[1] added in groups and combined the results according to the associative law. The modern method of reducing all of the fractions to a common denominator and adding their numerators was also recognized.[2] Tonstall[3] combined the first and the third methods. In adding $\frac{2}{3}$, $\frac{3}{4}$, and $\frac{4}{5}$ he suggested that the first two be added and that the third be added to this result, as:

$\frac{2}{3} + \frac{3}{4} = \frac{17}{12}$ and $\frac{17}{12} \times \frac{4}{5} = \frac{133}{60}$, or that they may be taken as $\frac{2}{3} = \frac{40}{60}, \frac{3}{4} = \frac{45}{60}, \frac{4}{5} + \frac{48}{60}$. The sum is $\frac{133}{60}$.

When the modern method was used, the product of the several denominators was often taken instead of their least common multiple. The following problem from Raets shows this:[4] To reduce $\frac{3}{4}, \frac{7}{8}, \frac{4}{5}$.

```
1.          4              160
            8               7
           ──              ───
           32               3
            5            1120(140
           ───           888
           160          
            3              160
           ───              4
          480(120          ───
          444               1
                          640(128
                          555
```

[1] Cardan, Practica Arithmetice (1539 ed.). "Exemplū volo agregare $\frac{2}{3}$, $\frac{3}{4}$, $\frac{4}{5}$, $\frac{5}{6}$ agrego p modū dictū Prima duo & fatiūt $\frac{17}{12}$ & reliq duo & fatiūt $\frac{49}{30}$, deinde agrego $\frac{17}{12}$ & $\frac{40}{30}$ & fiūt $\frac{1098}{360}$ & sūt integri tres & $\frac{1}{20}$ & hoc eſt facile." Fol. Bii recto.

[2] It was not customary, however, to use the least common denominator.

[3] Tonstall, De Arte Supputandi (1522 ed.). "Si vero plura fuerunt fragmēta: uti duae tertię. tres quartae. quatuor quintae. poſt duo priora fragmenta, ſicuti diximus, reducta, iterum denominator cōmunis prius inueſtigatus per tertij fragmenti denominatorem multiplicetur: et ſurgent ſexaginta, omnium denominator communis. $\frac{2}{3}$ $\frac{3}{4}$ $\frac{4}{5}$ *$\frac{7}{12}$ $\frac{4}{5}$ 60

* Should be 17 in the original, which shows that the fractions were added.

"Qꝯ si ſcire cupis: quot partes ſexageſimae ſint in quouis fragmento numeratorem ipſius fragmenti in denominatorem cōmunem multiplica: nempe ſexaginta: numerumqꝫ procreatū diuide per eiuſdem fragmenti denominatorem. Ita deprehendes in duabus tertijs quadraginta ſexageſimas . $\frac{2}{3}$ $\frac{40}{60}$ et in tribus quartis quadraginta quinqꝫ . ſexageſimas . $\frac{3}{4}$ $\frac{45}{60}$ et in quatuor quītis quadraginta octo ſexigeſimas." Fol. P₃ verso.

[4] Raets, Arithmetica Oft Een niew Cijfferboeck (1580 ed.), fol. Bvi verso to Bviii recto.

THE ESSENTIAL FEATURES

Therefore, the fractions become $\frac{120}{160}, \frac{140}{160}, \frac{128}{160}$.

2.
160(40	160(20	160(32
44 3	88 7	55 4
——	——	——
120	140	128

3.
5	4	4
8	5	8
——	——	——
40	20	32
3	7	4
——	——	——
120	140	128

This problem has an additional interest on account of its three solutions. In the first the common denominator is multiplied by each numerator, and the result is divided by the corresponding denominator. This is evidently the longest method. In the second the common denominator is divided by each denominator, and the results multiplied by the corresponding numerators. In the third the product of two denominators is multiplied by the numerator of the third fraction; this is the shortest process.

Mixed numbers were added in two ways: (1) By adding the integers and fractions separately and combining the results. (2) By reducing the mixed numbers to improper fractions and adding. The following example from Rudolff [1] shows a common form for arranging the work in adding by the first method:

$13\frac{1}{4}$		3	8	10	6
$7\frac{2}{3}$					
$12\frac{5}{6}$		$\frac{1}{4}$	$\frac{2}{3}$	$\frac{5}{6}$	$\frac{1}{2}$
$19\frac{1}{2}$					
$53\frac{1}{4}$			12	12	

The following shows the work of adding mixed numbers by the use of the second method: [2]

---

[1] Rudolff, Kunstliche rechnung (1534 ed.), fol. Dii recto.

[2] Ciacchi, Regole Generali D'Abbaco (1675 ed.). "Del secondo modo di sommare interi, e rotti. Supponga fi per efempio, che vno fi trouaffe debitore d'vn altro di diuerfe fomme di danari, cioè di lire 16$\frac{2}{3}$, di lir. 1$\frac{5}{8}$, di lir. 11$\frac{7}{8}$, di lir. 25$\frac{2}{3}$, di lir. 6$\frac{2}{3}$, di lir. 15.7.12 fimi, e di lir. 4.5.12 fimi, si domando di quanto fi douera afcriuere in vna fola partita; Si ponghino

$16\frac{1}{2}$	$4\frac{2}{3}$	$11\frac{1}{4}$	$25\frac{5}{6}$	$6\frac{4}{9}$	$15\frac{7}{12}$	$4\frac{5}{12}$
18	12	9	6	4	3	3
$\frac{33}{2}$	$\frac{14}{3}$	$\frac{45}{4}$	$\frac{155}{6}$	$\frac{58}{9}$	$\frac{187}{12}$	$\frac{53}{12}$

Somma prima	594
seconda	168
terza	405
quarta	930
quinta	232
ſeſta	561
settima	159
	3049

36] 84.13.10.⅔

The top row contains the numbers to be added. The third row is composed of the same numbers reduced to improper fractions. The middle row contains numbers of which the numerator of each fraction is to be multiplied to give an equal fraction with the denominator 36. The column which follows is the sum of these numerators. The result is expressed in lira, soldi, and denarii.

Under addition and other processes with fractions there generally were included problems in denominate numbers.[1]

Subtraction

The order in subtraction was naturally the same as that in addition. That is, the subtraction of fractions (1) with the

le ſomme per ordine, e ſi reduchino gl' interi a quella parte, con la quale ſi trouano copulati, e s'offerui il modo notato nell' antecedente." Fol. D₅ recto.

[1] This problem from Trenchant (L'Arithmetique, 1578 ed.) will illustrate:

$\frac{1}{2}$	10 ſ	0 δ
$\frac{2}{3}$	13 —— 4	
$\frac{1}{4}$	5 ——	
$\frac{5}{6}$	16 —— 8	
$\frac{3}{8}$	7 —— 6	
$\frac{7}{12}$	11 —— 8	
$3\frac{5}{24}$	3 l. 4 ſ. 2 δ	

The fractions represent parts of a lira, a money denomination, the second column contains the equivalent amounts expressed in the lower denominations, soldi and denarii.

like denominators, (2) with different denominators. Baker,[1] Gemma Frisius,[2] and Tonstall[3] emphasized the subtraction of a fraction from an integer, performing the process in two ways: By detaching one from the integer and subtracting the fraction from that, and by reducing the integer to an improper fraction of the same denominator as the given fraction and then subtracting.

The subtraction of mixed numbers was accomplished in two ways: by subtracting the fractions separately, adding one to the minuend when necessary, and by reducing both minuend and subtrahend to improper fractions. Theorists like Tonstall[4] who were fond of extreme classification gave three cases under mixed numbers:

1. Subtraction of a fraction from a mixed number.
2. Subtraction of an integer from a mixed number.
3. Subtraction of a mixed number from a mixed number.

The placing of (1) before (2) in this list is an example of the illogical order that characterized even the work of careful writers of this period.

[1] Baker, The Well Spring of Sciences (1580 ed.), fol. Ki recto, Kii recto.

[2] Gemma Frisius, Arithmeticae Practicae Methodus Facilis (1581 ed.), fol. Cv verso.

[3] Tonstall, De Arte Supputandi (1522 ed.). To subtract $\frac{4}{7}$ from 12, take 1 from 12 which leaves 11. $1 = \frac{7}{7}$ and $\frac{7}{7} - \frac{4}{7} = \frac{3}{7}$. Hence, $12 - \frac{4}{7} = 11\frac{3}{7}$.

Or, 12 may be reduced to sevenths, making $\frac{84}{7}$. $\frac{84}{7} - \frac{4}{7} = \frac{80}{7}$, $11\frac{3}{7}$.

"Quando minutiae fubducentur ab integris: fuffecerit eas ab uno integro, in minutias foluto, fubducere. et quod tam de integris q̃ de minutijs reftabit: totius fubductionis erit reliquum. Veluti fi $\frac{4}{7}$ fubtrahendae funt a 12. fumamus .1. de .12. et reftabunt .11. ab illo autem uno demptis $\frac{4}{7}$, relinquentur $\frac{3}{7}$. quę copulatae cum .11. reftare faciunt .11$\frac{3}{7}$. tantum fupereft: fi $\frac{4}{7}$ a. 12. fubducimus. Alij integra minutiarum more, fupra lineam notant: cui unitatem fubijciunt, ad integra defignanda. Deinde quafi minutiae a minutijs subducendae effent: poft obliquam numeratorum in denominatores multiplicationem, minorem productum a maiore fubducunt: et fupra lineam notant. cui denominatorem fubdunt. ita. 7. in 12. ducta creant .84. et. 4 in .1. ducta faciunt .4. quę fubducta ab .84. reliquunt $\frac{80}{7}$. Ea, fi reducas ad integra: hent .11$\frac{3}{7}$. ita res ad idem recidet. $\frac{4}{7}$ $\frac{8}{1}$ $\frac{80}{7}$." Fol. S₁ recto. Riese (1571 ed.) used this plan, fol. Dij verso.

[4] Tonstall, De Arte Supputandi (1522), fol. S₂ recto.

104   SIXTEENTH CENTURY ARITHMETIC

Among the works which correlate fractions and denominate numbers, it would be difficult to find a better specimen than that of Wencelaus. This is an example under subtraction of fractions:[1] "A silversmith had an amount of silver weighing 15 marc $1\frac{3}{4}$ once, he wished to make from it an article weighing 8 marc $5\frac{7}{8}$ once. The question is: How much silver is left?"

Multiplication

The multiplication of fractions was generally based upon the definition of a fraction. This statement, often included in the general definition of a fraction, gave the common rule for forming the product of two fractions. That the multiplication of one fraction by another does not require special emphasis was observed by Champenois:[2] " Fractions of fractions occur more rarely than the others (simple fractions), as two-thirds of three-fourths is written thus: $\frac{2}{3}$ of $\frac{3}{4}$. Likewise, three-fifths of a half, $\frac{3}{5}$ of $\frac{1}{2}$. Also, a half of two-thirds is $\frac{1}{2}$ of $\frac{2}{3}$. Two-thirds of three-fourths of five-sevenths is $\frac{2}{3}$ of $\frac{3}{4}$ of $\frac{5}{7}$." Calandri, who placed multiplication of fractions before addition, introduced the subject by finding the product of an integer and a fraction.[3] Though complicated by the use of

---

[1] Wencelaus, T'Fondament Van Arithmetica (1599 ed.).

Item eenen Silversmit heeft een Masse Silvers van 15. Marc/ inde 1. $\frac{3}{4}$. once/ daer wt wil hy een weeck toerichten van 8. marc. ende 5. $\frac{7}{8}$. oncen. De vraghe is: Hoe veel Silvers rester noch? P. 82.

Item vn Orsebure a vn masse dargent de 15. marc. & $1\frac{3}{4}$. d'once, il en veut faire vn ouurage de 8. marc. $5\frac{7}{8}$. once, la demande est, marc. $5\frac{7}{8}$. once, la demande est, 82.

[2] Champenois, Les Institvtions De L'Arithmetique (1578 ed.). "Les Fractions de Fractions aduinnêt plus rarement que les autres, & f' efcriuent par plufieurs fimples minutes, comme deux tiers de trois quarts ainfi figuré, $\frac{2}{3}$ de $\frac{3}{4}$. Item trois cinquiefmes d'vn demy, $\frac{3}{5}$ de $\frac{1}{2}$. Plus vn demy de deux tiers $\frac{1}{2}$ de $\frac{2}{3}$. Dauantage deux tiers de trois quarts de cinq feptiemes $\frac{2}{3}$ de $\frac{3}{4}$ de $\frac{5}{7}$." P. 88, fol. Giiij verso.

[3] Calandri, Arithmetica (1491 ed.). The problem is: "A man gained 45 ƴ 15 β 4 δ in one year, what will he gain in 23 years $3\frac{3}{5}$ months?"
Original. "Lhuomo guadagna lanno 45 ƴ 15 β 4 δ che ghuadagnera in 23 anni 3 mefi $\frac{3}{5}$." (See next page for the solution.)

denominate numbers it amounts to finding ⅗ of 45, 15, and 4. This is the appropriate phase with which to begin the multiplication of fractions and, as such, should precede formal work in addition and subtraction. Such a plan would be an improvement in modern arithmetic. The directions for forming the products of two fractions were the same as those in present use: Take the product of the numerators for a new numerator and the product of the denominators for a new denominator.[1] Thus, $\frac{2}{3}$ met $\frac{4}{5}$ comt $\frac{8}{15}$. Mixed numbers were usually reduced to improper fractions, as in:[2]

$$\frac{3\frac{4}{5}}{\frac{19}{5}} \text{ met } \frac{6\frac{7}{8}}{\frac{55}{8}}$$

A rare representation of the product of three fractions was given by Champenois:[3] I wish to reduce a half of two-thirds

He solves the problem thus:

45 —— 15 —— 4 ———— 23 —— $3\frac{3}{5}$

3 ——	16 ——	$3\frac{1}{3}$
0 ——	15 ——	3
920		12
115		5
17 ——	5 ——	0
0 ——	7 ——	8
9 ——	0 ——	0
2 ——	8 ——	0
0 ——	0 ——	9
0 ——	0 ——	1
2 ——	5 ——	0
0 ——	0 ——	9
1066 ℔	7 β	3 δ

He will gain in the time stated above ℔ 1066 β 7 δ 3.

"Guadagnera nel ſopra decto tempo diſopra ℔ 1066 β 7 δ 3 a pl'i." Fol. dvi recto, fol. 26 r. Another example from Calandri is: "El cogno de uino vale 37 ℔ 15 β 8 δ che uarranno 1 6 cogna 5 barili ⅔. Fol. d_{vi} recto.

[1] Van der Scheure, Arithmetica (1600 ed.), fol. E_7 recto.

[2] Van der Scheure, Arithmetica (1600 ed.), fol. E_7 verso.

[3] Champenois, Les Institvtions De L'Arithmetique (1570 ed.). "Ie veux $\frac{6}{7}$. Ie multiplie le premier Numerateur 1. par le secõd Numerateur 2. le reduire vn demy de deux tiers de ſix ſeptieſmes ainſi figuré $\frac{1}{2}$ de $\frac{2}{3}$ de pduict dõne 2. que ie multiplie par le troiſieſme Numerateur 6. le produict

of six-sevenths, represented in figures thus: $\frac{1}{2}$ of $\frac{2}{3}$ of $\frac{6}{7}$. I multiply the first numerator, 1, by the second numerator, 2, the product is 2, which I multiply by the third numerator, 6. This gives the product, 12, for the numerator of the reduction.

"I then multiply the first denominator, 2, by the second, 3, and obtain 6 as the product, which I multiply by the third denominator, 7, giving a product 42 for the denominator of the reduction. Then $\frac{1}{2}$ of $\frac{2}{3}$ of $\frac{6}{7}$ is reduced to one fraction, making $\frac{12}{42}$, or $\frac{2}{7}$."

The meaning of the above multiplication was shown graphically by the following diagram:[1]

P	Q					
M	N	O				
m	n	o				
i	k	l				
a	c	d	e	f	g	h
a	c	d	e	f	g	h	b

The base line, ab, represents a unit and ah is $\frac{6}{7}$ of it. Then af is $\frac{2}{3}$ of $\frac{6}{7}$, and ad is $\frac{1}{2}$ of $\frac{2}{3}$ of $\frac{6}{7}$.

Trenchant[2] gave a diagram, which actually demonstrated

donne 12. pour le Numerateur de la reduction. Apres ie multiplie le premier Denominateur 2. par le fecond 3. le produict donne 6. que ie multiplie par le troifiefme Denominateur 7. le produict dõne 42. pour le Denominateur de la reduction. Parquoy $\frac{1}{2}$ de $\frac{2}{3}$ de $\frac{6}{7}$ font reduicts en Vne Fractiõ fçauoir $\frac{12}{42}$iemes, ou $\frac{2}{7}$ieme." Page 89, fol. Gv recto.

[1] Champenois, Les Institvtions De L'Arithmetique (1578 ed.), p. 90, fol. Gv verso.

[2] Trenchant, L'Arithmetique (1578 ed.).

MULTIPLICATION OF FRACTIONS.

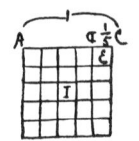

"Pour en auoir demonftration plus fuffifante: veyez cete fuperfice ou quarré A, B, qui eft le produit de la ligne A, C: multiplie en foy même, laquelle faut entendre vn entier diuifé en 5. Or eft il certain que 1 qu'elle reprefente multiplié en foy fét 1, denotant le total quarré A, B: mais le $\frac{1}{5}$ d'icelle, fçauoir eft, D, C, en foy multiplée,

the truth of the multiplication, a thing unique among the treatments examined. Thus he demonstrated that $\frac{1}{5} \times \frac{1}{5} = \frac{1}{25}$, $\frac{2}{5} \times \frac{1}{5} = \frac{2}{25}$, $\frac{2}{5} \times \frac{2}{5} = \frac{4}{25}$, and so on. It is evident that the products of other fractions may be found from similar diagrams. The applications of multiplication involving denominate numbers were of the type, — the product of an integer and a fraction,—as illustrated by this problem from Köbel.[1] "76 persons have 4698 gulden to be divided among them. The question is: 'How much belongs to each?' Solving by the Rule of Three, one finds that the share of each is $71\frac{12}{66}$ guldens. Reduce further this fraction and all resulting fractions according to the method described in the rule above and according to the example which follows, until the lowest denomination and the lowest fraction of that denomination is reached."

Division

The prevalent order in the treatment of the division of fractions was (1) to divide the numerators of fractions having a common denominator, (2) to reduce to a common denominator and divide the numerators, (3) to multiply crosswise the numerator of each fraction by the denominator of the other, (4) to invert the divisor and multiply. The third method is not so frequently used as the first and second, and the fourth is very rare. An excellent example of the fourth method is From Thierfeldern:[2] "When the denominators are different,

ne fét que le quarreau E: qui n'eſt que le $\frac{1}{25}$ du total & entier quarré A, B, qui en contient 25 ſemblables. Parquoy apert que $\frac{1}{5}$ par $\frac{1}{5}$ multiplié, ne fét que $\frac{1}{25}$ d'entier: comme auſſi $\frac{2}{5}$ par $\frac{1}{5}$ ne fét que $\frac{2}{25}$; & $\frac{2}{5}$ par $\frac{2}{5}$ font $\frac{4}{25}$.

"Semblablement ſe peut demontrer par vne autre ſuperficie, ayant 4 de long, & 3 de large: que $\frac{1}{3}$ par $\frac{1}{4}$, fét $\frac{1}{12}$; & $\frac{2}{3}$ par $\frac{3}{4}$, fét $\frac{6}{12}$: & ainſi des autres, ce qui nous a ſemblé bon de declarer en paſſant." Fol. H₃ recto.

[1] Köbel, Zwey rechenbůchlin (1537 ed.). "Auff das nim diß Exempel. 76. perſonen haben vnder ſich zu teylen 4698. gulden. Iſt die frag/ was vñ wie vil gebürt jr jeglichem. Machs nach der Regel de Tri/ ſo findet ſich das einem gebürt 71. gůldẽ/ vnd $\frac{12}{66}$ eines guldens. Diſe vnd all ander brüch reducier/ minder/ und bring ſie allo nach auß welſung obgeſchribner regel vnd Exempel/ wie nachuolgt/ in den kleyneren bruch oder in das kleyner theyl." Fol. H₈ verso.

[2] Thierfeldern, Arithmetica Oder Rechenbuch Auff den Linien vnd Ziffer/

invert the divisor (which you are to place at the right) and multiply the numbers above (new numerators) together and the numbers below (new denominators) together, then you have the correct result. As, to divide $\frac{3}{4}$ by $\frac{5}{8}$, invert thus $\frac{3}{4} \times \frac{8}{5} = \frac{24}{20} = 1\frac{1}{5}$." Thierfeldern used cancellation to simplify the work, as shown in the example[1] at the right. This was rarely done in the works of that time.

$$\frac{\overset{1}{7}}{\underset{12}{\cancel{}}} \text{ mit } \frac{\overset{3}{9}}{\underset{14}{\cancel{}}} \text{ facit } \frac{3}{8}$$
$$(4) \qquad (2)$$

Teachers often complain that their pupils do not readily pass to the multiplication by the reciprocal of the divisor after they have begun by using the common denominator method. The crosswise method of the sixteenth century forms a connecting link between these two plans, and it is possible that it could be used to advantage in making the transition in teaching. The relation is shown in this example from Baker.[2] The divisor was generally written first (which would not be done now) and the terms of the result above and below. If these fractions were changed to fractions with a common denominator, 12, the numerator would be found by multiplying the same numbers that are multiplied in the above work; and, since the result is the quotient of these numerators, Baker's process is the same as the one in which the common denominator is used, only the changed fractions are not in evidence.

$$\overset{9}{\frac{3}{4}} \times \overset{}{\frac{3}{8}}$$

The denominate number problems following division were of this type:[3] "At Breslau a man buys 3 sacks of wool weighing 14 stein, 12 stein, and 15 stein. How many centners is this, if one centner is equal to 5½ stein, and a stein is equal to 24 ℔.? Ans. 7 ceñ 2. stein 2 ℔."

(1578 ed.). "Da aber die Nenner vngleich/ ſo kehre allzeit den Theyler (welchen du zur rechten Hand ſetzen ſolt) vmb/ vnd multiplicir darnach die obern vnd vndern mit einander/ ſo haſt du es verricht/ Als: $\frac{3}{4}$ in $\frac{5}{8}$. stehet vmb gekehrt also:

$\frac{3}{4}$ in $\frac{8}{5}$ $\frac{24}{20}$ | $1\frac{1}{5}$ das Facit." Pages 64 and 65.

[1] Thierfeldern, Arithmetica (1578 ed.), page 63.

[2] Baker, The Well Spring of Sciences (1580 ed.), fol. Kviii recto.

[3] Rudolff, Kunstliche rechnung mit der Ziffern und mit den Zalpfennige/ (1534 ed.).

"12 Nuremberg pfennings equal what part of a pound? Ans. $\frac{2}{5}$."

"1 fl $\frac{3}{4}$ d is what part of 1 L? Ans. $\frac{17}{320}$ L."

Doubling and halving were often included under fractions with the same meaning as under integers and with as little use for independent existence. Baker, whose work is characterized by minute classification, devotes the eighth chapter in his book to duplation (doubling), triplation, and quadruplation of fractions. He gives these examples:[1]

(1) Duplation. To double any fraction, divide by $\frac{1}{2}$.

To double $\frac{3}{0}$. $\frac{1}{2} \times \frac{3}{8} = \frac{6}{8}$

(2) Triplation. To triple $\frac{3}{5}$, divide $\frac{3}{5}$ by $\frac{1}{3} = \frac{9}{5}$.

Proofs for the operations with fractions were far less numerous than for those with integers. One would expect this to be so. The work with fractions, having to do with small numbers, had usually been done mentally, without the use of the abacus, and so without proofs. Hence there were no proofs to carry over into figure reckoning, as there were in the case of integers. Only one-eighth of the writers gave proofs in fractions and commonly placed them at the close of the treatment of each operation, or in a list at the end of the chapter.

This table from Van der Scheure shows that each operation may be proved by applying the inverse operation.[2]

De proeve van	{ Additio Substractio Multiplicatio Divisio	Soubstractio Additio Divisio Multiplicatio

Commercial arithmetics, especially those which did not have denominate numbers under each operation with fractions, contained a section following the operations called the "Rule of Three with Fractions." Van der Scheure opens this section

---

[1] Baker, The Well Spring of Sciences (1580 ed.), fol. Liii verso, Liiii verso.

[2] Van der Scheure, Arithmetica (1600 ed.), fol. E$_8$ recto.

containing forty-one problems thus:[1] Having learned to use the species understandingly, do not fail to heed the advice to turn your thoughts quickly to the Rule of Three with Fractions.

The following serve to illustrate the application of this rule:[2]

"If a centner of anything costs 9¼ florins, how much does a pound cost?"

"If 45 ells of cloth cost 13 fl 17 gr., how much do 7 ells cost?" Ans. 2 fl 3 gr. 1 ᵈ 0 ⅔ hl'.

"4½ braza are worth 17 sol., what will 8 braza be worth?"[3]

"If a centner of wax is worth 13⅔ florins, how much are 17½ ℔. worth?"

PROGRESSIONS

Among those arithmeticians on whom tradition worked its spell, none failed to give progressions (Arithmetic, Geometric and often Harmonic) a place. This subject appealed to both the classical and the modern scholars of that time, since it was persistent in the few classical works that survived and in the more recent acquisitions from the Hindus. Theoretical writers did not attempt to justify the presence of Progressions in their text-books. That they were in existence was deemed sufficient reason why all educated persons should know of them.

Although their position in the list of species was variable, the favorite place for them was after the division of whole

---

[1] Van der Scheure, Arithmetica (1600 ed.).
"Die Specien gheleert.
Zijn nu met claer bedien,
Das laet den moet niet vallen,
Maer snel u sinnen keert
Toto den Reghel van Drien,
Ghebroken in ghetallen." Fol. E$_8$ verso.

[2] Riese, Rechnung auff der Linien und Federn/ (1571 ed.).
"Item/ Ein Centener für 9 floren/ vnd 1 orth/ Wie kompt ein pfund?" Fol. Dv recto.
"Item/ 45 Elln tuchs für 13 fl/ 17 gr/ Wie kommen 7 elln? Facit 2 fl/ 3 gr/ 1 ᵟ/ 0 hl'/ ⅔." Fol. Dvi recto.

[3] Borgi, Arithmetica (1540 ed.).
¶ E ſel te fuſſe detto ſe braza .4½. de tela val. fol. 17. che valera braza .8. Fol. E$_5$ recto.

numbers.[1] In some cases they followed proportion, in others roots.[2] Köbel and Van der Scheure reserved the subject for the latter part of their works, after practical arithmetic had been completed, and Noviomagus deferred it to his second book, entitled Liber Secundus Arithmeticae, qui est de numerorum Theorematis.[3]

The usual treatment consists in defining the series and in giving the rules for the last term and for the sum of a specific series. No proofs for these rules were attempted in arithmetic. This treatment of arithmetical progression from Tonstall[4] is more elaborate than those commonly given:

"Arithmetic progression is the collection, into one whole, of

[1] Riese, Baker, Tonstall, and Buteo.   [2] Finaeus.

[3] Noviomagus, De Numeris Libri II.

[4] Tonstall, De Arte Supputandi (1522 ed.). "Progressio Arithmetica est numerorū inter se equaliter distantium in unam summam collectio: - - - Eius autem duae sunt species. Altera est: in qua naturali numerorum serie seruata, numerus quilibet sequens sola unitate praecedentem superat: sicut in hoc exemplo. 1.2.3.4.5. 6.7.8.9. Altera in qua numeros quoslibet omittentes, et paria seruantes interualla, longam numerorum seriem connectimus. velutei. 1.3.5.7.9.11.13. - - -." Fol. M$_1$ verso.

"Ita fiet: vt numerus ex hoc productus summam omniū commonstret. veluti in hoc exemplo .1.2.3.4.5.6.7.8. primus numerus .1. ad postremum .8. addatur et fient .9. Cumq; in tota serie sint .8. loca. ducamus .9. in 4, eorum dimidiū. et prodibunt .36. quae omnium est summa. - - -." Fol. M$_2$ recto.

"Q7 si numerorū a se equaliter distantium atq; ordine continuo dispositorum series erit impar: tunc numerus indicans, quot loca sunt in serie, non in eum numerum ducatur: qui indicat quotus locus est in serie medius, sed in eum numerum qui in serie medius reperitur: atq; ab utroq; extremo aequaliter distat. Ita numerus procreatus omnium summa patefaciet. sicuti in hoc exemplo .1.2.3.4.5.6.7. quia loca seriei sunt .7. et medius numerus est .4.7. in .4. ducamus: et fient .28. quae suma est uniuersorum. Itidem si exempli causa sumantur. 1.4.7.10.13. quia loci serie sunt .5. et medius numer' est .7. 5. in .7. ducamus: et fient 35. quae summa est omnium." Fol. M$_2$ recto.

- - - - - - - -

"In omni progressione Arithmetica, siue series par., siue impar fuerit: numerus ab extremorum additione collectus in numerū indicatem, quot loca sunt in serie multiplicetur numerusq; productus postea dimidietur, et summa progressionis habebitur. Exemplum in serie pari. 1.3.5.7.9.11. primus numerus additus ad postremū facit .12. et quia .6. loca seriei sunt .12. per .6. multiplicemus. et surgent .72. quae si dimidientur: fient. 36. quae summa est progressionis." Fol. M$_2$ verso.

numbers equally distant from one another. There are two kinds, one is the natural number series, 1, 2, 3, 4, 5, 6, 7, where the numbers differ only by 1. The other in which any number of terms of natural series is regularly omitted, as 1, 3, 5, 7, 9, 11, 13. The sum of the series 1, 2, 3, 4, 5, 6, 7, 8 is found by adding 1 and 8, the first and last terms, and multiplying this result by half the number of terms, $\frac{8}{2}$, or 4. It gives 36, which is the sum of the series. Similarly in 1, 3, 5, 7, 9, 11; $(1 + 11) \frac{6}{2} = 12 \cdot 3 = 36$. In the case of an odd number in the series, the sum of the series is equal to the middle term of the series multiplied by the number of terms. Thus, in 1, 2, 3, 4, 5, 6, 7; $7 \cdot 4 = 28$, the sum of the series: and in 1, 4, 7, 10, 13, there are 5 terms and 7 is the middle one. Then $7 \cdot 5 = 35$, the sum of the series.

"In all cases of arithmetic progression, whether the number of terms be odd or even, the sum of the series may be found by adding the first and last terms, multiplying the result by the number of terms and dividing this result by 2. Thus, 1, 3, 5, 7, 9, 11; $(11 + 1) 6 = 12 \cdot 6 = 72$. $72 \div 2 = 36$, the sum of the series."

The following treatment of geometric progression from Adam Riese is a typical one from commercial arithmetic:[1]

"When numbers follow each other in twofold, threefold, or fourfold ratio, and so on, and you wish to find the sum, multiply the last number by the rate of progression, subtract the first term and divide this result by the rate of progression minus 1.

2, 4, 8, 16, 32, 64, 128, 256, 512, 1024, 2048.
$2048 \times 2 = 4096$ $\quad$ $4096 - 2 = 4094$.
$\frac{4094}{2-1} = 4094$, sum."

[1] Riese, Rechnung auff der Linien und Federn/ (1571 ed.).

"So aber eine zal die ander vbertrit/ zweyfeltig/ dreyfeltig/ vierfeltig/ ᴧc. vnd wolteſt die Summa wiſſen/ ſo multiplicire die letzte zal mit der vbertrettung/ nim von ſolchen die erſte/ was bleibt/ theil ab mit der vber trettung/ weniger 1/ Als hie in folgenden Exempeln.

"Item/ 2.4.8.16.32.64.128.256.512.1024.2048. duplir 2048/ komen 4096/ nim ab 2/ bleiben 4094/ die teil ab mit 2/ weniger 1/ als/ 1/ bleibt die zal an jr ſelbs." Fol. Cij recto.

Thierfeldern combines geometric progression with the extraction of roots.[1] "Hiernacht folget die Tafel/ dadurch ausgezogen werden alle Wurtzeln Geometrischer Progres."

ρ	χ								
2	2	χ							
cρ	3	3	χ						
ƺƺ	4	6	4	χ					
β	5	10	10	5	χ				
ƺcρ	6	15	20	15	6	χ			
ββ	7	21	35	35	21	7	χ		
ƺƺƺ	8	28	56	70	56	28	8	χ	
ccρ	9	36	84	126	126	84	36	9	χ

The characters in the left hand column represent the successive powers of a number from the first to the ninth; that is, these were algebraic symbols for x, x^2, and so on. The various lines are seen to be the binomial coefficients, and the form is essentially that of Pascal's triangle.

The traditional applications of the progressions were commonly given, but when an attempt was made to supply vital applications, the results were curious. The following are from Baker:[2]

"A marchant hath sold 100 kerſies after this manner following, that is to ſay, the first peece for 1 s̃, the second peece for 2 s̃, the thirde for 3 s̃, and so foorth, riſing 1 s̃ in every peece of kerſey unto the 100 peeces. The queſtion is to know how much he ſhall receiue for the ſayd 100 peeces of kerſeys." This is evidently an attempt at giving a practical problem.

" I woulde laye 100 ſtones or other things in a right line, of every of the ſayde ſtones to be a juſt pace one from an other, and one pace of from the firſt ſtone, there ſtandeth a baſket. I demaunde howe manye paces a man ſhall goe in gathering up the ſayde ſtones, and bearing them unto the

---

[1] Thierfeldern, Arithmetica Oder Rechenbuch Auff den Linien vnd Ziffern/ (1587 ed.), page 331.

[2] Baker, The Well Spring of Sciences (1580 ed.). Fol. Fiii recto.

baſket, the ſtone after the other." This was a puzzle problem of long standing.

" There is one man departeth from London to Cheſter, and ſo to Carnaruan, the diſtaunce beeing about 200 myles: He goeth the fyrſte day 1 mile, the ſecond day 2 myles, the thirde day 3: and so orderlye by natural progreſſion. An other man departeth at the ſame inſtante from Carnaruan to London, and goeth the fyrſte day 2 myles: the ſecond day 4 myles, the thyrde day 6 miles, and so encreaſing every day 2 miles. The queſtyon is to know in howe manye dayes they two perſons shall meete togither." This is a courier problem.

The following, though an artificial business problem, seems more plausible: "A man oweth me 400 l'i, to be payd in 10 yeares, by progreſſyon Arithmeticall, that is to ſay 40 l'i at the end of the fyrſte yeare, and euery yeare following 40 l'i, to the end of 10 yeares, hee offereth to pay me the ſayd 400 pound al at one paiment. The question is to know at what time hee ought to paye mee the ſame at one paimente, that I be not intereſſed in the time."

Only one problem in geometric progression was given. It is this:

"A marchante hath ſolde 15 yeardes of Satten, the firſte yarde for 1 s̃, the ſecond 2 s̃, the thyrde 4 s̃, the fourth 8 s̃, and so increaſing by double progreſſion Geometricall. The queſtyon is to know, how muche the ſayde marchant ſhal receiue for ẙ ſayd 15 yardes of ſatten."

Although the French writers were chiefly theorists, Champenois wrote to meet business needs, and his introduction to this chapter reads:[1] " Progression is a series of numbers in which there is a certain excess between the numbers, and the first is always exceeded by the second as much as the second

---

[1] Champenois, Les Inſtitvtions De L'Arithmetique (1578 ed.).

" Progreſſion eſt vne ſuite de nombre, qui ont vn certain excez les vns entre les autres, & touſiours le premier eſt autant excede du ſecond, que le ſecond du troiſieſme, & ainſi des autres. L'vſage de la Progreſſion eſt vn compendium d'Addition, & eſt fort vtile, tant eñ diuerſes queſtiõs d'Arithmetique, Geometrie, Muſique, qu' Aſtrologie, là où pluſieurs regles ſont faictes par la nature de la Progreſſion." Fol. Eviij verso.

is by the third, and so on with the others. The practice of progression is a summary of addition and is very useful in questions of arithmetic, geometry, music, and astrology, where many rules are made in the nature of progression."

Among his problems in progression are the following:

"A merchant has 60 horses and sells them to another merchant; he is to have 4 ecus for the first, 8 for the second, 12 for the third, and so on for the others. The question is: 'How much should he receive for the last, and how much should he receive for all?'"[1]

"A man about to die gives all his money to his relatives on the condition that the first should have 4 ecus, the second 6 more than the first, and the amount for the third and the others should increase at the same rate to the last. After the distribution was made, it was found that the last had 118 ecus for his part. The question is: 'How many relatives had he and how many ecus?'"[2]

"A merchant sells a piece of velvet containing 16 aunes to another merchant for which he shall give 2 sous for the first aune, 6 sous for the second, and for the others he shall give at the same rate up to the sixteenth aune. The question is: 'How much should he give for the 16 aunes?'"[3]

"A gentleman has 12 horses, which he wishes to sell, and

---

[1] "Vn marchant a 60 cheuailx, & les vend à vn autre marchant, par tel fi qu'il doit auoir 4 efcus du premier, 8 du fecond, 12 du troifiefme, & ainfi des autres. On demande combien il doit receuoir du dernier, & combien il doit receuoir du tout." Page 63, fol. Eviii recto.

[2] "Vn homme allant de vie à trefpas, donne tous fes efcus à fes parents, par telle côdition que le premier doit auoir 4 efcus: le fecond 6. plus que le premier, & ainfi du troifiefme, & autres iusques au dernier. Et apres le partage faict lon a trouué que le dernier a eu 118. efcus pour fa part. Lon demande combien il auoit de parents, & combien d'efcus." Page 64, Eviij verso.

[3] "Vn marchant vend vne piece de velours, qui contient 16. aulnes, à vn autre marchant, par tel fi qu'il donnera 2. fols pour la premiere aulne, & 6. fols de la feconde, & ainfi pourfuiuant la Progreffio des autres iufques à la feiziefme aulne. Lon demande combien il doit des 16. aulnes." Page 66, fol. F verso.

gives the first for 3 sous, the second for 12, the third for 48, and so on with the others up to the last." [1]

"A dealer wishes to sell a robe to a Master of Arts, who has little money. The Master of Arts, however, seeing himself without a robe, and that this one for which he was bargaining, seems to be well made, says to the dealer that he will give 4888 livres for it, reduced twenty times by half. The dealer is well satisfied and gives the robe to the Master of Arts, who does not refuse it, but joyfully putting it on his shoulders makes his reckoning with the dealer. At the end of the calculation he finds due to the dealer $2\frac{217}{10024}$ deniers, which is worth $\frac{3}{4}$ of a quarter of a pite, and $\frac{25}{64}$ths of $\frac{1}{16}$ of a pite. To pay this large sum he takes from his purse a piece worth 3 deniers, gives it to the dealer, and demands his change. The dealer driven to despair asks if he will put it at stake. The Master of Arts agrees. The dealer loses, the Master of Arts gains, and taking his 3 deniers he joyfully takes leave of the dealer. The dealer thanks him, saying that he is at his service. Thus, the Master finds himself well dressed at little expense by means of the cunning of an arithmetical rule." [2]

[1] "Vn Seigneur a 12 cheuaux, qu'il veut vĕdre, & donne le premier pour 3. ſols, le ſecõd pour 12. le troiſieſme pour 48. & ainſi des autres iuſques au dernier." Page 67, Fii recto.

[2] Champenois, Les Inſtitvtions (1578 ed.). "Vn frippier veut vendre vne robbe 58. lires à vn maiſtre és arts, qui n'auoit pas beaucoup de pecune. Toutefois ſe voyant ſans robbe, & que celle qu'il marchãdoit, luy ſembloit bien faicte, dict au frippier qu'il en dõneroit 4888 liures, en rabatant de moitié iuſques à 20 fois. Le frippier fut content, & dõna la robbe au maiſtre és arts: lequel ne la refuſa pas, mais d'vne gayeté de coeur la mit deſſus ſes eſpaules, & fit cõpte auec le frippier. Et à la fin du cõpte ſe trouua redeuable au frippier de 2. deniers & $\frac{217}{10024}$ieme d'vn denier qui vallet ¾ d'vn quart de pite, & $\frac{25}{64}$ieme d'vn quart de quart de pite. Et pour faire le payement de ceſte grande ſomme, prẽden ſa bourſe vne grande piece de trois deniers, & la done au frippier, & demande ſon reſte. Le frippier tout deſeſperé luy demanda ſ'il vouloit iouer ſon reſte à ſa grande piece de trois deniers. Le maiſtre és arts dict qu'il eſtoit cõtẽt. Le frippier perd: le maiſtre és arts gaigne, & prẽd ſa piece de trois deniers, & ioyeuſemẽt prend congé du frippier. Et le frippier le remercia, & luy dict que luy & ſon biẽ eſtoiẽt à ſon cõmandement. Monſieur le Maiſtre ſe trouua bien paré à peu de frais, par le moyen de la ſubtilité d'vne régle d'Arithmetique." P. 70, fol. Fiij verso.

RATIO AND PROPORTION

The treatment of this subject, more than that of progressions, followed the traditional lines of Greek and Hindu works [1] and occurred less often in the practical arithmetics of the period. The most useful tool in the solution of commercial problems, the Rule of Three, was, of course, proportion, but it was seldom connected with that subject.

It was the universal custom borrowed from the Greeks to use the terms, proportion and proportionality, for ratio and proportion until the latter part of the sixteenth century. Tonstall stated the Greek meaning of proportion in such a way as to enable one to recognize at once the corresponding modern ideas of Ratio and Proportion and gave an explanation that is more than a mere category. His treatment was as follows: [2]

"Proportion is nothing else than a comparison of things

[1] Unicorn, De L'Arithmetica vinversale (1598 ed.). "Che contien li altri 4. Algorismi della prattica di Arithmetica, cioe de radici, del piu, & men, de binomii, & recisi, & de proportioni, de radice uniuersali, & estrattioni de radici delli binomii, & recisi, quali sono il neruo del decimo libro de Euclide, & della proportione hauente il mezzo, & doi estremi, della qual il decimoterzo libro di Euclide." Fol. Fi recto. (Besides the four algorisms of practical arithmetic, this contains roots, positive and negative number, binomials, surds, proportion, roots in general, the extraction of roots of binomials and surds, which are contained in the tenth book of Euclid, and the extremes and means of proportion from the thirteenth book of Euclid.)

[2] Tonstall, De Arte Supputandi (1522 ed.). "Illa itaqȝ habitudo, qua fefe uel aequaliter, quando funt equales: mutuo refpiciunt. uel inequaliter, quando earum altera maior reliqua, aut minor eft: appellatur proportio. que nihil aliud eft: q̄ earum inter fe comparatio eiufdem quoqȝ generis quantitates effe debent: inter quas cadit proportio. Veluti duo numeri, duae lineae, due fuperficies, duo corpora duo loca, duo tempora. neqȝ enim linea maior aut minor fuperficie eft, aut corpora: nec tempus loco maius eft, aut minus. fed linea linea: fuperficies fuperficie: corpus corpore. lola enim, quae unius funt generis: inter fe comparabilia funt." Fol. i₁ verso.

"Quippe proportio apud ueteres in tria fecatur genera. quorum unum eft difcretorum, uidelicet numerorum: quod uocant Arithmeticum. Alterum continuorum: quod geometricum appellant. Tertium fonorum et concentuum: quod armonicū nuncupant, ex illorū utroqȝ mixtū: qȝ mufica in naufis et prolationibus tēnus fpectet: in uibrante nocū notarumqȝ diuifione, numeros." Fol. i₁ verso.

"Vnde fit: ut quęcumqȝ proportio occurrit in numeris: eadem reperiatur in omni genere continuorum. puta in lineis, fuperficiebus, corporibus, et temporibus." Fol. i₂ recto.

among themselves. Quantities which form a proportion must be of the same kind, as two numbers, two lines, two surfaces, two solids, two like orders, and not, a line is greater than a surface, or solid, or time is greater or less than a space, but line is comparable with line, surface with surface, solid with solid, and so on.

"Among the ancients proportion is divided into three classes, arithmetic, geometric and harmonic.

"Just as proportion occurs in numbers, so it is found in all continua, as in lines, surfaces, solids, and time."

Kinds of Rational Proportion [1]

"Any quantity compared with another is equal or unequal to it. A quantity is equal to another when it does not exceed that quantity, or is not exceeded by it, as a cubit to a cubit, or a foot to a foot, and so on. Unequal quantities are those in which one quantity exceeds the other. A series of numbers having a common difference such that the difference is an integral part of the first number is said to be composed of proportional numbers, and the series is classified according to the name of the part. They are called sequialteri, sequitertia, and so on. This is the origin of arithmetic progression."

Tonstall here gave the Pythagorean table again, showing ratio, proportion, multiplication, and division in their interdependence.[2] " Proportionality is the similarity of proportions among themselves." In this chapter Tonstall gave arithmetic and geometric proportionality and referred to

[1] Tonstall, De Arte Supputandi (1522).

"PROPORTIONIS RATIONALIS SPECIES."

"Omnis quātitas ad aliā cōparata aut ei equalis: aut inequalis reperitur. Quantitas equalis eſt: quae nec ſibi comparatam excedit: nec ab ea exceditur. Veluti cubitus ad cubitum collatus. pes ad pedem. numerus quaternarius ad quaternarium." Fol. i$_2$ verso.

"Inequalis autem quantitas, quae ſibi comparatam excedit: proportionem ad illā habet inequalitatis maioris: ueluti cubitus ad pedem. numerus quaternarius ad binarium." Fol. i$_2$ verso.

[2] Tonstall, De Arte Supputandi (1522). "Proportionalitas eſt proportionum inter ſe ſimilitudo." Fol. K$_4$ recto.

Jordanus as having given eight kinds. Vicentino gave four: arithmetic, geometric, harmonic, and contraharmonic.[1] This subject was given a more rigorous treatment by algebraists.[2]

Ratio and proportion in the modern sense came into arithmetic about 1550. Orontius Finaeus under Ratio, Proportion, and Rules of Proportion gave this definition:[3] "Ratio (as we shall use it) is the method of comparing two numbers of the same kind." The same conception of ratio will be recognized in this example from Buteo:[4] "When two numbers are proposed, as for instance, 12400 and 124, the ratio between them will be immediately shown by dividing the greater by the less; since it is 100 in this case, we shall call the ratio between the given numbers a hundredfold ratio."

[1] Vincentino, Proportione, et Proportionalita (1573 ed.).
"Proportionalità, fi dice la ugualità delle proportioni.
'La proportionalità, fi divide in Arithmetica, Geometrica, Harmonica, et Contraharmonica.

```
                     2 2
" La Arithmetica     5 7 9
                     ─────
                     6 9
"La Geometrica       4 6
                     ─────
                     2 1
"La Harmonica        6 4 3
```

"L'una ch'ha la differentia dello antecedente fopra il confeguente, alla differentia del confeguente fopra il terzo quanto, l'altra la proportione dell' antecedente al terzo quanto.

```
                     1 2
"La contraharmonic   6 5 3
```

"L'una che ha la differentia del confeguente fopra il terzo quanto, alla differentia dell' antecedente, fopra il confeguente, l'altra la proportione dell' antecedente, l'altra la proportione dell' antecedente al terzo quanto." Fol. G_1 verso.

[2] Tartaglia, La Prima Parte Del General Trattato (1556), Book 7.

[3] Finaeus, De Arithmetica Practica (1555 ed.). "Ratio igitur (ut ad remipfam deueniamus) eft duarum quantitatum eiufdem fpeciei adinuicem comparatarū habitudo." Fol. Q_1 recto.

[4] Buteo, Logistica, Quae Arithmetica vulgo dicitur (1559 ed.). "Propofitis duobis numeris, vt puta 12400, et 124, quaenā fit inter eos ratio, partitione maioris in minorem, ipfum prouenies ftatim oftendet, quod cum fit in hoc loco 100, dicemus inter datos huiufmodi numeros rationem effe centuplam." Fol. f_5 recto.

Ramus defined ratio as division.[1] He then added the old conceptions, as: "The ratio of 3 to 2 is sequialter, because 3 contains 2 one and a half times. The ratio of 5 to 3 is super biteria, because 5 contains 3 one and $\frac{2}{3}$ times." He defined proportion as the equality of two ratios.[2] Thus, proportion came to replace the old term proportionality, and at the beginning of the seventeenth century, the title, Ratio and Proportion, had taken the place of Proportion and Proportionality.[3]

Ludolf van Ceulen (1615) gave a chapter on proportion as applied directly to practical problems. He says that proportion is necessary in comparison of weights and measures,"[4] as when one says that a pound is heavier than a mark in comparing weight, or that the distance from Utrecht to Delft is farther than that to Leyden, in comparing length."

Ratio of fractions [5] and the Rule of Three [6] of fractions are

[1] Ramus, Arithmeticae Libri Duo (1577 ed.). "Ratio est comparatio, quoties terminus in termino continetur." Page 41.

[2] Ramus, Arithmeticae Libri Duo (1586 ed.). "Proportiono arithmetica fic est, geometrica fequitur in rationem acqualitate."

[3] Stevin, Les Oeuvres Mathematiques (1634 ed.). "Des definitions de la Raison et Proportion." "La proportion, pour en parler un peu en general, avant que parvenir au particulier, eft la fimilitude de deux raifons egales. Raifon eft comparaifon de deux termes d'une mefme efpece de quantite." Fol. Bi verso.

[4] Van Ceulen, De Arithmetische en Geometrische fondamenten (1615 ed.). "Alsmen spreeckt een pondt is svvaerder als een marcq dan verghelijcktmen ghevvichte, ofte van Delfft is Vtrecht verder als Leyden, hier vvert de lenghte vergheleecken." Fol. Biij verso.

[5] Buteo, Logistica (1559 ed.).
To find the ratio of $\frac{3}{5}$ and $\frac{4}{7}$:
$\frac{3}{5} \times \frac{4}{7}$ { The ratio is 21 to 20, or sesquivigesima. (See pages
21 20   33, 34 of this article.)
"De particularum fragmentorúmque rationibus, quomodo dignofcantur." "Non folum numeri conferuntur numeris, fed etiam particulis, atque fragmentis, & ipfae etiam inter fe particulae. Quarum rationem inuestigabis hoc modo. Sit propofitum dare rationem quam habet $\frac{3}{5}$ ad $\frac{4}{7}$. Difponātur datae particulae atque multiplicētur in decuſsim,
fiéntque producta 21 & 20. Quae eft igitur ratio 21 ad 20,   21   20
eadem eft $\frac{3}{5}$ ad $\frac{4}{7}$, hoc eft fefquiuigefima." Fol. f$_6$ verso. $\frac{3}{5} \times \frac{4}{7}$

[6] Ramus, Arithmetice Libri Duo (1577 ed.), Liber II, Chap. VI.

THE ESSENTIAL FEATURES

subjects sometimes met. The latter is generally characteristic of the commercial writers.[1]

INVOLUTION AND EVOLUTION

The commercial arithmetics naturally contain little concerning powers of numbers, and one might expect to find much less on evolution. But there was a large number of problems in mensuration, a subject of real interest at that time, which required a knowledge of roots. Consequently, most works of any pretension gave square and cube root. Theorists like Tartaglia[2] and Unicorn[3] explained evolution of orders higher than the third. It was quite common to preface the work on roots by a table of powers.[4]

---

[1] Thierfeldern, Arithmetica Oder Rechenbuch Auff den Linien vnd Ziffern/ (1587 ed.), Chap. IIII.

Baker, The Well Spring of Sciences (1580 ed.). "If one elle coſt me 17 s̄ what ſhall 15 elles ⅛ part coſte? which ⅛ is halfe a quarter of an elle." Fol. Qvii recto.

Köbel, Zwey rechenbůchlin (1537 ed.). "So einer dich fragt/ wañ einer 9. elen vnnd ¼. Tůchs vmb 7. gulden kaufft het/ was in 6. Elen koften."
"If a person bought 9¼ ells of cloth for 7 gulden, what will 6 ells cost?" Fol. I₂ recto.

[2] Tartaglia, La Seconda Parte Del General Trattato (1556), Book II, fol. Cvi verso.

[3] Unicorn, De L'Arithmetica vniverſale (1598), Book 2.

[4] Champenois, Les Institvtions De L'Arithmetique (1578). Champenois gives the squares of numbers from 1 - - - 9, inclusive, illustrating each by little squares beneath, thus:

Racines Simples	1	2	3	4	5	6	7	8	9
Quarrez	1	4	9	16	25	36	49	64	81

Page 258, fol. S verso.

The subjects of powers and roots were more generally treated in algebra or in algebraic chapters of the arithmetical works. The following

At that time roots were extracted by at least four methods, each subject to some variation.

1. Method of line reckoning.
2. Geometric method.
3. Scratch method.
4. Downward method.

Although the methods by the use of figures were not simple, the method by counters was still more difficult, and was rapidly superseded by the former. Examples solved by line reckoning were given by Köbel, Riese, and a few others. Geometric illustrations of square and cubic numbers were not uncommon, but graphical methods of extracting roots were rare. Trenchant in the third book of his Arithmetic gave the geometric demonstration commonly found in American arithmetics of the nineteenth century. In this he explained the construction of the diagram as here given and proved the equality of the rectangles, AF and FD, by reference to Euclid, Bk. II, Prop. 4. He then said: "From the above it is easy to see clearly and to demonstrate the logic of is a table from Ghaligai, Practica D'Arithmetica (1552 ed.), explaining his power symbols.

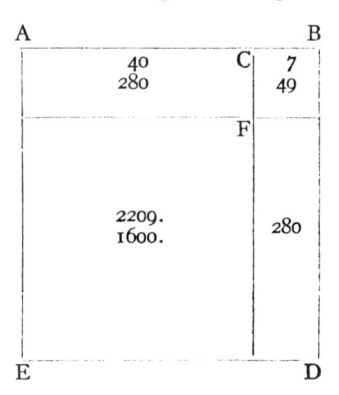

```
        n⁰  ---------  Numero  ------------------- 1
        o⁰  ---------  Cosa  --------------------- 2
        □   ---------  Censo  -------------------- 4
        ⌑   ---------  Cubo  --------------------- 8
      □ di □  -------  □ di □  ------------------16
        ☐   ---------  Relato  ------------------32
   *  ☐ di □  -------  ⌑ di □  ------------------64
        ☐   ---------  Pronico  ---------------- 128
   □di□di□  --------  □ di □ di□  ------------- 256
      ⌑ di ⌑  -------  ⌑ di ⌑  ------------- 512
      ☐ di □  -------  ☐ di □  ------------ 1024
        ☐   ---------  Tromico  --------------- 2048
   ⌑ di □ di □  ----  ⌑ di □ di □ -------- 4096
        ☐   ---------  Dromico  --------------- 8192
     ☐ di □  --------  ☐ di □  ----------- 16384
      ⌑ · ☐  --------  ⌑   ☐  -------------- 32768
```
Fol. Kii recto.

*Error in original. It should be turned horizontally. "di" indicates "to the power." Thus, □ di □ means 4, □□ di □ means 8 to the second power, □□ di □□ means 8 to the third power, and so on.

THE ESSENTIAL FEATURES

extracting square root: for let us take the same number, 2209 (which is the square on the whole line AB), to find the square root, the extraction of which we shall demonstrate from the figure and maintain the logic. First having separated the number into two periods (according to Article 4 of this chapter), I seek, according to Article 5, the root of the first period, 22: this is 4, which (because there is another root figure, or because it is of the tens' period) must be 40 and denotes the longer segment of the line, i. e., AC, and consequently, each of the sides of the square, EF, and also the longer sides of the supplementary rectangles, AF and DF. From 22 I subtract the square of 4, which is 16, and because 4 denotes 40, then its square 16 denotes 1600. This is the square EF. Then the remainder from 22 is 6, or from 2209 will leave 609, which is the area of the two rectangles, AF, DF, and of the small square, BF. But, if I divide the area of a rectangle by one of its sides, I obtain the other. That is, if I divide the product of two numbers by one of them, I obtain the other. So if I divide 280 (the product of 7 by 40) by 40, or 560 (the product of 7 by 80) by 80, I shall get 7. Therefore, knowing that 609 is the area of the two rectangles, AF, DF, and of the small square BF, and that 40 is the side of one of these rectangles, I double 40 making 80, denoting the side of the rectangles joined. Then I divide 609 by 80, so that I can also take away the square of the quotient, and obtain 7, which denotes the shorter sides of the rectangles, AF, DF, and consequently the side of the small square BF, which is BC. Finally, I multiply 80 by 7, and then 7 by 7, producing 560 and 49, which make 609; then I subtract the 609, and the remainder is zero. Thus, the square root of 2209 is 47." [2]

---

[1] It is well known that the Western Arabs used the sand-board in extracting roots; hence it is reasonable to suppose that they used the scratch method, whence the Italians obtained it. Cantor, Bd. I, p. 767 (1900 ed.).

[2] Trenchant, L'Arithmetique (1578 ed.), Book 3. "Par ce que deſſus ſe peut clerement veoir, & demontrer la raiſon des extractions quarées: pourquoy ſère prendrons ce même nombre 2209 (qui eſt le quarré de la totale ligne A, B) pour en tirer la racine quarrée: à l'extraction da laquelle monſtrerons ſur la figure la raiſon pretendue.

"Premierement ayant coupé iceluy nombre en deux ſections (ſelon le 4

The accompanying diagrams from Trenchant's pages, for extracting the cube root of 103,823, show that he used the modern block method.

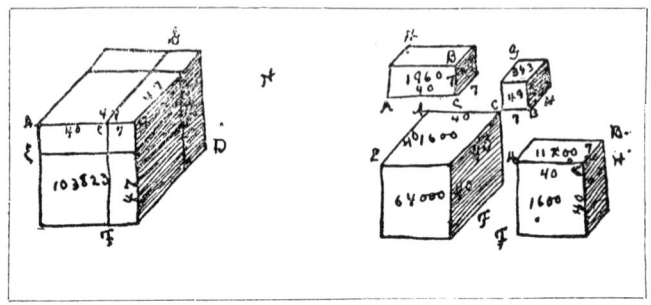

Fol. Q$_2$ verso.

The scratch method was the common algorism for this process. The following examples from Tonstall will illustrate it:[1] "The extraction of the square root is nothing else than the finding of a number which multiplied by itself will produce the proposed number, if it be a square, or the greatest square number contained in it, if it be not a square."

"Example in square root:

artic. de ce chap.). Ie cherche, felon le 5 art. la racine de la premiere fection 22: c'eft 4, lequel (à caufe de la figure radicale future, ou qu'il eft de la fections des dizeines) vaut 40 denotāt la maieure fection de la ligne A, C, & par confequent, chacun des cotez du quarré E, F, & auffi les plus grans cotez des fupplemens A, F, & D, F. En apres de 22, ie leue le quarré de 4, c'eft 16, lequel comme 4 denote 40, auffi fon quarré 16 denotera 1600, c'eft le quarré E, F. Par ainfi de 22 refte 6: ou de 2209, reftera 609 qui eft la fuperficie de 2 fuplemens A, F, & D, F, & du petit quarré B, F. Or qui diuife la fuperfice d'vn rectangle, par l'vn de fes cotez vient l'autre: ceft à dire, qui diuife le produit de deux nombres par l'vn d'iceux, vient l'autre: comme fi ie diuife 280 (prouenu de 7 foys 40) par 40, ou 560 (prouenu de foys 80) par 80 viendra 7. Parquoy fachant que 609 eft la fuperficie des deux fuplemens A, F, & D, F, & du petit quarré B, F, & que 40 eft le côté de l'vn d'iceux fuplemens, ie double 40 fét 80, denotant le côté des deux fuplemens affemblez. Donques ie diuife 609 par 80, de forte que i'en puiffe auffi leuer le quarré du quotient, vient 7 qui denote les moindres cotez d'iceux fuplemens A, F, & D, F, & par confequent ceux du petit quarré B, F, dont la fection B, C, en eft l'vn. Finablement ie multiplie 80 par 7, & encores 7 par 7, prouient 560, & 49, qui font 609, que ie leue de 609, & n'y refte rien. Ainfi la racine quarrée de 2209 eft 47." Fol. P$_6$ recto.

[1] Tonstall, De Arte Supputandi (1522), fol. N$_1$ recto *et seq.*

"The number given, 57836029, should be properly pointed off. Beginning at the left, we should search for the first number which multiplied by itself will give the first number marked off at the left, or, if it is not a perfect square, the number which multiplied by itself will give the nearest square which it can contain. The number is 7, and its square is 49, which subtracted from 57 leaves 8, and so 7 is placed between the parallel lines first made, 8 is put above the first point and crossed out. Then the 7 between the parallel lines is doubled, which makes 14, of which 4 is placed below and at the right, and the 10 left should be placed below the lines directly below the 8, which was the result of the former subtraction. Then again another number is to be found which, multiplied by 14, will give the number nearest to 88 (the 8 left from subtracting and the next figure of the given number.) This figure is 6, which multiplied by 14 gives 84; this taken from 88 leaves 4; then this number 6 multiplied by itself gives 36, which subtracted from 43 (the 4 left from the last subtraction and the next figure in the given number) leaves the number 7, which is written above the next point in the number given. The 6 is placed between the parallel lines as the next figure of the root, and so on."

"If one wishes to find out whether the number found is right, multiply the number found by itself and add the remainder, if there is one. If the work is correct, this result will be the given number."[1]

The example in cube root shown in the illustration is a reproduction from Tonstall's arithmetic:[2]

[1] Tonstall, *De Arte Supputandi* (1522), fol. N₂ verso.
[2] Tonstall, *De Arte Supputandi* (1522), N₄ verso.

A peculiar form in which the process is the same as the scratch method, only the numbers are not crossed out, is found in Cirvelo:[1]

```
                                             0                0  12   0
(a) 00|      (b) 00|    (c) 0  00|   (d)  03 | 00     (e)  1  28   0
    16|          25|        1  44|        67 | 24          5 | 47  56
     4|           5|        1  22|         8   162|        2 | 43 | 94 |
     4| Radix.    5| Ra.   *1| Ra.         8 | 2|           | 4 |
                                                           2 |  3 |  4 | Ra.
```
* The 2 is missing in the original.

Problem (a) is the process of finding the square root of 16, (b) of 25, (c) of 144, in this, however, the root is incomplete, (d) of 6724, and (e) of 54, 74, 756. The powers are written above the double lines and the roots below them.

A downward process resembling in many respects our present form is found in Widman:[2]

To extract the square root of 207936:

```
    (a)           (b)           (c)
   47936         47936          5436
     8             8             90
     4            45             45
```

The figures in the top row are the successive remainders with all periods brought down at each step. The last row is the root, the numbers in the root being repeated each time. The middle row is the trial divisor, not always having the zero added. Step (b) is really step (a) with the next figure, 5, of the root written down.

An interesting plan is given by Paciuolo, which has the principle common to all the other methods, but which differs from them in arrangement of calculation:[3]

[1] Cirvelo, Arithmetice practice seu Algorismi (1513 ed.), fol. b_i recto.
[2] Widman, Behend und hüpsch Rechnung (1508 ed.), fol. di recto.
[3] Paciuolo, Sũma de Arithmetica (1523 ed.).

"De aproximatione .R. in furdis."

"Apresfo per le. R. forde: cioe q̃lle che nõ fonno difcreta: qui fequente mettaro vna reᵃ. p laquale femp̃ tu piu chel cõpagno te porrai aproximare: vnde a voler trouare ditte. R. fempre troua prima la fua. R. derita de põto: como fai laltre d fopra. E qñ tu hai trouato la prima. R. fanne pua. e vedi quanto la pasfa el detto nº. Alora torrai quel piu: cioe la dria e ptirala per lo doppia dɔ q̃fta prin̊e. R. che te la data: e quello che virra de ditto ptimento cauaraio de ditta pina . R̃. el remanente fera la

THE ESSENTIAL FEATURES

To find the square root of 6:

(1) $\sqrt{6} \dots 2 + \dfrac{6-4}{4} = 2\frac{1}{2}$. (2) $\sqrt{6} \dots 2\frac{1}{2} + \dfrac{6 - 6\frac{1}{4}}{5} = 2\frac{9}{20}$.

(3) $\sqrt{6} \dots 2\frac{9}{20} + \dfrac{6 - 6\frac{1}{400}}{4\frac{9}{10}} = 2\frac{881}{1960}$, and so on.

This agrees with the general formula:

$$a = \dfrac{A - a^2}{2a} = a_1, \qquad a + \dfrac{A - a^2_1}{2a} = a_2, \text{ and so on.}$$

It is easy to recognize in every method the plan of dividing the remainder by twice the part of the root found and adding the result to the root for the next figure.

Square and cube roots of fractions were common. Widman gives these examples: Find the square root of $\frac{36}{49}$ and the cube root of $\frac{27}{729}$." "Give a number, $\frac{1}{2}$ of $\frac{1}{3}$ of $\frac{1}{5}$ of $\frac{1}{7}$ of which is its own quare root." Ans. $\frac{44100}{208849}$.[1]

APPLIED ARITHMETIC

The authors of arithmetic of the sixteenth century may be classified into three groups: writers of theoretic arithmetic,[2]

.R. fcda. de ditto n . afai piu p fimana che la p*. poi p aproximarte piu: farai la pua ancora di q̃fta. e vederai quãto e la fupchia ditto n°. E anche quel piu che te dara q̃fta feconda. R. ptiralo pure per lo dopio de esfa .R. 2ª. che te la dato: e q̃llo auenimento cauafo de ditta .2ª. R. el remanẽte fia. . 3ª. piu pximana de ditto m°. Poi a mõ ditto: farane proua. e vederai quanto la pasfi ditto n°. e pigliarai anche quella dr̃ia e ptira la per lo doppio pure di quefta. R. 3ª. che tal dr̃ia te dette: e lauenimento de lei: caua el rimanente fera. R. quarta piu pfimana de ditto n°. E cofi fempre in infinitũ andarai facẽdo: e guarda fempre de cauare li ditti auenimẽti de le R. fchiette: e nõ delle duplate verbi gra. R. pª. di 6. ene. 2½. E q̃fta pasfa de. ¼. pche. 2½. via. 2½. fa. 6¼. parti quel. ¼. quale e la dr̃ia p lo doppio di la R. prima che la dato: cioe p .5. neuẽ $\frac{1}{20}$. qual caua de .2½. che e la. R fchietta resta .2$\frac{9}{20}$ e quefto di co che. 2ª. R. di 6 piu pximana che la prima, cioe 2¼. E cofi andarai fequitando a modo ditto e trouerai che qfta 2ª. R. pasfa .6. de .$\frac{1}{400}$. la terza R fera .2$\frac{881}{1960}$. E quefta pafsara .6. de $\frac{1}{3831600}$. la quarta .R. fera fecondo che vedi q de fcripto in margine. e cofi la quinta al medifimo modo trouato. E quefto fin qua e detto fe habia intendere de li numeri fani. Fol. 45 recto, F, recto.

[1] Widman, Behend und hüpsch Rechnung (1508 ed.) "Gyb ein zal welch mit irm ½, ⅓, ⅕, ⅐ sey ir selbst qdrata radix. Ans. $\frac{44100}{208849}$. Fol. E₇ recto.

[2] De Muris (1538), Maurolycus (1575).

writers of arithmetic primarily theoretic and secondarily practical,[1] and writers of arithmetic primarily practical and secondarily theoretic.[2] The first class is the smallest, and the second is the largest. Taking the three classes in order of their size, their numbers are approximately proportional to 1, 4, 6, as the lists given below suggest. It was common usage to divide arithmetic into theoretic and practical. For example, Trenchant, in the beginning of his arithmetic, defined these divisions thus:[3] "Theory is the speculation through which one becomes acquainted with the property of numbers. Practice is the performing of the operations which arise from such knowledge and speculation."

As would be expected, practical arithmetic was about the same in its general features wherever found. The exceptions are due to local influence or to eccentricity of authorship. For example, Champenois drew his problems mainly from military affairs. Thus:

"The Commissary-General had four stewards; the first had 7,836 loaves of bread, the second 6,342 loaves, the third 5,424 loaves, and the fourth 6,398 loaves. The question is: How much bread did they have altogether?"[4]

"A squadron contains on the front 312 men and on the side 232. The question is: 'How many men are there in a squadron?'"[5]

[1] Tonstall (1522), Paciuolo (1494), Cardan (1539), Noviomagus (1539), Tartaglia (1556), Gemma Frisius (1540), Riese (1522), Ramus (1567), Trenchant (1571), Champenois (1578), Unicorn (1598).

[2] Borgi (1484), Calandri (1491), Widman (1489), Cirvelo (1505), Rudolff (1526), Köbel (1531), Baker (1562), Raets (1580), Van der Schuere (1600).

[3] Trenchant, L'Arithmetique (1578). "La Theoreque eſt la ſpeculation par laquelle l'on vient a connoêtre la proprieté de leur ſugét. Et la pratique, eſt l'operation & eſſét qui prouient de telle connoeſance & ſpeculation." Fol. A$_4$ verso.

[4] Champenois, Les Inſtitvtions De L'Arithmetique (1578). "La Commis general des viures a quatre prouiſeurs de pain. Le premier a 7838 pains : le ſecond, 6342 : le troiſieſme, 5424 : & le quatrieſme, 6398. Lon demande combien il y de pain en tout." Page 10, fol. Bv verso.

[5] Champenois, Les Inſtitvtions De L'Arithmetique (1578 ed.). "Vn eſca-

"A captain with 4,000 soldiers is besieged in a fortress by the enemy for seven months; they have food for five months and are without hope of obtaining any during the period of the siege, which is seven months. The question is: 'How much should the captain diminish the rations of the soldiers that the food may last through the time of the siege, which is 7 months?'"

Another writer who used peculiar problems was Suevus. His interest inclined to history. In the dedication of his arithmetic he named the following applications:[1] "To reckon feast days of the church, also many mysteries and secrets of the church. For use in schools, which Cicero, that learned pagan, called the foundation of the whole republic, as all other arts are learned so much better through arithmetic. Also in the army; among merchants; among manual workers, as artists, goldsmiths, mint masters, watchmakers, painters, builders, masons and others; and in housekeeping."

The subject-matter of the book presents a most remarkable collection of historical material. Some of the problems illustrate a tendency not uncommon at that time to correlate religious teaching with school instruction. Under Numeration the first example is: "The number of years from the beginning of the world to the birth of Christ, our Saviour, and the Incarnation was:

3970.

"That is, Three thousand nine hundred seventy years.

"That was the time decided upon when God promised to send his Son. This promise he had fulfilled (Galat. 3), by which we may know his truth and uprightness, and putting aside all sorrow and doubt, we may sing cheerfully with the dear David from the 33d Psalm, and we may say: 'The

---

dron contient en front 312 hommes, & en flanc 232. Lon demande combien il y a d'hommes en l'efcadron." Page 27, fol. Cvi recto.

"Vn Captaine auec 4000. foldats eft affiegé en vne forterelle, de l'ennemy pour 7. mois, & n'ont de viures que pour 5. mois, & sans efperance d'en pouuoir recouuir durant le temps de l'affiegement qui elt 7. mois? Lon demande combien le Captaine doit apetiffer la penfion du foldat, afin que le viure puiffe durer le temps de l'affiegement, qui eft 7. mois." Page 83, fol. Gij recto.

[1] Suevus, Arithmetica Historica (1593 ed.).

word of the Lord is true, and that he hath promised will he surely fulfil."[1]

Other examples under Numeration are:

"According to the statements of Theodore Bibliander, the cost of building Solomon's temple was 13,695,380,050 crowns."[2]

"The yearly cost of maintaining the wars of the Emperor Augustus, especially in holding the Roman borders, was 12,000,000 crowns."

"The annual income of King Ptolemy Auletes was 7,500,000 crowns."[3]

Addition finds application in determining the age of Methuselah:

"Methuselah was 187 years old when he begot Lamech; after that he lived 782 years. What was his age? Ans. 969 years."[4]

Division is applied thus:

"In his thirty-fourth Book, Livy informs us that 1,200 Gallic prisoners were released with 100 talents. The question is: 'How much should each receive?'"[5]

---

[1] Suevus, Arithmetica Historica (1593). "Die Jarzal von anfang der Welt/ biss auff Christi vnsers Heylandes Geburth vnd Menschwerdung.
3970.
"Das sind: Drey tausend/ neun hundert vnd siebentzig Jar.
"Das ist die bestimpte zeit/ darin Gott seinen Son zu senden verheissen/ auch seine zusage kreffigerfüllet hat/ Galat. 3. daraus wir seine Trew vnd Warheit kennen lernen/ vnd wir allen kummer vnd zweiffel/ mit dem lieben David aus dem 33. Psalm getrost singen und sagen mügen: Des Herrn Wort ist warhafftig/ vnd was er zusagt/ das helt er gewiss." Fol. Aij verso.

[2] "Des Tempels Salomonis vnkosten zu bawen/ nach des Theodori Bibliandri verzeichnis. 13695380050 Cronen." Fol. Aij verso.

"Des Keysers Augusti Järlich Kriegs vnkosten/ sonderlich des Romischen Reichs Gretzen zu halten. 12000000 Cronen." Fol. Aiij recto.

[3] "Des Königs Ptolomei Auletis Jahrlichs Einkommen. 7500000 Cronen." Fol. Aiij recto.

[4] Methusalem war hundert vnd sieben vnd achtzig Jahr alt/ vnd zeugete Lamech/ vnd lebete darnach sieben hundert vnd zwey vnd achtzig Jahr. Wie gros ist denn sein gantzes Alter geworden? Antwort, neun hundert und neun vnd sechzig Jahr." Page 22.

[5] "Liuius Lib. 34 meldet: 'Das zwölff hundert Welche gefangene Kriegsleute mit hundert Talentis sind ausgelöset worden.'"
"Ist die Frage: 'Wie viel für eine Person gegeben sey?'"

The following problems occur under the Rule of Three:

"In the 7th Chapter of his 12th Book, Pliny tells us that a pound of black pepper was bought for 4 denarii—that is, for a half Taler. Here is the question: 'If $3\frac{3}{4}$ pounds cost $12\frac{4}{5}$ denarii, what will $14\frac{2}{3}$ pounds cost?'"[1]

"Martial (the poet) informs us that an amphora of wine was sold for 20 asses, that is, for 2 denarii, which is as much as a quarter of a Taler. The question is: 'At this rate how much should a Roman sextarius cost, if it takes 64 sextarii to fill a Greek amphora?'"[2]

In the early printed arithmetics, as in those of Borgi[3] and Calandri,[4] the number of problems is meagre, each problem usually being followed by its solution. In the arithmetics of a date later than 1525 problems for practice are numerous. The explanation is probably to be found in the fact that the cost of paper and printer's composition rapidly decreased.

Although, as we have said, applied arithmetic was generally thought of as a department by itself, certain applications were distributed among the simple operations. The most important of these are the problems of denominate numbers (pp. 77-85 of this article), which were real applications and not mere exercises in manipulating symbols often found in modern arithmetics. But, passing to that department commonly called practical arithmetic by sixteenth century authors, we find that it was generally composed of a list of rules of operations under

---

[1] Suevus, Arithmetica Historica (1593). "Plinius Lib. 12. Cap. 7. meldet: Das man ein Pfund schwartzen Pfeffer vmb vier Denarios gekaufft habe/ das ist vmb einen halben Taler.

"Hier ist die Frage: Wenn drey Pfundt/ vnd drey viertel eines Pfundes vmb zwolff Denar/ vnd vier Fünffiel eines Denarij gekaufft würden: Wie tewr vierzehen Pfund vnd zwey Drittel eines Pfundes im Kauff sein würden?" Page 250.

[2] Suevus, "Martialis meldet, Das ein Amphora Wein sey vmb 20. Asses verkaufft worden/ das ist vmb 2 Denar/ so viel als ein Ort eines Talers. Ist die Frage: Wie thewr ein Romisch Sextarius oder Nössel/ deren vier vnd sechtzig auff ein Griechische Amphoram gehen/ zu rechnen sey?" Page 256.

[3] Borgi, Arithmetica (1488 ed.).

[4] Calandri, Arithmetica (1491),

SIXTEENTH CENTURY ARITHMETIC

which are grouped the corresponding problems of business concern.

The following may be taken as a typical category:

Rule of Three (Two and Five).	Exchange and Banking.
Welsch Practice.	Chain Rule.
Inverse Rule of Three.	Barter.
Partnership (with and without time).	Alligation.
Factor Reckoning.	Regula Fusti.
Profit and Loss.	Virgin's Rule.
Interest, Simple and Compound.	Rule of False Assumption, or False Position.
Equation of Payments.	

Besides these more general rules, the following were often added:

Voyage.	Rents.
Mintage.	Assize of Bread.
Salaries of Servants.	Overland Reckoning.

Gemma Frisius recognized the dependence of most of the rules given in the above list upon the Rule of Three:[1] "From this one rule, which in fact may be called 'The Golden Rule,'[2] grow many different rules or methods of work, as the branches of a tree grow from its trunk, so much so that it has place in nearly all questions, and all canons lean upon it as a foundation, or base, one of which is the Double Rule, which you will understand from the following example."

The Rule of Three [3] was the method of simple proportion.

---

[1] Gemma Frisius, Arithmeticae Practicae Methodus Facilis (1575 ed.).
De Regulis vulgaribus.

"Ex una hac regula (quam verè auream licet appellare) multae diuersaeq; regulae, siue Canones operandi tanquam rami ex trunco oriuntur, adeo vt in omnibus ferè quaestionibus locum habeat ac omnes Canones hinc innitantur, tanquam fundamento seu basi, quarum vna est regula duplex, quam ex tali exemplo intelliges." Fol. D_8 recto.

[2] Jacob, Rechenbuch auf den Linien und mit Ziffern/ (1599 ed.). "So viel hat ich von den progreffionen erzehlen und fetzen wollen/ Folgt/ ferrner die Regel De tri/ von etlichen/ Proportionum, auch fonften Aurea Mercatorum genannt." Fol. D_6 recto.

[3] Aryabhatta (c. 500 A. D.) used Rule of Three. See Rodet's Leçons de Calcul d'Aryabhata.

Its explanation was sometimes expressed in general terms by the writers of arithmetic, as in Heer's Arithmetic:[1]

"I am composed of three parts; always place the question last; whatever number is like the question put in the first place. Multiply together the last and middle numbers and divide the result by the first number. The quotient will be of the same kind, or denomination, as the middle number. Thus is the question solved."[2] Such generality, however, was unusual, the solution of a typical example ordinarily served as a guide without the aid of a general theory or formula.

This statement of the rule was given by Borgi:[3]

"A Rule Pertaining to Trading."

"Three quantities are known to find the other. Multiply the second by the third and divide the result by the first."

"Example. The three numbers are 2, 3, 4.

$3 \times 4 = 12 \qquad 12 \div 2 = 6$."

[1] Heer, Compendium Arithmeticae (1617 ed.).
"Von dreyen bin ich zufamm gefetz
Die Frag fetz alle mal zu letzt
Vnd was die Frag für Namen hat
Das ordne an die vorder ftatt
Das hinder vnd mitler Multiplicir.
Was komt durchs vorder Dividir
Der Quotient bringt dir zur frift
Den Nam/ fo mitten geftanden ift
Damit ift der Frag auffgelöft du wift?"
Fol. Avii verso and Aviii recto.

[2] It is clear from this rule that, if the unknown term had been written, it would have taken the fourth place in the proportion, whereas in the modern form it takes the first place.

[3] Borgi, Arithmetica (1540 ed.).
"Como fi procede in tutte rafon merchadantefche per ditta regola"
"Altro non ci refta fe non a ueder in che modo per la precedête regola fe die proceder in el far delle rafon merchadantefche, cominciando in quefto modo, fel te fuffe detto, fe .2. val .3. che valera .4. prima metti quefte tre cofe vna drieto a laltra, cioe 2. val .3. che valera .4. prima metti quefte tre cofe vna drieto a laltra, cioe .2. 3. & .4. fi come tu vedi, poi moltiplica la feconda in la terza, cioe .3. via .4. e fara .12. el qual .12. parti per la prima, cioe per .2. & in fira .6. e tanto val el 1 adonque achi ti diqaffe fe .2. val. 3. che valera 4. tu hai a rifponder che 1 val. 6.
"Se braza .3. de tela val fol. .15. che valera el brazo.
"Se braza .4½. de tela val fol. 17. che valera braza. 8." Fol. E$_5$ recto.

Problems: 1. If 3 braza cost 15*p*. what does 1 braza cost?

b | 3   *p* 15   *b* | 1

2. If 4½ braza are worth *p* 15, what will 8 braza be worth?

b | 4½   *p* 17   *b* | 8

Problem 1, of course, is a direct case of division. Problem 2 is the usual type of proportion. It was not unusual to preface problems like the second by some like the first.

It has been explained on pp. 119-120 of this chapter that proportion came to have its present meaning in the sixteenth century. Consequently one would expect to find some use of proportion in solving problems and its relation to the Rule of Three. This connection is supplied by Buteo in the following treatment:

"Three numbers being given, to find a fourth proportional number, called the Rule of Three."

"By many, indeed, it is called the Regula trium, or, as a certain contemporary foreigner wrote it, regula de tri. By others it is called 'The Rule of Four Proportional Numbers.'"[1]

Ramus also combines the rule with proportion, for after applying it to problems involving integers and fractions in the usual way, he gives the following chapters:

Chap. VII. Golden Rule requiring Antecedent Proportion.

A typical problem is: "The lion on a fountain had 4 pipes, of which the first fills the pool below in 24 hours, the second in 36 hours, the third in 48 hours, and the fourth in 6 hours. If they flow simultaneously, in how many hours will they fill it? Add in turn the four ratios, 1 pool to the 4 periods of time, and the total will be 37 pools and 144 hours, antecedents of the proposition. Since 37 pools are filled in 144 hours, therefore 1 pool is filled in $3\frac{35}{37}$ hours."[2]

---

[1] Buteo, Logistica, Quae & Arithmetica vulgò dicitur (1559). "A multis fiquidem dicitur regula trium, vel ficut quidam Barbarus fcripfit tempore noftro, regula de tri. Ab aliis regula quatuor proportionalium." Fol. g₄ recto, p. 104.

[2] Ramus, Arithmeticae Libri duo. Liber II, Cap. VII.

"Leo fontis 4 fistulas habet, quarum prima implet fubjectum lacum 24 horis, fecunda 36, tertia 48 quarta 6: fi fimul fluant, quot horis implebunt?

Chapter VIII. Concerning Reciprocation.

A typical problem is: "When a measure of wheat is sold for 5 aurei, a loaf of bread weighs 4 unciae; when, however, it is sold for 3 aurei, a loaf of bread will weigh 6⅔ unciae." [1]

Chapter IX. Composite Proportion through Addition.

Chapter X. Alligation.

Chapter XI. Composite Proportion through Multiplication only.

"A piece of tapestry 2½ ells long and 2 ells wide was sold for 50 libelli, therefore a piece of tapestry of the same quality 1 ell long and ⅚ of an ell wide will sell for l. 8 s. 6 d. 8." [2]

Chapter XII. Composite Proportion through Multiplication and Addition.

Chapter XIII. Continuous Proportion for Finding the Smallest Term in a Given Series.

In the fifteenth century the Italians originated a modification of the Rule of Three for certain problems involving denominate numbers. This method was first published in Germany by Schreiber (Grammateus) in 1518 [3] under the name of Welsch Practice. At that time the people of southern France and northern Italy were often called Welsch by the Germans, whence the name given to the process. Italian writers refined the processes in arithmetic in many ways,

Adde rurfum quatuor rationes 1. lacus ad quadruplex tempus, tota ratio erit 37 lacuum 144 horas antecedens propositionis. Dic igitur 37 lacus implentur 144 horis, ergo 1. lacus impletur horis $3\frac{35}{37}$ fic:

1.	24
1.	36
1.	48
1.	6
37.	144, 1 $3\frac{35}{37}$."

[1] Ramus, Arithmeticae Libri duo (1577 ed.). "Cum modius tritici vaenit 5 aureis, tum panis est 4 unciarum: ergo cúm vaenit 3, panis erit unciarum 6⅔." Page 59.

[2] Ramus, "Aulaeum longum ulnas 2 & ½, latu 2 emitur 50 libellis: ergo tapetum ejusdem generis alterum longum ulnam 1, latum ⅚ emetur l. 8. s. 6. d. 8." Page 73.

[3] Schreiber, Ayn new Künstlich Buch welcher gar gewifs vnd behend/ lernet nach gemainen regel Detre/ welschen practic/ (1518 ed.), fol. D₁ verso.

which led to the custom of designating any ingenious operation originating with them as Welsch Practice. Thus, the name became widely used in the broader sense, occurring in the titles of many arithmetics of the sixteenth and seventeenth centuries.

The technical difference between the Rule of Three and Welsch Practice in the original narrow sense may be seen from two examples from Riese.

1. Problem. "If 1 pound costs 3 groschen 9 denarii, how much will 3 centner 2 stein 7 pounds cost?"[1]

Solution by the Rule of Three:

1 : 3 groschen 9 denarii = 3 centner 2 steins 7 pounds : ( ). Since 1 centner = 110 lb., 1 stein = 22 lb., then 3 cent. 2 stein 7 lb. = 381 lb. Reduce the 3 gr. 9 d. to denarii. The result is 45 d.

Then 1 : 45 = 381 lb. : ( )

Reduce 381 × 45 d. to florins, groschen, and denarii.

2. Problem. If $5\tfrac{5}{6}$ lb. cost 32 fl. 13 gr. 12 d., what will 47 lb. 25 lot cost?

Then $5\tfrac{5}{6}$: 32 fl. 13 gr. 12 d. = 47 lb. 15 lot : ( ).

He now has to multiply the means together as in the Rule of Three, but instead of reducing each compound number to one denomination he performs the work as follows:

```
 5⅚ lb. kosten   32 fl. 13 n gr. 12 δ.      was 47 lb. 25 lot?
      6                                         16 ½ lb.
    ───         ─────────────────               8  ½
    35           194 fl. 22 n gr.               1  ⅛
                1358 fl.      10 | ⅓ fl.
                 776          10 | ⅓
                               2 | ⅕  aus ⅓
                 15 fl. 20 n gr. ⎤
                 15  "  20   "   ⎬ = 22 gr., mal. 47
                  3  "   4   "   ⎦
                 97  "  11   "
                 48  "  20   "    9  δ. ⎤
                  6  "   2   "   10½  " ⎦ = Preis für 25 Lot
                ──────────────────────
                9304 fl. 18 n gr. 1⅛ δ.  Summa
              5)
                1860  "  27   "   11 1/40 "
              7)───────────────────────
                265 fl. 25 n gr. 6 201/280 δ.
```

[1] Riese, Rechnung auff der Linien vnd Federn/ (1571 ed.), Unger, p. 92.

Explanation. 1. Multiply the terms of the first ratio by 6 to avoid fractions.

Then, 35 : 194 fl. 22 gr. = 47 lb. 15 lot: ( ).

The equivalents here are 1 fl. = 30 gr., 1 gr. = 18 d., and 1 lb. = 32 lot.

2. Multiply 194 fl. by 47. The result is 1358
776

3. Multiply 22 gr. by 47. To do this separate 22 gr. into 10 gr. + 10 gr. + 2 gr., which equals ⅓ fl. + ⅓ fl. + ⅕ of ⅓ fl., and multiply each by 47. The result is 15 fl. 20 gr. + 15 fl. 20 gr. + 3 fl. 4 gr. (Note that 10, 10, 2 are parts of 30 gr. (= 1 fl.) expressed by unit fractions.)

4. Multiply 194 fl. 22 gr. by 25 lot. To do this separate 25 lot into 16 l. + 8 l. + 1 l. = ½ lb. + ½ of ½ lb. + ⅛ of ½ of ½ lb. and multiply 194 fl. 22 gr. by each term. The result is 97 fl. 11 gr., 48 fl. 20 gr. 9 d. by taking ½ of the last result, and 6 fl. 2 gr. 10⅛ by taking ⅛ of the last result. (Note again the unit fractions.)

5. The partial products are now added and divided by 5 and 7, or 35.

It is the ingenious method of separating the multipliers in order to avoid reduction to one denominator, as in the solution by the Rule of Three, that constitutes the characteristic feature of Welsch Practice; a good example of how the shortest process may become the longest.

Problems then solved by the Rule of Three are now solved by unitary analysis or by the equation, and Welsch Practice has lost its virtue on account of the comparative simplicity of the modern denominate number systems. It is interesting to note that Welsch Practice in its early form exactly coincides with our present unitary analysis. This may be seen by an example from Calandri:[1] "If a cogno of wine is worth 33 ɣ 11 β 4 δ, what are 5 barili worth?"

[1] Calandri, Arithmetica (1491 ed.). "El cogno del ulno uale 33 ɣ 11 β 4 δ che narranno 5 barili." Fol. 28 verso.

138 SIXTEENTH CENTURY ARITHMETIC

SOLUTION.

10) 33 — 11 — 4 —— 5
     3 — 7 —————— 1⅜

     15
     1 —— 15 —— 0
     0 —— 0 —— 5
     0 —— 0 —— 3
     ─────────────
     16 ℣ 15 β 8 δ

EXPLANATION.

The top line is the statement of the problem, namely, 10 barili : 33 ℣ 11 β 4 δ = 5 barili : ( ). This is evident, since 1 cogno = 10 barili. The second line is found by dividing the first two terms by 10. This gives the cost of 1 barili. The other lines are the results of multiplying the denominators of the second line by 5, the relations being 20 β = 1 ℣, 12 δ = 1 β.

Thus, the whole solution is briefly, if 10 barili cost 13 ℟ 11 β 4 δ, 1 barili costs $\frac{1}{10}$ of this. 5 barili cost 5 times the latter result. This process we call unitary analysis.

In the Double Rule of Three, also called the Rule of Five, are recognized the problems of compound proportion. Five quantities are given to find a sixth. A typical example from Gemma Frisius is:

" If 4 aurei must be paid for transporting 20 pounds of merchandise 30 miles, how much must be paid for transporting 50 pounds 40 miles?"[1]

The Rule of Two was the process of dividing the product of two numbers by the sum, and was applied to problems whose solution could thus be obtained. In the Treviso book[2] it is applied to certain courier problems.

Inverse Rule of Three

The Inverse Rule of Three is explained by Baker thus:

" Of the Backer Rule of Three."

" The backer rule of three is so called because it requireth a contrarye working to that, which the Rule of three direct doeth teache, whereof I have nowe treated."[3]

[1] Gemma Frisius, Arithmeticae Practicae Methodus Facilis (1581 ed.). "Pro 20 Libris cuiufuis mercis, aductis per 30 milliaria, foluendi funt 4 aurei, quantum pro 50 lib. aducctis per 40 milliaria?" Fol. E$_8$ verso.

[2] See p. 9, bibliographical note.

[3] Baker, The Well Spring of Sciences (1580 ed.), fol. Gvi recto.

Example. "If 15 shillinges worth of Wyne will serue for the Ordinary of 46 men when the Tonne of wyne is woorth 12 pounds: for howe many men will the same 15 shillinges worth of wine suffice; when the ton of wine is woorth but 8 pounds."

Partnership

The first kind, simple partnership, was concerned with dividing a gain or loss proportional to a given set of numbers. The following is an example from Suevus prefaced by an introduction resembling a Herbartian Preparation:[1]

Introduction. "In the first chapter of the Prophet Jonah we read how God enjoined upon the Prophet to proclaim to the Ninevites his righteous anger against their sins; this Jonah refused to do, and for this reason betook himself to a ship and departed with the sailors. But Almighty God arrested the progress of the Prophet Jonah by a mighty tempest which greatly frightened the sailors. As soon as they had

---

[1] Suevus, Arithmetica Historica (1593). "Im Propheten Jona Cap. 1. lesen wir/ wie GOTT der HERR dem Propheten aufferleget hat/ den Niniuiten seinen gerechten Zorn wider ihre Sûnde zuuerkundigen/ des sich der Prophete gewegert/ vnd sich derhalben auff ein Schiff begeben hat/ vnd mit den Schiffleuten dauon gefahren ist/ aber der Allmachtige GOTT hat den *Propheten Jonam,* durch einen grossen Sturmwind auff dem Meer arestiret vnnd auffgehalten/ darûber die Schiffleute sehr erschrocken sind/ als bald das Schiff zu/ leichtern/ etlich Gerethe aussgeworffen/ auch darumb (sonder zweiffel aus sonder schickung GOTTES) das Loss geworffen haben/ zu erkûndigen/ umb wen es doch mûsse zu thun sein/ und weil das Loss den *Propheten Ionam* getroffen/ hat er sich willig darein begeben/ das sie ihn aus dem Schiffe ins Meer gestûrtzet haben/ welchen als bald ein grosser Wallfisch auffgefangen vnd verschlungen/aber noch dreyen tagen vnd nachten wieder zu Rande vnd Lande gebracht hat/ das er nach dem befehl das *Herrn* den Niniuiten die Busse gepredigt hat.

"Dauon wollen wir auch ein nûtzlich Exempel nemen.
"Wan vier Kauffleuthe ein Schieff mit Gûttern beladen hatten/
"1. Einer mit vier und funfftzig Lasten:
"2. Der ander mit zwey vnd Siebentzig Lasten:
"3. Der dritte mit Hundert vnd vier vnd zwantzig Lasten:
"4 Vnd der vierde mit Hundert vnnv Funfftzig Lasten: Jeder Last auff 12 Tonnen zu rechnen/ dauon die Schieffleute inn grossem vngewitter das Schiff zu Leichtern,/ haben Sechs Last vnd vier Tonnen auswerffen mussen. Ist die Frage: Wie viel ein jeder Kauffman in sonderheit habe schaden Leiden mûssen." Pages 339-340.

thrown over some of their wares to lighten the ship, they cast lots (without doubt by the special Providential arrangement of God) to find for whose sake the calamity had to happen, and because the lot fell to the Prophet Jonah, he voluntarily gave himself up that they might cast him from the ship into the sea: as soon as they did this a great fish seized and swallowed him. After three days and nights, however, he was brought to the shore again that he might preach of repentance to the Ninevites."

Problem. " From this we also wish to take a useful example:

" Four merchants loaded a ship with goods; the first furnished 54 Lasten, the second 72 Lasten, the third 124 Lasten, and the fourth 150 Lasten. Each Last is to be considered as 12 tons. In a violent storm the sailors had to throw overboard 6 Lasten and 4 tons to lighten the ship. The question is: ' How much must each mercant share in the loss?' "

The second kind, Partnership with Time, may be illustrated by the following from Riese:[1]

" Three men formed a partnership. The first gave 20 florins for 4 months, the second 24 florins for 3 months, and the third 40 florins for 1 month. They made 101 florins; how much belonged to each?"

$$\begin{array}{lllll} \text{Ans.} & \text{1st.} & 42 \text{ fl.} & 1 \text{ ß} & 8 \text{ heller.} \\ & \text{2d.} & 37 \text{ fl.} & 17 \text{ ß} & 6 \text{ heller.} \\ & \text{3d.} & 21 \text{ fl.} & & 10 \text{ heller.} \end{array}$$

$$192 \longrightarrow 101 \text{ fl.} \longrightarrow \begin{array}{l} 80 \\ 72 \\ 40 \end{array}$$

[1] Riese, Rechnung auff der Linien und Federn/ (1571 ed.). "Item/ Drey machen ein Gefelfchafft alfo/ Der erft legt 20 floren/ 4 monat/ Der ander 24 floren drey monat/ Vnd der dritte 40 floren ein monat/ Haben 101 fl gewunnen/ wie viel gebûrt jglichem? Facit dem erften 42 fl/ 1 ß/ 8 heller/ Dem andern 37 fl/ 17 ß/ 6 heller/ Vnd dem dritten 21 fl/ 10 hl'.

"Machs alfo/ multiplicir jglichs Geld mit feiner zeit/ Summir/ wird dem Theiler/ Vnd fetz darnach in maffen/ wie du oben gethan haft/ Stehet alfo." Fol. Hviii recto.

$$192 \longrightarrow 101 \text{ fl} \longrightarrow \begin{array}{l} 80 \\ 72 \\ 40 \end{array}$$

The problems in partnership reflect real conditions of that time, although they seem artificial now, for there was a popular prejudice among Christians against taking interest, and usury laws were made to prevent it. Hence, merchants pooled their money in enterprises for various periods, often very brief, and shared the profits in proportion to the amounts invested and the times for which they were furnished.[1]

The problems concerning pasturage (pasturing partnership[2]) are relics of the days of commons and shepherds. Contractors rented large sections of the estates, which had been farmed out to them by the state, to the owners of stock, and these paid in proportion to the numbers in their herds.[3] Such problems may be found in a few arithmetics at the present time.

Tonstall gives a third case of partnership in which, while different times intervene, money is drawn out also.

Example. "Four merchants formed a partnership for two years. The first contributed 30 aurei at the beginning, and after 8 months drew out 10 of them. At the beginning of the twentieth month he contributed 12 aurei to the partnership. At the beginning the second contributed 24 aurei, and at the beginning of the sixteenth month he contributed 14 more aurei. The third contributed at the beginning 20 aurei, at the beginning of the seventh month he withdrew all his money, and at the beginning of the eighteenth month contributed 16 aurei. The fourth at the beginning of the seventh month contributed 18 aurei, and at the beginning of the fourth month after drew out 9 of these; again in the seventeenth month he added 15 aurei to the business. How should a gain of 100 aurei be divided among them?"[4]

He gives the following solution with a careful explanation:

[1] W. Cunningham, The Growth of English Industry and Commerce during the Middle Ages (London, 1896), p 364.

[2] Ortega's Arithmetic (1515 ed.), fol. 762, has the expression "compagnia pecovaria."

[3] Ramsey, Manual of Roman Antiquities (London, 1901), p. 548.

[4] Tonstall, De Arte Supputandi (1522), fol. Z_2 verso.

$$\begin{array}{ccc} & 620 & 35\frac{205}{437} \\ & 558 & 31\frac{403}{437} \\ 17480 & & 100 \\ & 252 & 14\frac{182}{437} \\ & 318 & 18\frac{84}{437} \end{array}$$

Factor Reckoning corresponds to the modern topic of commission, as shown by the following problems from Baker:

"A marchant hath delivered to his Factor 1200 li. to gouerne them in the trade of marchandiſe, upon ſuch condition, that he for his ſeruice ſhall have the ⅓ of the gaine, yf anything be gained, and he ſhall beare the ⅓ of the loss if any thinge be loſte: I demaunde for how much his person was esteemed." [1]

"A marchante hath delivered unto his Factor 1200 l'i and the Factor layeth 500 l'i and his person. Nowe, because hee layeth in 500 li. and his person, it is agreed between them y̓ he shall take ⅔ of the gaine: I demaunde, for how much his person was esteemed?" [2]

Profit and Loss

Problems of this kind were often unclassified and used as applications of the Rule of Three. But some writers grouped them under a separate title, thus setting the precedent followed until the present time.[3]

A type example and the plan of solution is seen in the following from Riese:

"A man bought a centner of wax for 16¾ florins. How many pounds will he sell for 1 fl. if he wishes to make 7 fl. on 100 florins? Answer, 5 pfund 29 loth 3 quintle 2 pf. gewicht o$\frac{1684}{6741}$ heller." [4]

(Reckon first how much wax was bought for 100 florins,

[1] Baker, The Well Spring of Sciences (1580 ed.), fol. Wii recto.

[2] Baker, The Well Spring of Sciences (1580 ed.), fol. Wv recto.

[3] Sfortunati's Arithmetic (1545 ed.), fol. 47 recto, has "di guadagni e perdite."

[4] Riese, Rechnung auff der Linien und Federn/ (1571 ed.). "Item/ Ein Centner Wachs für 16 floren/ 3 ort/ Wie viel pfund komen für 1 fl/ ſo man an 100 gewinnen wil 7 floren? Facit 5 pfund/ 29 loth/ 3 quintle/ 2 gewicht/ o heller/ vnd $\frac{1684}{6741}$ teil. Machs alſo rechne zum erſten wie viel Wachs für 100 floren kömpt/ Als denn addir die 7 floren zu 100/ vnd ſprich/ 107 floren geben ſo viel Wachs/ als hierin 634$\frac{58}{63}$ ℔/ Was gibt 1 fl? Brichs/ ſtehet alſo."

6741 —— 40000 ℔ —— 1 fl. Fol. Evii verso.

then add 7 florins to 100, for which he will sell the same amount of wax, or $634\tfrac{58}{63}$ lb.) How much does he sell for 1 *fl*?

$$6741 \longrightarrow 40{,}000 \text{ lb.} \longrightarrow 1 \text{ } fl.$$

It was common to speak of the gain per hundred, or per cent, as it is now, for per cent always meant a rate in that period. Thus, in Rudolff:

"A piece of velvet cost 36 flo.; it contained $15\tfrac{2}{3}$ ells, for how much should 6 ells be sold so as to gain 10 florins on a hundred?

Gain was also reckoned with time. The first example in Tonstall is:

"A merchant gained 5 aurei in 3 months from 70 aurei. At this rate what would he gain from 70 aurei in 13 months?"[1]

The other cases treated by Tonstall were: To find the time when the gain is given. To find the gain from a larger amount when the gain on a small amount is given. To find the time in which a gain greater than the money invested can be found.

Simple Interest

Van der Schuere began the subject thus:[2] Simple interest is much like gain and loss with time, so that if you can work one subject, you can easily understand the other.

"A man placed 100 L at simple interest for 4 years at $6\tfrac{1}{4}\%$; how much did he have at the end of the time?"[3]

The rates varied from 6 per cent to 12 per cent, although there were exceptional extremes.[4]

[1] Tonstall, De Arte Supputandi (1522). "Mercator ex avreis septvaginta per menses tres lucri fecit quinq;. quātum lucri tredecim mensibus ex aureis septuaginta obueniet?" Fol. a₁ verso.

[2] Van der Schuere, Arithmetica, Oft Reken = const/ (1624 ed.).
  "Den simp'len Int'rest, is, Winst end Verlies met Tijdt,
  Ghelijckend' een groot deel, dus van het werck subijt
  Suldy veel haest verstant ghecrijghen door u vlijt."
  Fol. Pv recto.

[3] Van der Schuere, Arithmetica (1624 ed.) "Eenen gheeft op Interest 100 L voor 4. Jaer/ om daer voor te hebben simpeleln Interest/ teghen 6¼ ten 100 t's Jaers/ Hoe veel ontfang hy dan ten eynde des tijdts." Fol. Pv recto.

[4] Raets mentions 14%, and Trenchant 10% (1578 ed.), p. 300.

Jean solved problems of interest from a table. This example will illustrate:

"I wish to find the interest on 720 livres at 16 deniers per livre. On line 16 I search for the sum, and when I find it I refer to the number at the top of the column, where I find 45 which is the interest on 720 livres."[1]

Trenchant gives the following interest table with interest at 12 per cent on sums from 10,000 livres to 1 sou.[2]

Principal.	Interest.	Principal.	Interest.
10000 l'.	1200 l'.	9 l'.	1 l'. 1 f. $7\frac{1}{5}$ d.
9000	1080	8	19 — $2\frac{2}{5}$
8000	960	7	16 — $9\frac{3}{5}$
7000	840	6	14 — $4\frac{4}{5}$
6000	720	5	12 —
5000	600	4	9 — $7\frac{1}{5}$
4000	480	3	7 — $2\frac{2}{5}$
3000	360	2	4 — $9\frac{3}{5}$
2000	240	1 l'	2 — $4\frac{4}{5}$
1000	120	19 f	2 — $3\frac{9}{25}$
900	108	18	2 — $1\frac{23}{25}$
800	96	17	2 — $0\frac{12}{25}$
700	84	16	1 — $11\frac{2}{25}$
600	72	15	1 — $9\frac{3}{5}$
500	60	14	1 — $8\frac{4}{25}$
400	48	13	1 — $6\frac{12}{25}$
300	36	12	1 — $5\frac{7}{25}$
200	24	11	1 — $3\frac{21}{25}$
100	12 l'. 0 f.	10	1 — $2\frac{2}{5}$
90	10 — 16	9	1 — $0\frac{24}{25}$
80	9 — 12	8	— $11\frac{13}{25}$
70	8 — 8	7	— $10\frac{2}{25}$
60	7 — 4	6	— $8\frac{16}{25}$
50	6 —	5	— $7\frac{1}{5}$
40	4 — 16	4	— $5\frac{19}{25}$
30	3 — 12	3	— $4\frac{8}{25}$
20	2 — 8	2	— $2\frac{22}{25}$
10	1 — 4	1	— $1\frac{11}{25}$

The following is an example worked from the above table: "To find the interest on 16,097 livres 8 sous."

[1] Jean, Arithmetique (1637 ed.). "Ie veux tirer l'interest au denier 16 de la somme de 720 liures: le cherche donc ladite somme dans la ligne 16, & l'ayant trouuée, ie regarde directement au dessus en la ligne capitale, où ie trouue 45, qui est 45 liures de rente que donnent lesdites 720 liures." Fol. Aiiij recto.

[2] Trenchant, L'Arithmetique (1578 ed.), fol. M₆ recto.

(Soit maintenant qu'il faille fçauoir les interefts de 16097 liures, 8 fouz de principal.)

```
   10000 l'      1200 l'      0 ſ      0 den.
    6000          720
      90           10 ——— 16
       7
                    ——— 16 ——— 9⅗
    0 — 8 ſ                  ——— 11 13/25
    ─────────────────────────────────
    1931 l'        13 ſ       9 8/25 δ
```

Compound Interest

Compound interest was commonly called Jewish interest, or profit, as is shown by the following from Van der Schuere:[1]

"When one wishes to gain money more quickly than can be gained in the usual time, then one must learn to reckon well what is his just due according to the Jewish profit."

The same tendency to associate compound interest with Jewish practice is seen in Riese:[2]

"A Jew lent a man 20 florins for 4 years, every half-year he added the interest to the principal. Now I ask, how much will the 20 florins amount to in 4 years, if every week the interest on 1 floren is 2 denarii? Answer, 69 florins 15 gr. 9 $\frac{2125648028045}{39389806391 67}$ δ."

Equation of Payments

This topic was not commonly given. A few authors gave it separate treatment, but most of them condensed it into a few problems and placed them under other rules, as that of interest. Trenchant states the object of the process thus: To

---

[1] Van der Scheure, Arithmetica, Oft Rcken—const/ (1600 ed.).
  "Soo yemandt van t'ghevvin oock vvinst vvil heben snel,
   Als vvinste niet betaelt en vvordt ter rechter tijdt,
   So moet hy leeren hier berekenen seer vvel,
   Wat hem met recht toecomt, al ist een Ioodtsch profijt."
                                                          Fol. Q₈ recto.

[2] Riese, Rechnung auff der Linien und Federn/ (1571 ed.). "Item/ ein Jüde leihet einem 20 floren 4 Jar/ vnd alle halbe Jar rechnet er den gewin zum hauptgut/ Nu frage ich/ wie viel die 20 floren angezeigte vier Jar bringen mügen/ fo alle wochen 2 δ von einem fl gegeben werden? Facit— gewin vnd gewins/ ℞ 69 floren/ 14 gr/ 9 δ/ vnd $\frac{2125648028045}{39389806391 67}$ teil."
Fol. Gv verso.

reduce to a single payment at one time several items payable at different times.[1]

Exchange and Banking

Exchange as a business custom existed among the Greeks, from whom it was communicated to the Romans. It is known with certainty that Bills of Exchange existed about 309 B. C. and were introduced into Italy from Greece. In Rome private bankers were known as "Argentarii," and the practice of Exchange as " Permutatio."[2] The subject as it has appeared in arithmetics was developed by the Italians in the sixteenth century. According to Unger (Die Methodik, p. 90) the earliest appearance of a bill of exchange was in Borgo's (Paciuolo's) Summa (1494), fol. 167. The earliest Italian bank was a kind of subtreasury of the Mint and was located at Venice. Public banking took its rise in that city in 1587.[3] Tartaglia gave four kinds of Exchange[4] and explained the conditions for acceptance, protestation, and return. The problems of exchange are chiefly concerned with the translation of money units, weights and other denominate number tables from one system to another, as shown in Adam Riese:[5]

" 894 Hungarian florins are equal to how many Rhenish florins, when 100 Hungarian florins equal 129 Rhenish? Ans. 1153 fl. 5 β 2⅔ heller. Proceed thus: Add the exchange to 100 Rhenish and say that 100 Hungarian florins make 129

[1] Trenchant, Arithmetique (1578 ed.). "Remettre à vn iour de payment vne ou pluſieurs parties payables à diuers termes." Page 316.

[2] See "Exchange, Roman," in Harper's Dict. Classical Lit. and Antiq. (N. Y., 1897), 2:1597.

[3] C. A. Conant, A History of Modern Banks of Issue (N. Y., 1896).

[4] Tartaglia, Tvtte l'Opera (1592 ed.), II, fol. 174 recto.
Cambio (Exchange).
1. Minuto = common, meant changing money from one system to another.
2. Reale = chief, meant expressing the value of a sum of money in different places and covered remittances.
3. Secco = dry, treated of drafts drawn on the maker.
4. Fittitio = special kind of secco, meant bills drawn with various devices to prevent fraud.

[5] Riese, Rechnung auff der Linien und Federn/ (1571 ed.). "Item/ 894 Vngeriſch floren/ wie viel machen die Reiniſch/ 29 auff? Facit 1153 Reiniſch/ 5 β 2 heller/ und ⅖ teil. Thue jm alſo/ Addir den Auffwechſſel zu 100 Reiniſch/ und ſprich/ 100 Vngeriſch thun 129 Reiniſch/ wie viel 894 Vngeriſch? Facit wie oben." Fol. F verso.

Rhenish. How many Rhenish florins will 894 Hungarian florins make? Ans. Same as above."

The questions often included the matter of remittances also. Thus, a person in Paris wishes to order the payment of 1200 crowns in Augsburg; how many florins must be paid in Augsburg?

Since in the sixteenth century nearly every principality had its own mint and its own system of coinage, a treatment of exchange required a statement of the equivalents of many systems. Thus, Tartaglia treats of exchange between these places:

	Rome		Venice
	Naples		Pisa
	Lyons		Siena
	Antwerp		Naples
	London		Bologna
	Paris		Milan
Venice	Milan		Barcelona
and	Pisa		Provence
	Perugia		Aquila
	Bologna	Florence	Sicily
	Genoa	and	Perugia
	Florence		Rome
	Valencia		Geta
	Palermo		Avignon
			London
	Barcelona		Genoa
Avignon	Paris		Flanders
and	Florence		Majolica
			Apulia
	Venice		Rhodes
Pisa	Perugia		Constantinople
and	Rome		
	Barcelona		Venice
			Genoa
	Venice	Milan	Avignon
	Milan	and	Pisa
	Genoa		Paris
	Paris		
Bologna	Pisa		Venice
and	Rome		Pisa
	Perugia	Genoa	Rome
	Ferrara	and	Palermo
	Siena		Barcelona
			Paris
Paris	Bruges		
and	Pisa		

It is easy to note from the problems of exchange the various articles of trade. A few are: saffron, wax, wool, soap, tin, sable, tallow, pepper, skins, furs, grain, ginger, cloves, camlet, caps, fustian, tapestry, taffeta, worsteds, musk, linen, satin, velvet, lead, iron, steel.

The following is a partial list of articles which were items of exchange between the cities named:[1]

Place sent from.	Article.	Place sent to.
Breslau	garments	Vienna
Bohemia	wool	Breslau
Prague	cloth	Ofen
Venice	cloves	Nuremberg
Eger	tin	Nuremberg
Venice	saffron	Nuremberg
Nuremberg	pepper	Vienna
Nuremberg	pepper	Breslau
Basel	paper	Nuremberg
Breslau	wax	Nuremberg
Posen	wax	Nuremberg
Augsburg	almonds	Vienna
Nuremberg	tin	Augsburg
Venice	soap	Augsburg
Venice	cloves	Vienna
Vienna	wine	Nuremberg
Augsburg	silver	Vienna

No adequate idea of the subject of Exchange can be given in a brief general article, for when the equivalents for weights, measures, and moneys of different systems are considered the matter increases to volumes. For a work of two hundred pages on this subject see Pasi, page 83 of this monograph.

Chain Rule

Although the name of this rule had a curious origin,[2] the

[1] Rudolff, Künstliche rechnung mit der Ziffer und mit den zalpfennige/ (1534 ed.). Under Chapter on Wechfel.
See also Exempel Bůchlin (1530 ed.), fol. d_8 recto.

[2] According to Cantor this term has its origin thus: In Menelaus's proposition in which a line divides the sides of a triangle into six segments, the transversal was called sector (cutter). The Arabs translated this

meaning given to it in the sixteenth century was peculiarly appropriate. In the Arithmetics of that period it meant a rule to find the relation between two denominate numbers measured in different units by means of a series of intermediate denominate numbers. The following example from Riese will illustrate: 7 pounds at Padua make 5 pounds at Venice, 10 lb. at Venice make 6 lb. at Nuremberg, and 100 lb. at Nuremberg make 73 lb. at Cologne; how many pounds at Cologne do 1000 lb. at Padua make?

The work is arranged thus:

7 lb. Padua = 5 lb. Venice
10 lb. Venice = 6 " Nuremberg   1000 Padua
100 lb. Nuremberg = 73 " Cologne

Then, 7,000 lb. Padua = 2190 lb. Cologne, multiplying in columns. Therefore, 1000 lb. Padua = 1000 lb. $\times \frac{2190}{7000} = 312\frac{6}{7}$ lb. Cologne.

The Italian plan of arranging the work brought out more clearly the significance of the name, Chain Rule. By their method the above problem would be solved thus:

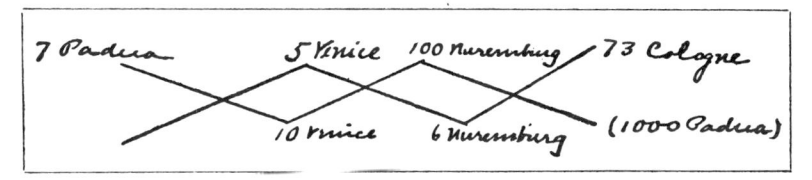

```
7 Padua          5 Venice   100 Nuremberg   73 Cologne
                 10 Venice   6 Nuremberg   (1000 Padua)
```

Divide the product of the numbers on the broken line from Padua to Padua by the product of the numbers on the line from Cologne to Venice. Then 1000 lb. Padua = $\frac{7 \cdot 10 \cdot 100 \cdot 1000}{73 \cdot 6 \cdot 5}$ lb. Cologne = $312\frac{6}{7}$ lb.

Examples of this nature were given by Brahmagupta[1] (c. 700 A. D.) and by Leonardo of Pisa[2] (1202). In Germany they were usually solved until 1550 by repeated application of the Rule of Three. Widman,[3] however, gave the

ál-kattâ, which appeared in the Latin of Leonardo of Pisa's Liber Abaci, as figua cata. Cantor, Geschichte der Mathematik, 2: 15.

[1] Unger, Die Methodik der praktischen Arithmetik, p. 91.
[2] Scritti di Leonardo Pisano, I, pp. 126, 127.
[3] Widman, Behēde Rechnung (1489 ed.), fol. 152.

Italian form, Apianus (1527) explained the difference between the Chain Rule and the Rule of Three, Rudolff (1540) gives some examples, and Stifel (1544) made a clear and formal explanation. The method reached England in the seventeenth century, for it appears in Wingate's Arithmetic [1] (1668).

The rule has several names, "Vom Wechsel," because of its connection with exchange, "Vergleichung von Mass und Gewicht," "Verwechselung von Mass und Gewicht," [2] "figua cata," [3] "regula del chatain," [4] "Regula pagamenti, [5] and "Kettensatz," the name that became general in Germany in the eighteenth century.

Barter [6]

Although Barter was an extensive custom among primitive peoples,[7] it may seem strange that it should find place as a subject of instruction up to the last century.[8] There are two reasons why the subject was of sufficient importance in the sixteenth century to have given rise to a chapter in the arithmetics.[9] First, the scarcity of coined money,[10] and second, the custom of holding interstate fairs.[11] Not until the discovery of large quantities of gold in the New World was there a suitable metal in sufficient quantities to supply the demands of trade; hence, the direct exchange of goods was

[1] Villicus, Geschichte der Rechenkunst, p. 101.

[2] Widman.

[3] Leonardo of Pisa.

[4] Ghaligai, Practica D'Arithmetica.

[5] Widman.

[6] Often called Stich Rechnung. Heer, Compendium Arithmeticae (1617 ed.). Fol. Giij recto.

[7] W. Cunningham, The Growth of English Industry and Commerce (London, 1896), p. 114.

[8] It persisted in holding a place in the Arithmetics of the nineteenth century. See Pike's Arithmetic, 8th ed. (N. Y., 1816), p. 221.

[9] Ciacchi, Regole generali d'abbaco (Florence, 1675), p. 114.

[10] See "Barter," New International Encyclopedia (New York, 1901-4). Cunningham, Cambridge Modern History, I, Chap. XV (London, 1902).

[11] Cataneo, Le Pratiche (1567 ed.), fol. 49 verso.

essential to commercial progress. The great fairs which corresponded to the International Expositions of the present time served to encourage this form of trade. Thus, the many technical questions about the expressions of values of goods in different systems and the methods of calculating the amount of one product to be exchanged for another necessitated a treatment of the subject in the arithmetics of that time. In barter the prices of articles were usually placed higher than in selling for cash. An example in barter from Baker reads:[1]

"Two marchants will change their marcâdise, the one with the other. The one of them hath cloth of 7 š 1 d. the yard to sell for readye money, but in barter he will sell it for 8 š 4 d. The other hath Sinamon of 4 š 7 d' the li. to sell for readye moneye. I demaunde how he shall sell it in barter that he be no loser."

Alligation

In the sixteenth century alligation found application chiefly in problems of the mint. Among others Rudolff gave these two problems:[2]

"A man has refined silver containing $14\frac{1}{2}$ lot per marck and coins containing $4\frac{1}{2}$ lot per marck. How much of each will he need to make 40 marcks in which each marck will be 9 lot fine? Ans. 18 m of silver and 22 m of coins."

"A mint-master has some refined silver containing $14\frac{1}{2}$ lot per marck. How much silver and how much copper must he take in order to have 45 m̃, each marck being 9 lot fine? Ans. Pure silver, 27 m̃ 14 lot 3 qñ 2 $\frac{1}{29}\vartheta$; copper, 17 m̃ 1 lot 0 qñ $\frac{18}{29}\vartheta$.

The following is from Thierfeldern:[3]

---

[1] Baker, The Well Spring of Sciences (1580 ed.), fol. Wv verso.

[2] Rudolff, Künstliche rechnung mit der Ziffer und mit den zalpfennige/ (1534 ed.).

Similar problems are found in Rudolff's Exempel Büchlein (1530), fol. F_8 verso and G recto.

[3] Thierfeldern, Arithmetica (1587 ed.). "Item/ ein Herr hat dreyerley Gold/ wegen/ das erste 15 marck/ helt ein marck 15 karat/ 3 gran/ das ander 21 marck/ helt die marck 17 karat 2 gran/ das dritte 48 marck

"A man had three qualities of gold, the first contained 15 marcks, each marck containing 15 karats 3 grains, the second contained 21 marcks, each marck containing 17 karats 2 grains, the third contained 48 marcks, each marck containing 12 karats 1 grain. What is the greatest weight the metal resulting from a mixture of these can have so that each marck may contain 14 karats 3 grains? Ans. The resulting metal will weigh $56\frac{1}{10}$ marcks, for which he takes the first two and from the third takes $29\frac{1}{10}$ marcks."

Regula Fusti

The Regula Fusti is an application of the Rule of Three to problems involving a reduction for impure or damaged goods. The problems refer to such commodities as spices, gold, silver, honey, and oil. Thus:[1]

"A sack of pepper weighs 3 centners 50 lb. The tare for the sack is $3\frac{3}{4}$ lb., each centner contains 11 lb. of fusti. One pound of fusti cost 4 gr. and a centner of pure pepper $72\frac{1}{2}$ fl. The question is: What is the pepper worth?"

Another example is from Simon Jacob:[2]

"A merchant bought at Frankfurt a sack of cloves weighing 2 centners $45\frac{1}{4}$ lb. The tare was $8\frac{1}{2}$ lb., and each centner contained 16 pounds of fusti. A pound of pure cloves cost 21 β, and a pound of fusti 6 β. He then went to Nuremberg. His expenses were $5\frac{1}{2}$ fl. For how much must he sell the cloves

helt 1 marck 12 karat/ 1 gran/ wie vil mag er von difen am meyften befchicken/ das ein marck halte 14 karat/ 3 gran? facit/ das Werck wird $56\frac{1}{10}$ ms. dar zu nimpt er die erften zwey/ vnd von dritten $29\frac{1}{10}$ marck." Page 193.

[1] Thierfeldern, Arithmetica (1587 ed.). "Item/ ein Sack Pfeffer wigt 3 cr. 50 lb. Thara fûr den Sack/ $3\frac{3}{4}$ lb. helt der cr. 11 lb. Fufti/ kost 1 lb. Fufti 4 gr. vnd ein cr. lauter $72\frac{1}{2}$ fl. Ift die Frag/ was der Pfeffer geftehe? Fa. 231 fl. 0 gr. 8 δ $0\frac{19}{20}$ hr." Page 119.

[2] Jacob, Rechenbuch auf den Linien und mit Ziffern (1599 ed.). "Item/ einer laufft zu Franckfurt einen Sack mit Någlin/ der wigt 2 centner $45\frac{1}{4}$ lb. tara $8\frac{1}{2}$ pfundt/ helt der centner 16 pfund Fufti/ das lb. lauter vmb 21 β. das lb. Fufti vmb 6. β. die bringet er gehn Nûrnberg/ geftehen mit vnkosten dahin $5\frac{1}{2}$ fl. wie soll er da selbst 1 lb. durch einander verkauffen/ das er vber allen kosten 30 gûlden gewine. Vnd ich setze das Frankforter gewicht gleich dem Nurnberger?" Fol. Mv verso.

a pound that he may gain 30 guldens above all costs? And I reckon the Frankfurt weight equal to that of Nuremberg."

Virgin's Rule, also called Rule of Drinks.

This rule (Regula Virginum, or Regula Cecis)[1] grew out of the custom of charging men, women and maidens different prices for their drinks. Riese explains it thus:[2] "At times it chances that many people of different kinds are included in one bill and the reckoning is obscure as when men, women, and maidens are included in a reckoning for money spent in drinking and they are not to pay equally. To make such a reckoning you must study industriously this excellent rule, called the Rule of Drinks."

Thierfeldern gives this example:[3]

"47 people, men, women, and maidens together spent 47 gr., each man gave 5 gr., each woman 3 gr., and each maiden 1 hr. How many persons of each kind were there? Ans. 3 men, 4 women, and 40 maidens."

Rule of False Position (Single; Double)

The Rule of False Position (Regula Falsi), essentially an algebraic process, is as old as Egyptian mathematics. It was used to solve various indeterminate problems.[4] Gemma Frisius explains the name thus:[5] "This rule which we are

[1] This name is derived from the Arabic cintu Sekês, according to Zeuthen in L'Interm., 1896, p. 152 (quoted by Enestrom B. M., 10(2) : 96).

[2] Riese, Rechnung auff der Linien und Federn/ (1571 ed.). " Es begeben fich zu zeiten viel und mancherley rede unter den Leyen/ und unverftendigen der Rechnung/ Als wenn Menner/ Frawen/ und Jungfrawen in einer Zeche verfamlet/ ein anzal gelds vertrincken/ und nicht zu gleich bezahlen/ Solches zu machen/ foltu mit fleis diefe hübfche Regel mercken/ welche Cecis genant wird" Fol. Lvii recto.

[3] Thierfeldern, Arithmetica Oder Rechenbuch (1587 ed.). "Item/ 47 Perfonen/ Mann/ Frawen und Jungfrawen/ haben verzehrt 47 gr. ein Mann gibt 5 gr. ein Fraw 3 gr. ein Jungfraw 1 hr. Wie vil find jeder Perfon in fonderheit. facit/ 3 Man/ 4 Frauwen/ vnd 40 Jungfrawen." Page 215.

[4] The Arabs called it the operation with scales, because of the figure, $\underline{\quad}\times\underline{\quad}$, used in the method. Steinschneider, Abhandlungen 3; 120

[5] Gemma Frisius, Arithmeticae Practicae Methodus Facilis (1575 ed.). "Vocatur autem regula quam iam docemus, Falsi, non quod falsum doceat, sed ex falso verum elicere, fit ꝗ in hunc modum." Fol. F_a recto.

now teaching is called the Regula Falsi, not because it teaches what is false, but because it teaches to find the true through the false."

Tonstall [1] says of the name that the Arabs and Phoenicians, celebrated merchants, from whom arithmetic is thought to have originated, called this method of finding the truth by the foreign word, cathaym. The Latin races called it either the Rule of False Position or the Rule of False Assumption.

Variations of this word are Kataim used by Cardan [2] and Helcataym used by Tartaglia.[3] Baker [4] speaks of this rule as the "Rule of Falsehoode, or false positions."

Under applications of this rule Widman gives many number puzzles, as:[5] "You are to find for me a number to which if I add ⅔ of itself and divide the result by 4½, the answer will be 12."

"Divide for me 15 into two unequal parts so that if I divide the larger by the smaller, the result will be 19."

The following example from Onofrio will illustrate the method of working: [6] "This principle is illustrated by several

[1] Tonstall, De Arte Supputandi (1522 ed.). "Arabes et Phoenices mercatura celebres, et a quibus Arithmetica profecta primum putatur: artem illam ueritatis inueniende barbaro uocabulo Cathaym appelant. Latini fiue falfarū pofitionū, fiue falfarū cōiecturarū regulas uocāt. Fol. r₃ recto.

[2] Cardan, Practica Arithmetica (1539 ed.), Chap. 47, Lii verso.

[3] Tartaglia, La Prima Parte Del General Trattato (1556 ed.), Book 16.

[4] Baker, The Well Spring of Sciences (1580 ed.), fol. Zv verso.

[5] Widman, Behend und hupsch Rechnung (1508 ed.). "Du solt mir sůchē ein zal wen ich ⅔ der selben zal dar zů addir/ vñ darnach das aggregat in 4½ partir/ das mir 12 kūmen." Fol. e₃ recto.

"Diuidir mir 15 in 2 teil die vngleich sein/ vnd wē ich dz gröst diuidir durch dz kleinst das 19 kūmē/.

[6] Onofrio, Arithmetica (1670 ed.). "E per dar principio à gl' effempij fia quefto il primo. Ottauiano Semproni comprò tre diamanti; il fecondo li coftò on. 4. piú del primo, & il terzo quanto il primo, e fecondo, & on. 5 piú; in tutto fpefe on. 81. quanto dunque li coftò ciafcun diamante? Per folutione della prefente domanda, fupponi il primo diamante efferli coftato on. 24. il fecondo, perche dice la domanda, che li cofto on. 4. piú del primo; li fará coftato on. 28. & il terzo, perche coftò quanto il primo, e fecondo, & on. 5. piú, dunque coftò on. 57. la fomma delli quali tre numeri s'è on. 109. & eglino coftarono on. 81. dunque la noftra pofitione

examples, of which this is the first: Ottaviano Semproni bought three jewels, the second of which cost 4 on. more than the first, the third cost 5 on. more than the first, and the third cost 5 on. more than the first and second together, and all three cost 81 on. Required the cost of each. In order to solve, suppose for the present that the first jewel cost 24 on., the second, because it was to cost 4 on. more, cost 28 on., the third, because it was to cost as much as the first and second together and 5 more, cost 57 on. The sum of these make 109, and since they are to cost 81 on., then our position is false by excess; this excess (since 28 is the result of taking 81 from 109) will be designated by the letter, P, in this manner 24 P. 28.

fù falſa per ecceſſo, quale ecceſſo (che ſono on. 28. perche tanto auanza il numero 109. al numero 81.) ſi noterà con la lettera P, in queſta maniera. 24. P. 28.
 "Facciſi vn' altra nuoua poſitione e ſuppongaſi il primo diamante hauêr coſtato on. 20. il ſecondo, perche coſtò onze 4. piú, ſara conſtato on. 24. & il terzo, perche coſtò quanto il primo, e ſecondo, e 5 piú, haueráa coſtato on. 49. ſommati queſti tre numeri fanno on. 93. & eglino
doueano fare on. 81. dunque habbiamo di nuouo auanzato dalla   24. P. 28
verità per on. 12. e però noteremo queſt' errore parimente con   20. P. 12
la lettera P, così dunque ſtara l'eſſempio.
 "Hor per trouare la verità mediante la proportionalità della poſitioni con quella degl' errori, coſí s'operira. Perche l'vna, e l'altra poſitioni haue auanzato la verità, ſi ſottrarrà il minore errore dal maggiore, cioè 12. da 28. e rimarra 16. quale ſi noterà ſotto per partitore: doppo ſi moltiplice in croce la prima poſitione, cioè 24. per il ſecondo errore 12. & il prodotto 288. ſi ſcriuerà alla parte deſtra del medeſimo errore 12. come in queſt' eſſempio appare: parimente ſi moltiplicherà la ſeconda poſitione 20. per

il primo   24. P. 28   560
             ＞＜
            20. P. 12   288

      Partitore   16.   272 Partitione
      Quotiente 17.   112
                        —0

errore 28. & il prodotto 560. ſi ſcriuera dalla parte deſtra del medeſimo errore 28. delli quali due prodotti ſottratto il minore dal maggiore, cioè 288. da 560. reſterà 272. da partirſi al partitore 16. ſi che partendo 272. a 16. il quotiente ſara 17 & onze 17 coſtò il primo diamante, il ſecondo on. 21. cioe on. 4. piu, che il primo, & il terzo on. 43. cioè quanto il primo, e ſecondo, e 5 più, quali tre numeri inſieme vniti fanno on. 81. come nella domanda ſi cercaua." Fol. Ee₃ verso.

"Take a new position and suppose that the first cost 20 on., the second, since it cost 4 on. more, would cost 24, and the third, because it was to cost 5 more than the first and second together, would cost 49 on. The sum of these would then be 93, where it should be 81, then we have the new variation from the truth, 12, which error we designate by the letter, P, as in the example.

24. P. 28
20. P. 12

"The truth is found by finding the mean proportionals between these positions together with their errors.

"Since the former and the latter positions vary from the truth, if the smaller group is subtracted from the larger, as 12 from 28, there remains 16, which we place below for a divisor. Then we multiply crosswise the first position, 24, by the second error, 12, which gives the product, 288, which we place at the right of the error, 12, as shown in this example:

```
       24. P. 28        560
          ><
       20. P. 12        288
       ──────────    ──────────
     Partitore   16.   272 Partitione
     Quotiente 17.     112
                       ──0
```

"Then multiply the second assumption, 20, by the first error, 28, and the product is 560, which is placed at the right of the error, 28, then the difference between these products is found which is 272. When this remainder is divided by 16, the quotient will be 17, therefore the first jewel cost 17 on., the second 21, 4 on. more than the first, and the third, 43, equal to 5 more than the first and second; the three together make 81, as the problem required."

Most of the minor rules, mentioned p. 132, are special cases of other rules. That is, they designate more minute divisions used by a few authors for particular problems and included by most writers under more general rules. Thus, voyage[1] was commonly used to stand for courier problems.

Problems of the mint were very important at that time, be-

[1] Van der Schuere, Arithmetica, Oft Reken = const (1600 ed.), fol. Ziiii recto, gives the Hound and Hare problem, the Mule problem, and other courier problems.

cause the coinage of money was delegated to local auth rities and on account of the multiplicity of standards. Although these questions were often treated under Alligation, many authors grouped them under the title Mintage.[1]

Certain practical arithmetics emphasized solutions of questions of householders and landlords and designated the problems by such titles as Salaries of Servants and Rents.[2]

Among the many safeguards which European nations have thrown about general public interests for centuries is the legal standardizing of bread. The weight of a loaf of bread which sold for a fixed price was regulated according to the price of the grain from which it was made. The earliest regulation yet found is the Frankfurt Capitulare (794 A. D.). London regulations are found as early as the twelfth century. Another good specimen is the "Assize of Bread" of the time of Henry II. The general law which was practically followed was: The weight of the loaf varies inversely as the price of wheat.[3] The following from Finaeus is a typical bread problem, as found in the arithmetics of the sixteenth century:[4] "When a bushel of wheat is sold for 34 shillings (for example), and the bread made from it is sold at 6 denarii per loaf, one observes that the weight is 12 ounces; if the same bushel of wheat is sold at 28 shillings, how many ounces must be put into each loaf to sell for 6 denarii?"

Overland Reckoning

The title, Rechnung Über Land, really a synonym for Ex-

[1] Van der Schuere, Arithmetica Oft Reken = const (1600 ed.), fol. Yiiii recto.

[2] Unicorn, De L'Arithmetica universali (1598 ed.), fol. Ccccc$_4$ verso.

[3] W. Cunningham, The Growth of Industry and Commerce during the Early Middle Ages (London, 1896), p. 68.

An excellent explanation of the English Law in 1800 is found in Nasmith, An Examination of the Statutes now in Force Relating to the Assize of Bread (Wisbech, 1800).

[4] Finaeus, De Arithmetica Practica (1555 ed.). "Cùm medimnus tritici, uaenit (exempli gratia) duodenis 34, & confectus ex illo panis 6 denariorū turonen obferuat pōdus 12. unciarum: fi idem medimnus tritici, uenerit ad pretium 28 duodenorum, queritur quot unciarū formandus erit idem panis 6 denoriorū?" Fol. Sij recto.

change, was used by some writers in a broader sense, namely, to include problems concerning the purchase of foreign goods as well as the methods of remitting money. Trenchant [1] gave twenty-three pages to the subject as well as several appendices and included in it the treatment of Exchange, explaining four cases similar to those of Tartaglia. See page 146, note 4 of this monograph.

Because problems on gain and loss, interest and discount were abundant, one naturally seeks for a treatment of percentage. But percentage as a separate subject did not appear until the end of the sixteenth century. There appeared, however, under the various subjects, problems of that nature. The symbol, %, although not in the text-books of that period, originated about the beginning of the fifteenth century.[2]

The following are among the various expressions used for *per cent*:

p cr.[3]	von 100 [4]	pour 100 [5]	ten 100 [6]
mt hundert[7]	int hundert[8]	met 100 [9]	mit 100 [10]
per cento[11]	pro 100 [12]	p 100 [13]	uppon the 100 [14]
an 100 [15]	p $\frac{0}{0}$ [16]	auff 100 [17]	per C.[18]

[1] Trenchant, L'Arithmetique (1578 ed.), p. 340.

[2] The origin of the present sign, %, as an abbreviation for per cento has recently been traced by Dr. David Eugene Smith, Columbia University, New York, to a manuscript of the first half of the fifteenth century.

[3] *E. g.*, Heer, Compendium Arithmeticae (1617), fol. F recto *et al.*

[4] *E. g.*, Heer, fol. Fv verso. Jacob, Rechenbuch auf den Linien und mit Ziffern (1599 ed.), fol. Mv recto.

[5] *E. g.*, Wenceslaus, T'Fondament Van Arithmetica (1599 ed.), under Interest.

[6] *Ibid.*

[7] *E. g.*, Van der Schuere, Arithmetica (1600 ed.), under Gain and Loss.

[8] *Ibid.*   [9] *Ibid.*   [10] *E. g.*, Jacob, under Gain and Loss.

[11] *E. g.*, Chiarini and Jacob, under Gain and Loss.

[12] *E. g.*, Finaeus, De Arithmetica Practica (1555 ed.), fol. Si verso.

[13] *E. g.*, Unicorn, De L'Arithmetica vniuersali (1598 ed.), under Interest.

[14] *E. g.*, Baker, The Well Spring of Sciences (1580 ed.), fol. Riiii verso.

[15] *E. g.*, Heer, fol. Fiij recto.

[16] *E. g.*, Giocomo Filippi Biórdi, Arithmetica et Prattica (MS.) (1684). He uses "12 p $\frac{0}{0}$ + $\frac{4}{5}$" for $12\frac{4}{5}$%.

[17] Jacob, "Setz 93 fl. losung (verſtehe auß 100 fl.) gehen $3\frac{7}{8}$ fl. wie viel 117 fl." Fol. Mv recto.

[18] Chiarini, Qvesta e ellibro che tracta de Mercatanti et vsage de paesi."

Puzzles

Besides the practical problems which were classified under the general rules, there were many problems famous as puzzles or amenities. The work of Bachet de Méziriac [1] (1624), a book now generally accessible through modern editors, is a collection of such problems known in his time. The following list is incomplete, but it contains the most interesting of those contained in the arithmetics consulted in preparing this monograph; the writers mentioned are those in whose arithmetics the problems appeared, but not the originators of the problems. Only the essential feature of each problem is stated:

Potato Race. One hundred stones (or potatoes) are placed in a row, the adjacent stones being 1 yard apart; how many yards will one have to travel in starting with the first and bringing each stone separately to the position of the first? (Trenchant).

Snail in the Well. There is a well 20 fathoms deep. Every day a snail climbs 7 fathoms and at night falls back two fathoms. In how many days will he come from the well? Ans. $3\frac{5}{7}$ days. (Rudolff, Riese, and others).

Chess-board Problem. Required the number of kernels of wheat needed in order to place 1 kernel on the first square of a chess-board, 2 on the second, 4 on the third, and so on for the 64 squares. Given by Masudi, (Cairo, 950) in "Meadows of Gold." See Bonc. Bull., 13:274.

Eating and Drinking Problems. Some hunters with loaves of bread and bottles of wine meet at a spring; they seek to divide the refreshments so that each shall share according to what he brought. (Ghaligai, fol. 66 recto).

Similar problems about drinking wine were given by Recorde. In the Dutch arithmetics this problem takes the form of a dispute between a lion, a wolf, and a dog over their prey.

Horseshoe Problem. A man agrees to pay one penny for the first nail, 2 pence for the second, 4 for the third and so on

---

[1] Claude Gaspard Bachet de Méziriac, Problèmes plaisants (1624).

for all the nails used in shoeing his horse; how much does he pay? This is similar to the Chessboard problem.

Courier Problems. The name is now used to represent the whole class of problems that concern the movement of bodies at given rates in which some position of these bodies is given and the time required before they will assume another given position. The name originated with the French to designate problems about messengers delivering despatches in connection with military service.

The problems of the clock hands and the times of conjunction of the planets fall into this general class.

Courier problems appear in the Bamberg Arithmetic (1483) under the title, "Van Wandern." They are found in Calandri, Tonstall, Köbel, Cardan, and Trenchant.

Three Casks. Three casks together contain 79 gal.; the second contains 3 gallons more than $\frac{1}{2}$ as much as the first, and the third contains 7 gallons less than the second; how many gallons are there in each? (Trenchant, Baker, Köbel.)

THREE JUGS.[1]

God Greet You Problem. God greet you with your 100 scholars! We are not 100 scholars; but our number and the number again and its half and its fourth are 100; how many are we? (Rabbi Ben Ezra, Alcuin, Leonardo, Grammateus, Riese, Köbel and Van der Schuere.)

Thief Problem. A thief having robbed a castle met a guard in trying to escape whom he bribed with $\frac{1}{2}$ of his plunder; at the next gate he met a guard whom he bribed with $\frac{1}{3}$ of what he has left; he escaped with 15 lb. How much did the owner of the castle lose? (Tonstall and Köbel.)

This problem ran through many variations as the plundering of gardens and the stealing of apples.

Reed Problem. A reed standing in the center of a circular pond 12 feet deep projects 3 ft. out of water; when the wind blows it over to the side of the pond, it just reaches the surface; what is the distance across the pond?

[1] This illustration is from a fourteenth century manuscript.

Tree Problem. A tree 50 ft. high was broken so that its top touched the ground 30 ft. away from its base. How much was broken off and how much remained standing? (Calandri).

Mill-Wheel Problem. A mill has 5 wheels, the first wheel grinds 7 staria of wheat in 1 hour, the second 5 staria, the third 3 staria, the fourth 2, and the other 1. In how many hours will they altogether grind 50 staria?

Jealous Husband Problem. A boatman has his wife, two strangers, and their wives to ferry across a stream. His boat will carry only two persons. Being jealous of his wife he is not willing to leave her with either of the strangers. How many trips must he make to ferry the party across and not leave his wife with a stranger?

BOAT AND DOCK.[1]

A familiar form of this problem is that of the boatman with a fox, a goose and some corn, or with a wolf, a goat and some cabbage.

Cistern Problem. See page 134. Many variations of this problem are still found in text-books concerning the building of walls, digging of trenches, and the famous "If A can do a piece of work in 5 days, and B can do it in 8 days, how long will it take both working together to do it?"

Market Problem. A woman going to market with a basket of eggs found that when she counted them by twos there was one over, but when she counted them by threes there were two over. The whole number was between 50 and 60; how many were there in the basket? (Baker.)

Mule and Ass Problem. A mule asked an ass whether his load was heavy; the ass replied: "My load is thrice as heavy as yours, but, if I had yours and mine together, it would be only half a ton; find the result yourself." (Gemma Frisius.)

Servant Problem. A master bargained with a servant to give him 10 guldens a year and a coat. The servant remained only 7 months. At that time the master said: "Leave my house and take the coat that I gave you; I owe you noth-

---

[1] This illustration is from a fourteenth century manuscript.

ing more. How many guldens was the coat worth?" (Unicorn and Köbel.)

Casket Problem. A jewel casket and lid weigh 27 oz.; the lid is ⅔ as heavy as the casket; what is the weight of the lid?"

Striking of Clock. Venetian clocks strike from 1 to 24; how many days and nights go by for 300 strokes of the clock?

Tower Problem. One-third of a tower is hidden under the earth, a fourth is submerged under water. 60 cubits rise above the water. It is desired to know how many cubits are under the earth and how many are submerged under water. (Tonstall.)

Garrison Problem. A captain with 4000 soldiers was besieged in a fortress by the enemy for 7 months. They had only provisions for 5 months and were without hope of receiving any during the siege of 7 months. It is required to know how the captain shall apportion the rations that they may last during the siege. (Champenois.)

Will Problem. A man on his death-bed made his will thus: If his wife (about to be confined) should bear a son, he should receive ½ of the property valued at 3600 aurei, if she should bear a daughter, the daughter should receive a third. She gave birth to a son and a daughter; it is required to know how much each should receive. This question was also known as the Widow Problem and the Problem of Inheritance and dates back to the Greeks and Romans. It was stated by Salvianus Julianus in the reign of Hadrian. (Given by Gemma Frisius, Tartaglia, Rudolff, Trenchant, Widman.)

Hiero's Crown. Vitruvius relates in Book 9, Chapter 3, that when Hiero, the king, had decided to make an offering to the gods of a crown of pure gold, he entrusted it to a workman, who (as they are always wont to do) mixed a portion of silver with the gold. A fraud was suspected when the crown was finished and Archimedes of Syracuse detected it thus: He obtained a mass of pure gold of the same weight as the finished crown and another mass of pure silver of the same weight. He placed each separately into a vessel filled with water saving the water which flowed out each time from the vessel and thus found the amount of gold and silver. Let us suppose the weight of the crown and the two pieces of metal to have been 5 lb. each; 3 lb. of water overflowed from the immersion of the gold, $3\frac{1}{4}$ lb. from that of the crown, and $4\frac{1}{2}$ from that of the silver. Therefore the question is: how much gold and how much silver were there in the crown? (Gemma Frisius.)

Statue of Minerva Problem. I am the statue of Minerva; my gold, however, is the gift of the youthful poets. Charisius furnished $\frac{1}{2}$, Thespis $\frac{1}{8}$; Solon, $\frac{1}{10}$, Themison, $\frac{1}{20}$; the remainder, nine talents, was the gift of Aristodicus. (Ramus.)

Herds of Alcides. To one asking the number in the herds of Alcides it was replied that $\frac{1}{2}$ were near the gently flowing Alpheus, $\frac{1}{8}$ grazed on the hill of Saturn, $\frac{1}{12}$ on the mountain of Tarixippus, $\frac{1}{20}$ near the divine Elides, and $\frac{1}{30}$ in Arcadia. The rest of the herd is 50.

Beggar Problem. Three mendicants approached a priest holding a purse of money to be distributed among the poor. Having compassion for their poverty he gave to the first one-half of what he had in the purse and 2 nummi; to the second he gave half of what was left and 3 nummi besides; to the third he gave 4 nummi more than half of what was left. Only one nummus remained in the purse. It is required to find how many nummi were in the purse at first. (Tonstall.)

Ring problem. To find who has a ring in a company. If one person in a company standing in line has a ring on a certain finger and you wish to know which one has it and on which finger it is, have one of the company silently double the number denoting the order of the one who has the ring, add 5, multiply this by 5, add the number of the finger on which the person has the ring, and tell the result. Take away 25 and the tens' digit will be the number of the person and the units' digit the number of the finger. (Trenchant.)

Mensuration

Besides the commercial applications, arithmetic of the six-

164   SIXTEENTH CENTURY ARITHMETIC

teenth century was very serviceable in the field of mensuration. Practical arithmetics commonly contained a section devoted to mensuration. The combination of the Reckoning Book (Rechenbüch) and the Mensuration book (Visirbüch) by Köbel [1] represents the two forms of arithmetic at that time. The Visirbüch was better illustrated than any of its contemporaries. The name, Visir, means gauge and Visirbüch, technically gauge book, means a book to teach gauging of casks. Its contents, however, were concerned with all forms of practical mensuration.

The following list given by Cataneo furnishes an idea of the extent of the subject of mensuration: [2]

The Measurement of Wood.[3]
The Measurement of Solid Bodies.[4]
The Measurement of Triangular Prisms.[5]
The Measurement of Square Prisms.[6]
The Measurement of Square Pyramids.[7]
The Measurement of Parallelepipeds.[8]
The Measurement of Walls.[9]
Another Method of Measuring Walls, Floors, Surface to be Whitewashed.[10]
The Measurement of Casements.[11]
The Measurement of the Scarp of a Wall.[12]

[1] Köbel, Zwey rechenbûchlin. "Uff der Linien vnd Zipher/ Mit eym angehenckten Visirbůch/ so verstendlich für geben/ das iedem hierauß on ein lerer wol zulernen" (1531).

[2] Cataneo, Le Pratiche Delle Due Prime Matematiche (1567 ed.).

[3] Del Misvrar De I Boschi, fol. W$_4$ verso.

[4] Del Qvadrar Le Cose Corporee, fol. Xi recto.

[5] Del Qvadrar Le Colonne Triangulari, fol. Xi recto.

[6] Del Qvadrar Le Colonne Qvadrangulari, fol. Xi verso.

[7] Del Qvadrar Le Piramide Qvadrangulari, fol. Xi verso.

[8] Del Riqvadrar I Vasi Qvadrangulari, fol. Xi verso.

[9] Del Riqvadrar Le Muraglie, fol. Xij recto.

[10] Altro Modo Di Riquadrar Muraglie, palchi, sciabli, e legnami, fol. Xij recto.

[11] Del Misvrar I Casamenti, fol. Xij verso.

[12] Del Riqvadrar Le Scarpe De I muri, fol. Xij verso.

Further subjects are:

The Measurement of Bodies with Square Surfaces.

The Measurement of Floors and the Number of Bricks Necessary for a Square Surface.

The Method of Finding the Number of Bricks in a Wall.

The Measurement of Round Bodies, first the Measurement of a Ball.

The Measurement of a Cistern.

The Measurement of a Cylinder.

The Measurement of a Cone.

The Measurement of a Pile of Grain.

Another Method of Finding the Contents of a Pile of Grain.

A still different Method of Finding the Contents of a Pile of Grain.

The Method of Finding the Capacity of a Cask.

The Method of Finding the Capacity of a Barrel.

Another Method of Finding the Capacity of a Barrel.

The Method of Finding the Capacity of a Bin of Grain.

The Measurement of a Small Cylinder.

The Measurement of Cylindrical Walls.

Besides the guage which served to measure the capacities of castes and small receptacles, another instrument, called the quadrans, or quadrant, was used to measure cisterns, walls, and distances. There were two forms of the latter instrument, one a square with graduated sides and the other a quarter of a circle with a graduated arc. Although the proportionality of the corresponding sides of similar triangles was the chief principle used in the solution of problems, the graduated arc in connection with the plumb-line made possible the measurement of angles. In this form of the quadrant we recognize the beginnings of the modern theodolite.

The following page from Finaeus (1532) illustrates the method of finding heights and distances by use of each form of the *Quadrans*.

A typical problem of this kind is the following from Belli:[1]

[1] Belli, Silvio, Qvattro Libri Geometrici (1595 ed.). "La ragione è qvesta, l'angolo del triangolo AEB, èguale al l'angolo B del triangolo CEB, perche l'vno, e l'altro d'essi è retto, & l'angolo E è commune ad amendue i detti triangoli: Onde per la trigesima seconda del primo libro de gli elementi d'Euclide, il restante angolo del l'altro. Et per la quarta del sesto i lati, che riguardano gli angoli vguali sono proportionali. Adun-

Required to find the distance from point E to point A and the distance from B to A as shown in the figure. The explanation is as follows: The angle (B) of triangle AEB equals the angle B of the triangle CEB, because they are right angles; and the angle E is common to both of these triangles. Then by the thirty-second proposition of the First Book of Euclid's Elements the remaining angles are equal, and by the fourth proposition of the Sixth Book, the sides opposite to the equal angles are proportional. Then BC is to BA as EC is to EA, as the side BE of the small triangle is to the side BE of the large triangle. And the side BE of the small triangle, as was presupposed, occupies as many small divisions of the square as there are paces in the side BE of the large triangle, wherefore the small divisions of the side BC of the small triangle are as many as the paces of the side BA of the large triangle which was the first thing sought. And in the same way the

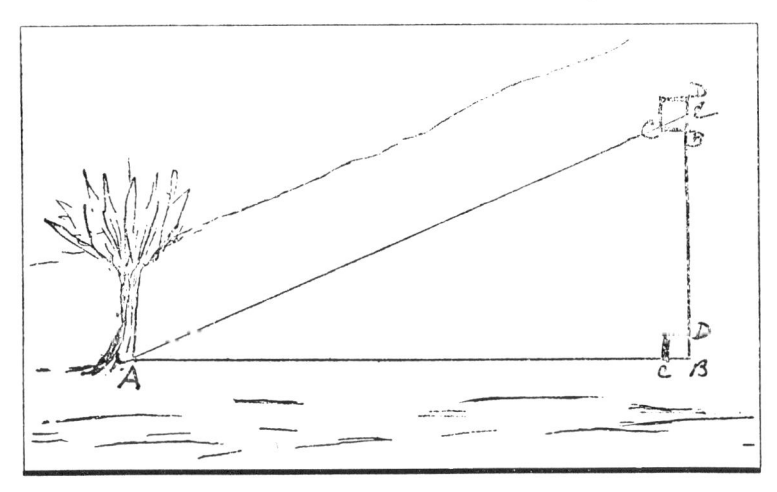

que la proportione del lato BC al lato BA, & dello EC allo EA, fi come del lato BE del picciolo, al lato BE del grande, & il lato BE del picciolo, dal prefuppofito ha tante delle particelle del lato del Quadrato quante fono le paffa del lato BE del grande: per la qual cofa ancor le particelle del lato DC del picciolo fono quante le paffa del lato BA del grande, che è il primo intento. Et per lo medefimo modo le particelle del lato CE del picciolo triangolo fono vguali per numero alle paffa del lato AE del grande, che e il fecondo." Fol. A$_4$ verso.

number of small divisions of the side CE of the small triangle is equal to the number of paces of the side AE of the large triangle, which was the second thing sought.

Thus applied arithmetic represented the vital commercial interests of that period; it naturally contained some traditional and artificial problems, but in the main it expressed the quantitative side of contemporary trade and industry.

Summary

The foregoing exposition of the subject matter of arithmetic belonging to the first century of printed books shows that this was an important period in perfecting the algorisms, or the processes of present day arithmetic with the Hindu numerals. From the treatment of processes (pp. 36-37) it appears that the addition, subtraction, multiplication, and division of integers reached their highest development in the sixteenth century. Some forms of these processes have since been discarded,[1] but all that are in current use to-day are an inheritance from that period. All processes with common fractions now used, including some graphical methods, were practiced in the sixteenth century (pp. 85-110). Some methods, however, were rare, as multiplying by the reciprocal of the divisor in division (p. 107). Arithmetic, geometric and harmonic progressions (pp. 110-116) as finite series, were commonly explained by particular examples. The processes of involution and evolution were practically complete (pp. 121-127). Even the use of tables to save calculation was a common practice. (Tartaglia, p. 58; Trenchant, p. 144, and Jean, p. 82.) Thus the elementary processes reached their maturity except in the case of decimals and logarithms. The decimal fraction, the prefection of the processes with decimals, and logarithms were contributions of the seventeenth century.

The constructive period of applied arithmetic began about 1400 and lasted for more than a century. Mensuration

[1] For example, addition and subtraction in which the result was placed above the addends or above the minuend; multiplication by complements; multiplication by tables above 12 × 12; multiplication by fancy geometric forms; division by galley and other methods.

THE ESSENTIAL FEATURES 169

(p. 163) and commercial problems (p. 132) received exhaustive treatment at the hands of Paciuolo, Borgi, Tartaglia, Rudolff and Riese. Little has been added to the work of these writers from that time to the present, except in such particulars as industrial problems, insurance, compound interest and exchange. There are few problems found in present school arithmetics whose types were not foreshadowed in the arithmetic of that century. The sixteenth century problems in accounts, exchange, transportation, gain, loss, percentage, discount, salaries, rents, taxes, interest, tare, duties and partnership testify to this fact (pp. 132-139).

Even the methods of solution were more like those now in use than is generally supposed. Besides the solution of indeterminate problems, which were really solved by algebra in the form of rules as now, there were two methods of solving business problems: the method of unitary analysis (pp. 137-138) and the Rule of Three (pp. 132-139).

The actual contributions to the theory of arithmetic made in the fifteenth and sixteenth centuries were few. The first great arithmetic printed in Europe, that of Paciuolo (1494), doubtless possessed some originality, but its chief merit consisted in its being a systematic and exhaustive summary of all the pure mathematics known at that time, and little was added to Paciuolo's arithmetic by way of theory in the sixteenth century. There were certain variations in processes, as the reduction of the number of species (pp. 36-37), different orders of presentation, and graphical illustrations (pp. 104-106) which may be called improvements, but the processes with integers and common fractions were practically complete before the era of printed books. With symbolism the case was different, for the improvements in methods of notation of whole numbers (pp. 37-39) and of decimal fractions (p. 72) and in the symbols of operation (p. 53) show that arithmetic was in a rapid state of development. Besides the advance in notation and symbolism, great progress was made in applied arithmetic; the cumbersome form of unitary analysis (as used by Calandri, p. 138) developed into the equational form seen in Thierfeldern; the arbitrary Rule of Three came to be simple proportion; exchange came to embrace a comparison of the denominate number systems of all Europe and the Levant; and finally, many processes were superceded by tables of reference (pp. 82, 144).

The Place of Arithmetic in the Schools of that Period

Arithmetic in the Latin Schools

The Latin Schools were the chief agency through which the great reformers and teachers of the Renaissance reconstructed and extended elementary education. Seventy gymnasia[1] were founded in the kingdom of Prussia during the sixteenth century. These were not everywhere known, as in Germany, by the name of "Latin Schools," for in England they received the name, "Grammar Schools," and in France and Italy they were known as the "Schools of the Teaching Orders."

The chief functions of these schools were to teach the Latin language and to furnish general culture. A knowledge of Latin was necessary at that time for one who wished to be educated, for the standard works of literature, science, philosophy, law and theology were all expressed in the classical languages.

The courses of instruction in these schools were not uniform. Many of the greatest scholars and teachers of that period advocated the study of philology to the exclusion of history, geography, physics and mathematics. In his school laws Trotzendorf prescribed: "The students are never to use their mother tongue with teachers, fellow students or learned people." It was boasted of Trotzendorf's teaching:[2] "He has so thoroughly instilled the Latin language in all, that it is considered a disgrace to speak in the German language; to hear the servants speak Latin, one would believe that Goldberg lay in Latium." The school regulations[3] for Stuttgart in

[1] Unger, Die Methodik der praktischen Arithmetik, p. 1. Leipzig, 1888.
[2] *Ibid.*, p. 5. [3] *Ibid.*

1501 commanded the school master to punish with scanty food the students who spoke German to one another. Even Melancthon, who did much through lectures to encourage the study of mathematics, laid special stress upon language. "The school master, so far as possible, is to speak nothing but Latin with the boys in order that they may become accustomed to it." The early Jesuit schools in France were likewise closely confined to the Latin language. In England Roger Ascham, though at one time a lecturer in mathematics at Cambridge, expressed his views thus:[1] "Some wits, moderate enough by nature, be many times marred by overmuch study and use of some sciences, namely, music, arithmetic and geometry. These sciences, as they sharpen men's wits overmuch, so they change men's manners oversore, if they be not modestly mingled and wisely applied to some good use in life." But in all of these countries there were men who took a broader view of education. Martin Luther encouraged the extension of the course of study. He said:[2] "If I had children, and if it were possible, they would not only learn language and history, but also music, singing and mathematics." Michael Neander, head of the Latin School of Ilfield, contrary to the practice of Sturm and Trotzendorf, taught geography, history and the natural sciences.[3] Père Lamy, a leader of the Oratorians, exerted a similar influence in France. He said:[4] "I know of nothing of greater use than algebra and arithmetic." And Rabelais,[5] the great Benedictine, advocated the learning of mathematics "through recreation and amusement."

In all of the Latin Schools the study of Latin consumed the most time. Mathematics seldom extended over more than half of the course, and in some schools it was not taught until the fifth or sixth year, and then only an hour weekly.

[1] The Scholemaster.
[2] Unger, Die Methodik, p. 5.
[3] Seeley, History of Education, p. 179.
[4] Compayré, History of Pedagogy, p. 151.
[5] *Ibid.*, p. 98.

The plan of individual instruction used in these schools tended to discourage the teaching of arithmetic in the first years of the course. For each pupils had to prepare his lessons from a text-book in Latin, hence he had to master the language before he could read his book. Classes which read Terence and Cicero and studied syntax and prosody, learned only the four operations with whole numbers. The full course seldom advanced beyond fractions and the Rule of Three. The following extract from a curriculum of a six-class Latin School of the sixteenth century gives some idea of the studies pursued:[1]

"The practice of the sixth class; figures and numbers; of the fifth, common reckoning; of the fourth, not given; of the third, music, arithmetic and astronomy; of the two highest classes, second and first, not given."

The following is from the curriculum of a five-class Latin School of the same period:

"On Friday from 12 to 1 the arithmetic shall be read. The preceptors shall use no other arithmetic than that of Piscator (John Fischer), and in the fourth class (the next to the highest in which Terence and Cicero are read) the species alone, in the fifth (highest class) the whole arithmetic is read.'"

The courses of the early English Grammar Schools were very similar to those of the Latin Schools. About three-fourths of the time was given to the study of the classics. Few head masters paid any attention to mathematics. The Writing Master usually taught some arithmetic in the forms below the fifth and sixth.[2]

Since Latin was prescribed as the language of instruction in the Latin Schools, it was necessary to provide reckoning books in that language. Among the most important writers of these text books were: Michel Stifel, Hieronymus Cardanus, Gemma Frisius, Peter Ramus, Christopher Clavius, Simon Stevin, Piscator (John Fischer).

[1] Unger, Die Methodik, pp. 24-25.
[2] W. H. D. Rouse, History of Rugby School, p. 130.

Michel Stifel (1487-1567), an Augustinian monk, escaped from a monastery and went to Wittenberg in 1523, where he became a friend and follower of Luther. The last years of his life were spent at Jena as a private teacher of mathematics. Not only was Stifel interested in serious theological and mathematical subjects, but also in visionary fancies about the secrets of number. These fancies led him to write " Ein Rechen Büchlein von End. Christ. Apocalysis in Apocalysim, Wittenberg, 1532." He reckoned the last day of the world to be October 19, 1533, and imparted this knowledge to his parishioners at Lochau, who consumed their fortunes and goods. Stifel's life was endangered by this false prophecy and was saved only by the personal intervention of Luther. He then gave himself up to serious study and in 1544 wrote "Arithmetica integra," a work which gave him a place among the leading mathematicians of the sixteenth century.

Hieronymus Cardanus (1501-1576) taught mathematics in many Italian towns. He wrote " Practica arithmeticae generalis et mensurandi singularis 1537," and "Ars magna arithmeticae. Artis magnae sive de regulis algebraicis liber unus, 1545."

Gemma Frisius (1508-1558) was Professor of Medicine at the University of Lourain and the author of "Arithmeticae Practicae Methodus Facilis, 1540." This book, small in compass, but rich in contents, was as popular in the Latin Schools as Adam Riese's was in the Reckoning Schools. It is composed of rules with an example to illustrate each.

Peter Ramus (1515-1572), an anti-scholastic, was a professor at the University of Paris; but on account of his affiliation with the Huguenots, he was obliged to leave France in 1560. He returned to Paris (1571) and was slain in the St. Bartholomew massacre (1572). Ramus was more important as a philosopher than as a mathematician. He was the author of " Scholarum mathematicarum libri XXXI, Basel, 1569 " and "Arithmeticae libri duo" (1567.)

Christopher Clavius (1537-1612), a Jesuit, became a teacher

of mathematics in the Jesuit College at Rome. He assisted in a revision of the calendar under Gregory XIII (1582), and wrote Opera Mathematica, 1611," 5 vols., and " Christophori Clavii Bambergensis e societate Jesu Epitome Arithmeticae Practicae, Rome, 1583." This was to be only the predecessor of a complete arithmetic, which, unfortunately, did not appear. In the subject matter of his works Clavius did not approach Tartaglia, but in methodical treatment was his peer.

Simon Stevin (1548-1620) was a book-keeper at Antwerp, a revenue officer at Bruges, and a teacher and favorite of Prince Maurice of Nassau, by whom he was appointed inspector of the dikes in Holland. He discovered decimal fractions and published the oldest discount table. His works were edited by Girard: " Les oeuvres mathematiques de Simon Stevin de Bruges. Le tout revu, corrigé et augmenté par Albert Girard, Leyden, 1634." The arithmetical part, written in the form of Latin compendia, is characterized by complete definitions and the development of processes from concrete problems.

Piscator (John Fischer) was the author of Arithmeticae Compendium (1545). The school regulation of Kursachen (1580) prescribed this arithmetic of Piscator to be used in the school. He also wrote reckoning books in the German language.

Thus, the writers of Latin School arithmetics, with few exceptions, were instructors in private schools, in Latin Schools, or in Universities. Their activities, however, were not confined to mathematics; for example, Ramus achieved fame as a philosopher; Frisius as a physician, and Stifel as a theologian. Hence, although the arithmetic of the Latin Schools was meagre, the text-books were written by the foremost scholars in medicine, science, engineering and philosophy.

Since the essential features of the arithmetic produced by the above writers have been noted (pp. 23-170) it is necessary only to summarize them here. These works are characterized by a prominence of pure arithmetic, somewhat precise definitions (pp. 29-35), rules and explanations of processes with examples. Although one can recognize few principles of method consciously applied in mathematical instruction at that time, the arithmetics of certain Latin School writers contain material classified and organized with a view to facilitating the educational process; for example, the graded treatment of the cases in the multiplication of integers (p. 61), in the validity and sufficiency of the proofs of sevens, nines and elevens (pp. 44, 66), and the recognition of the relation of inverse processes (p. 109). The subject matter was usually organized on the following plan: The whole realm of integers was presented at the outset (pp. 36-77) and represented under each operation. The four processes were repeated with fractions and often with denominate numbers. There were no stages based on the size of numbers, no concentric extension of operations, and no limits corresponding to the different ages of pupils. The following examples illustrate the rapid plunge into large numbers in the addition of integers:[1]

4	309	59	389	7389	7389	20
3	204	34	204	1264	6264	10
7	13	93	93	8653	13653	30

402	4052	4321	73005894	69001303
301	3601	10	60203643	69000000
				69008000
				79017100
				79000003
				79006000
				89004000
				89026200
				89008000
				89005000
				99002400
				99017002
				1008095008

[1] Cuthbert Tonstall, De Arte Supputandi (1522), fol. C₃ recto, *et seq.*

The applications of the processes given in the Latin School books were not numerous. The tendency was towards puzzles, and factitious and traditional problems. For example, Ramus [1] gave the courier, the tower, statue of Pallas, the herds of Alcides, the mill-wheel, the fountain, the architect, and the widow problems (pp. 138-9). In all of the Latin School arithmetics there was a dearth of business problems. The rule of three, partnership, alligation, rule of false position and a few others were generally included, but the practical problems characteristic of the commercial world of that time were generally ignored. The arithmetic of Gemma Frisius, which ran through some fifty-five editions, and which is probably the best example of Latin School text-books, contains for its applications artificial problems of this kind: [2]

"A man having a certain number of aurei bought for each aureus as many pounds of pepper as equaled half of the whole number of aurei. Then upon selling the pepper he received for each 25 pounds as many aurei as he had at the beginning. Finally, he had 20 times as many aurei as he had at first. The number of aurei and the quantity of pepper are required."

"Three men together have a certain amount of silver, but each one is ignorant of the amount he has. The first and second together have 50 aurei, the second and third, 70 aurei, the third and first, 60 aurei. It is required to know how much each one has."

The reasons for teaching arithmetic in the Latin Schools must be deduced from indirect evidence, for discussions of courses of study or of educational values were so rare in that period that history gives little direct evidence on the subject. One must look to the scholars and leading educators of that age, as of every age, and not to the directors and teachers of schools, to learn of the ideals and purposes of education. The scholars and educators of the sixteenth century were

---

[1] Peter Ramus, Arithmeticis Libri Duo (1586 ed.), fols. M_4 recto, M_5 recto.

[2] Gemma Frisius, Arithmeticae Practicae Methodus Facilis (1540).

enthusiasts for classical studies and the schools reflected their tastes. There was much of grammar, rhetoric, and literature in the Latin language, hence there was much of grammar, rhetoric and literature in the schools. There was little of physical science and mathematics available in Latin, hence there was little of these subjects in the schools. Greek mathematics, however, including the works of Euclid, Ptolemy, Archimedes and Diophantus were of great interest to scholars, and, being early made available by translation, gradually found place among school studies.

That the arithmetic of the classical languages did leave its stamp upon the works of the sixteenth century writers is evident from the Greek classifications of numbers found in the extended treatments of proportion of the Latin School Arithmetics. Gemma Frisius treats at length harmonic and arithmetic proportion, proportion of equal and unequal numbers, multiplex, superparticular, superpartiens, multiplex superparticulare and multiplex superpartiens proportion, proportion of fractions, mean proportional, and addition and subtraction of proportion. The extent to which the classics influenced Maurolycus, a contemporary, is shown by this partial bibliographical list:[1]

Euclidis elementa.
Theodosij Sphaerica elementa.
Menelai Sphaerica.
Apollonij Conica elementa.
Sereni Cylindrica.
Archimedis opera.
Jordanj Arithmetica.
Theonis Data geometrica.
Rogerii Bacconis. & Io. Pelsan Perspectivae breuiatae cum adnotation
    ibus errorum.
Ptolemei Specula.
Autolyci de sphera.
Theodosii de habitationibus.
Euclidis Phaenomena brevissimè demonstrata.
Aristotelis problemata mechanica, cum additionibus complurimis, & iis,
    quae ad pyxidem nauticam, & quae ad Iridem spectant.

[1] Franciscus Maurolycus, Arithmeticorum Libri Duo (1575), fol. Hh recto.

Therefore, one reason for the teaching of arithmetic in the Latin Schools was that it formed at least a small part of the classical inheritance. Another reason why arithmetic was taught in the Latin School was for its culture value. It was believed by the writers of arithmetical text-books to be an essential part of knowledge and of an education. The preface to nearly every arithmetic contains a eulogy on the importance of the science and its functions. The authors referred to the opinions of Greek philosophers, as Plato, who held that arithmetic alone distinguished men from the unreasoning beasts. They quoted from the Church Fathers and Holy Writ. They declared arithmetic to be valuable not only as an art, but as an essential to philosophical attainment and to an understanding of the mysteries of the Scriptures. That arithmetic was not taught in the Latin Schools in order to make proficient reckoners is shown by the lack of practice problems in their text-books; and, likewise, the lack of vital commercial problems of that day show that it was not taught in order to prepare for a business life. It is evident from such considerations that these scholars and writers neglected the applications of the subject and believed theoretic arithmetic to be an essential in producing mental efficiency.

Arithmetic in the Reckoning Schools

The Reckoning School was born of necessity and owed its origin to the commercial development of the thirteenth century. The schools conducted by the clergy taught chiefly reading and writing. Instruction in book-keeping and reckoning, the necessary equipment for a business career, was not found in the schools. Hence, merchants were obliged to instruct their sons and to take others as apprentices who wished to enter commercial life. Under the direction of the Hanseatic League commerce grew so rapidly that merchants had to employ assistants to give instruction in reckoning. These teachers were the forerunners of the Reckoning Masters. As the merchant leagues increased in importance, municipal governments conferred upon them privileges relating to the management of trade; and this connection between government and private enterprise accounts for the official position and title, " Privileged Town Reckoning Master," to which the teacher of commercial arithmetic arose. As a public officer he usually acted as town clerk, inspector of weights and measures, shipping master, notary, and sometimes as surveyor. In his capacity as teacher he often monopolized the secular instruction of his town. Thus, were founded the Reckoning Schools, which sprang up in the towns along the trade routes of the Hanseatic League, and, with certain modifications, throve in Italy, Germany, France, the Netherlands, and possibly in England. The Reckoning Master became such an important factor in education toward the end of the sixteenth century that he was even called upon to supplement the work of the Latin Schools. A record of appointment of a Reckoning Master at Rostock in 1627 contains the following:[1] " We, the Burgermeisters and members of the council at Rostock, announce hereby that we have appointed the honorable and well educated Jeremias Bernsterz for our common Town Writing and Reckoning Master, until one party or the other shall give notice a half-year in advance. In this document we also command him to attend the Latin School every week an hour each on Mondays, Tuesdays, Thursdays and Fridays and there to teach the youths without discrimination, and for a moderate monthly or weekly salary to teach others outside of the school, whether they be boys or girls who desire instruction, Latin and German writing, reckoning, book-keeping and other useful arts and good manners, he is also to do with greatest industry and according to the best of his knowledge and ability all other things which are properly the duties of an industrious and honest Writing and Reckoning Master. That his honest service may be properly rewarded, we shall pay him 400 marks a year from the common treasury at four quarterly payments; we also promise him exemption from taxes, excises, hundred penny tax, soldier money and all other con-

[1] Unger, Die Methodik der praktischen Arithmetik, pp. 26-27.

tributions, whatever they may be; we grant him the freedom of the city and a free dwelling. We promise all in honor and good faith."

As the number of Reckoning Masters increased, especially in the larger commercial centers, guilds, regulated by a constitution and by-laws, were formed. Boys who wished to become Reckoning Masters served an apprenticeship of six years, after which, by successfully passing a prescribed examination and signifying their allegiance to the constitution of the guild, they were admitted to membership. There is preserved in Nuremburg school history the record of a diploma certifying that a candidate had passed the required examination, July 12, 1620.[1] Among the signatures is that of Johann Heer, Reckoning Master and author of an excellent reckoning book (p. 12 Bibl.). Although these guilds were of great service in the sixteenth century in furnishing the common people a practical education, they later became a serious hindrance to public instruction, because they were not obliged to follow the advances in educational methods.[2]

The function of the Reckoning Schools was to teach reckoning, business forms and the solution of commercial problems. But, since individual instruction from a text-book was the prevailing method of teaching, the pupil was obliged to read and write in his native tongue before he could study arithmetic.

The courses of study, as verified by the above record of appointment consisted of the vernacular, writing, business forms, arithmetic, and sometimes Latin. Arithmetic was the chief subject, and language a secondary one, in contrast with the Latin Schools, where language held the major place and arithmetic a minor one.

The authors of arithmetical text-books for Reckoning Schools wrote in German, Dutch or Italian to correspond to the language of their readers; an occasional one, as Piscator (John Fischer) also wrote books for the Latin Schools. Similar books for the use of merchants appeared in other coun-

[1] Unger, Die Methodik der praktischen Arithmetik, pp. 31-32, 33.
[2] *Ibid.*

tries, as in France and England. The most important writers of reckoning books were: Ulrich Wagner, Johann Widman, Jacob Köbel, Adam Riese, Christopher Rudolff, Peter Apianus (Bienewitz), and Simon Jacob.

Ulrich Wagner, a Nuremberg Reckoning Master, was the author of the first arithmetic published in Germany [1] (1482).

Johann Widman entered the University of Leipzig with a certificate of poverty and took the degree of Bachelor of Arts in 1482 and that of Master of Arts in 1485 without cost. He became a teacher, lectured at Leipzig, and probably held a professorship. His chief work was his reckoning book: "Behend und hupsch Rechnung uff allen Kauffmanschafften," Leipzig, 1489. Five other editions are known, Pforzheim, 1500, 1508; Hagenau, 1519, 1521; Augsburg, 1526.

Jacob Köbel (1470-1533) studied jurisprudence, mathematics and astronomy at Heidelberg. He made a special study of mathematics at Krakau (1490), where he was a fellow student of Copernicus. After his return to southern Germany, Köbel became town clerk at Oppenheim (1511) where he passed the remainder of his life. He is best known as a poet, designer, wood carver, printer, publisher and mathematician. His fame as a reckoning book writer rests upon these works: "Eynn newe geordent Rechebüchlein vf den Linien mit Rechepfenigen (1514); Das new Rechepuchlein Wie mann vff den Linien und Spacien/ mit Rechepfenning/ kauffmanschaft (1518)"; "Mit der krydê od' schreibfedern/ durch die Zieferzal (1520);" "Ein new geordêt Visirbüch (1515)." In 1531 Köbel combined the last three books into one which was designed for self-instruction.

Adam Riese, also Ries, Rys, Ryse (1492-1559), Germany's most famous Reckoning Master, taught at Erfurt (1522) and at Annaberg (1525). His reckoning books are: I. "Rechnung auff der linihen gemacht durch Adam Riesen vonn Staffelsteyn/ in massen man es pflegt tzu lern in allen rechen-

---

[1] A book published by the same printer, Petzensteiner (1483), probably was also a work of Wagner. This is known as the Bamberg Reckoning Book.

schulen gruntlich begriffen anno 1518," Colophon: " Getruckt tzu Erffordt durch Mathes Maler M. CCCCCXXV Jar."; II. Rechenung auff der linihen vnd federn in zal/ mafs, vnd gewicht auff allerley handierung/ gemacht vnd zusamen gelesen durch Adam Riesen von Staffelstein Rechenmeister zu Erffurdt im 1522 Jar. Itzt vff sant Annabergk durch in fleyssig vbersehen/ vnd alle gebrechen eygentlich gerechtfertigt/ vnd zum letzten eine hübsche vnderrichtung angehengt." III. " Rechnung nach der lenge/ auff den Linihen vnd Feder. Darzu forteil vnd behendigkeit durch die Proportiones Practica genant/ mit grüntlichem vnterricht des visirens. Durch Adam Riesen im 1550 Jar." Colophon: " Gedruckt zu Leipzig durch Jacobum Berwalt." IV. Ein Gerechent Büchlein/ auff den Schöffel/ Eimer vnd Pfundt gewicht/ zu ehren einem Erbarn/ Weisen Rathe auff Sanct Annaberg durch Adam Riesen, 1533. Zu Leiptzick hatt gedruckt diss gerechent Büchlein Melchior Lotter. Volendet vnd aufgangen am abendt des Newen Jars. 1536." The picture of the author appears in his third book with the legend, "Adam Riese in the year 1550 at the age of 58," which furnishes the date of his birth. Riese's reckoning books were for a century the most popular books of the people and were reprinted many times in several combinations.

Christopher Rudolff was educated at the Vienna Hochschule. His writings were a Coss (1525), Künstliche Rechnung mit der Ziffer vnd mit den Zalpfennigen sampt der Wellischen Practica/ vnd allerley vortheyl auff die Regel de Tri/ allen Liebhabern der Rechnung vnd sonderlich derselbigen kunst anfahenden Schülern zu nutz/ Wien 1526," and "Exempel Buchlin" (1530). The second, a reckoning book, was his most popular work. Three later editions were published (1546, 1574, 1588). Rudolff was one of the few writers of that time who did not copy Riese.

Peter Apianus (Bienewitz) (1495-1552), a scholar of great breadth, was educated at Leipzig and became the professor of Astronomy at the University of Ingolstadt and teacher of Kaiser Karl V. His interest included astronomy, geography, philology and mathematics. Besides a work on the Coss and one on astronomy, for which the emperor presented him with 3,000 gulden, Apianus wrote " Eyn newe vnd wolgegründte vnderweysung aller Kauffmannſsrechnung in dreyen Büchern mit schönen Regeln vnd fragstucken begriffen, Sunderlich was fortl vnd behendigkeit in der Welschen Practica vnd Tolleten gebraucht wirdt. Desgleichen fürmalſs weder in Teutzcher noch in Welscher sprach nie gedruck. Durch Petrum Apianum von Leyſsnick d'Astronomie zu Ingolstadt Ordinariû verfertigt." Colophon: " Gedruckt vnd volendt zu Inglostadt durch Georgium Apium von Leyſsnick im Jar. nach der geburt Christi 1527 am 9. tag Augusti." Thus he deprived Grammateus of the honor of being the only University teacher who had written a German reckoning book.

Simon Jacob of Coburg (died, 1564), was the most important reckoning master of the last half of the sixteenth century. He wrote a reckoning book as well as a work on geometry.

The first German work on book-keeping was written by Heinrich Schreiber, (Grammateus).

Corresponding to the German writers there was a school of writers of practical and commercial arithmetics in other countries. Among the Italians were the author of the Treviso book (1478), the first printed arithmetic, Philip Calandri and Piero Borgi; among the Dutch a century later, Willem Raets, Jaques Van der Schuere, Martin Wencelaus and Ludolf van Ceulen; among the French, Savonne and Trenchant; among the Spanish, Juan Perez de Moya, Ortega, and among the English, Robert Recorde and Humphrey Baker. Most of the authors of reckoning school arithmetics, like the writers of Latin School arithmetics, were scholars of high rank. But they were in closer touch with the needs of the schools for which they wrote, for many of them served as Reckoning Masters, while the Latin writers more often were professors in the Universities.

It is noticeable that the contents of the reckoning school arithmetics were deficient in pure arithmetic. Little attention was given to definitions; the operations were stated dogmatically; few attempts were made to grade any operation into steps; and numbers larger than those commonly used in business were avoided. Numerous examples for practice were given in connection with the processes or in separate chapters. Rudolff's book, for example, was divided into three parts, Book of Elements, Book of Rules, and Book of Examples. Much importance was attached to rules, and several writers resorted to verse in order to render them more effective (p. 133). The following subtraction rule by Reichelstain (1532) is a popular illustration:

> So du magst von der obern nit
> Ein ziffer subtrahirn mit sitt,
> Von zehen sollt sie ziehen ab,
> Der nechst under addir eins knab.

Thus, the theory of arithmetic was treated less scientifically in these books than in the Latin School books.

The reckoning book, in harmony with its purpose, was rich in applied problems. Problems involving denominate numbers, exchange and merchants rules occupied the greater part (pp. 77-85, 132, 158). Besides commercial problems, mensuration received much attention, because the Reckoning Master, who often performed the duties of surveyor in his town, included in his reckoning book the methods for finding heights and distances (pp. 163-7); and, since as inspector of imports he had to measure the bales and casks, he gave in his books the theory and practice of the gauge.[1] It was usual for the applications to follow directly the explanation of the processes, although in several works a problem was proposed before the process required had been taught (p. 48), a plan revived in the eighteenth century by Sturm and Wolf.

The reasons for teaching arithmetic in the reckoning schools scarcely need to be stated. The origin and function of these schools and the interests of their teachers leave no doubt as to why arithmetic was taught. Utility was their shibboleth. They sought to make good computers and to give a thorough training in industrial and commercial arithmetic.

[1] Jacob Köbel, Ein new geordēt Visirbüch (1515).

CHAPTER II

Educational Significance of Sixteenth Century Arithmetic

We have set forth in Chapter I the contents of sixteenth century arithmetic. We have seen that it was produced by the leading scholars and teachers of that period, and that the chief influences responsible for this product were: the demands of the commercial and industrial world, the educational ideals and practices, the restraint of traditional customs, and the demands of science. We have seen that the purposes or aims of the writers of arithmetic were: to furnish useful information, to provide material for mind training, and to advance human knowledge for its own sake. And, furthermore, since the leading spirits among the authors of arithmetic in that period were also the leading spirits among the teachers of the subject, the teacher's aims corresponded to those of the author; namely, to furnish the mind with useful information, to exercise it in mathematical thinking, and to interest it in arithmetic for the sake of knowledge getting.

We recognize in these influences and aims the same forces and purposes that control the present day production and teaching of arithmetic. Hence, a study of the questions which arose and were solved at that time in relation to the corresponding questions now pressing for an answer will show to what extent we may profit from this inheritance; in other words, it will show the educational significance of sixteenth century arithmetic from the point of view of the present time.

Both the problems of that period and those of to-day concerning the teaching of arithmetic may be classified under the heads: subject-matter, method, and mode.

Subject-Matter

We have seen that the subject-matter of arithmetic consisted of rules for reckoning with counters (line reckoning, pp. 25-26), rules for reckoning with the Hindu numerals (figure reckoning, pp. 27-29), a body of properties and relation of numbers (pp. 29-77), a system of denominate numbers (pp. 77-85), and a heritage of amenity or puzzle problems (p. 159).

The chief question relating to subject-matter which confronted sixteenth century writers was the basis of its selection. The few who wrote in an encyclopedic fashion, Paciuolo and Tartaglia for example, tried to furnish arithmetic of all kinds and suited to all purposes; but most writers grasped a special need or set up an ideal and formulated their works in harmony with it.

We have seen in the cases of Riese and Köbel and other reckoning masters that the basis of the selection of subject-matter was *the need of the trader*.[1] By them, processes and number relations were reduced to those only which were of use in solving commercial problems. The simple operations with comparatively small integers and fractions were briefly explained but elaborately applied to business questions; and denominate numbers, because of their variety and complexity, were made a prominent feature. In the cases of Cardan, Unicorn, Ramus, and other Latin School writers the basis of selection of subject-matter was *the need of the scholar*. Consequently, these authors gave a more elaborate treatment of processes covering a larger number field, emphasized theoretic subjects, like proportion, progressions, and roots, extended arithmetic to the solution of equations, retained the puzzle problems, but neglected the business applications. In the

---

[1] This is seen from such dedications as: "Prepared for merchants" (Borgi), "For business purposes" (Riese), "For merchants, bookkeepers and beginners" (Van der Schuere), "To the right worshipfull, the governoure assistentes, and the rest of the companye of Marchants adventurers: Humfrey Baker Lōdoner wisheth helth with continuall increase of comodity by their worthy travail." Baker.

cases of still others the basis of selection seemed to be *a preference for the traditional*. What had attracted Nicomachus and other Greeks, what had seemed to Boethius worth while, appealed to these authors and caused them to perpetuate and extend the fanciful classifications of numbers handed down from antiquity (pp. 32-35).

The same ideas control the selection of material in the preparation of arithmetics to-day. The needs of the trader inspire the " commercial arithmetic," the needs of the scholar inspire the " disciplinary school arithmetic," and the influence of tradition is responsible for the retention in both of these books of much formal arithmetic long since obsolete.

A comparison of the conditions which made the " Rechenbuch " of the sixteenth century, with the corresponding conditions of to-day, indicates that we are entering upon a new era of commercial arithmetic; for, when a nation passes from pastoral and agricultural pursuits to those of manufacture and trade, the transition seems to be reflected in the subject-matter of its arithmetic. It was true of the European nations of the fifteenth and sixteenth centuries. The fall of Constantinople (1453) and the consequent westward movement of Christian civilization initiated the educational and industrial awakening of Italy. This movement was reflected in the first printed arithmetic (Treviso, 1478) and in the subsequent Italian works of Calandri (1491), Borgi (1484), Paciuolo (1494), and Tartaglia (1556). The Hanseatic League by opening trade routes developed the commercial possibilities of Germany. The establishment of reckoning schools along these routes provided the opportunities by which the great German Reckoning Masters, Ulrich Wagner, Adam Riese, and Christopher Rudolff rose to fame. The spirit of enterprise invaded France in 1553, and Savonne ushered in commercial arithmetic. The Netherlands awoke to her maritime possibilities under the Inquisition through the oppression of the Spanish king, and practical arithmetic immediately found expression in the works of Van der Schuere and Raets. England, feeling the pulse of continental commerce, increased her trade, and Recorde and Baker founded her practical arithmetic. The conditions in America to-day are somewhat similar to those of the European countries of the sixteenth century. The United States has built up a vast industrial system on the basis of its natural resources. It has recently taken the position of a world power through commercial and political expansion, and the teaching of arithmetic is just beginning to respond to this movement. Teachers and educators are demanding that the subject-matter of arithmetic shall meet the needs of the present. The school cannot prepare for life unless it reflects the interests of the people. It must recognize in its teaching the quantitative aspect of such far-reaching enterprises and industries as our railways, steamships, telegraphs, telephones, mines, quarries, ranches, plantations, and factories. The following is a broad classification of the type of problems that are beginning to appear in the arithmetics of the twentieth century:

Problems of Resources: Products of soil and mine; supply of timber and water power; capacity of development and consumption.

Problems of Industries: Labor and capital, production of food products, clothing, tools, and luxuries.

Problems of Transportation: Express rates, freight rates by railroad and steamships, capacities of carriers, and storage.

Problems of Communication: Postal rates, telephone, telegraph, and cable rates.

Problems of Government: Expenses, revenues, enterprises, imports and exports, immigration, and employees.

Problems relating to Education: Schools, libraries, printing, and cost of public instruction.

Problems of Science and Art: Domestic economy and nature study.

This, however, does not mean that twentieth century arithmetics are to be a revival of the Reckoning Books of the sixteenth century. The Reckoning Book owed its existence to the exclusion of commercial arithmetic from the schools of the Church, the Municipality, and the Teaching Order. No compromise was possible, the educational ideal of the school men of that day was too limited to appreciate the needs of the merchant. Modern systems of education on the other hand welcome utilitarian arithmetic. The business men of to-day are not obliged to found special schools and seek special books in order to promote elementary business knowledge. The business college is a convenience and short cut to certain vocations rather than a substitute for public school instruction. Modern education tends toward uniformity and toward a correlation of interests, hence twentieth century arithmetic will not be wholly utilitarian like that of the Reckoning Books, but will be a composite of materials chosen on all three bases, the needs of the business man, the needs of the scholar, and the influence of tradition.

Another modification of the subject matter of arithmetic in the sixteenth century due to the commercial ideal was the transition from line (abacus) reckoning to figure reckoning (algorism). This change in the subject matter of arithmetic was hastened by the conviction that the Hindu reckoning was a more efficient system of calculation than the abacus in solving business problems. The abacus was not discarded because it was a machine, but because a better method was found to do its work. A similar tendency exists to-day through the introduction of the calculating machine. Although the modern tendency is to change from head work to automatic machinery, which seems to be exactly opposite to the change in the sixteenth century, it is, nevertheless, similar in being a change from the difficult to the more easy method of practical calculation. If the cost of a reliable machine for performing the four fundamental operations did not prevent its use from becoming universal, one might reasonably predict the disappearance of the formal processes from business arithmetic before the end of the present century. But this is certain, that the mechanical calculator by decreasing the need for expert accountants will lessen the amount of abstract drill matter in arithmetic and will limit the treatment of the operations to the field of small numbers.

The needs of the trader affected the selection of subject matter in another way. No business arithmetic could be efficient without a thorough treatment of contemporary denominate numbers, and a glance at the practical arithmetics of the sixteenth century conveys the impression that an elaborate and exhaustive treatment of such numbers was essential. But a careful inquiry into the weights, measures, and moneys of that time shows that the variety in use was so great and the awkwardness of the systems so extreme that even a conservative exposition of them occupied a large share of the text-book (pp. 83, 147). This necessary prominence given to denominate numbers in the first printed books initiated a custom which for centuries led writers to compile tables of weights and measures long after they had ceased to be useful. The lesson which the sixteenth century has for modern writers on this point is that they should present only the contemporary systems, taking full advantage of their simplicity and uniformity.

We have shown what lessons concerning the selection of the subject matter of arithmetic may be drawn by comparing the influence of the sixteenth century commercial renaissance with that of the present industrial development. Similarly, we may obtain further suggestions by comparing the effects of the educational ideal then prevalent with the effects of our own. The scholar's need of arithmetic at that time was thought to depend upon three things, mental discipline in the narrow sense of logical thinking, culture in the broad sense of information and pleasure in knowledge getting, and propædeutics, or preparation for scientific research.

The teaching of arithmetic at the opening of the twentieth century is in much the same condition that it was at the beginning of the sixteenth. The nineteenth century was an epoch of mental discipline, and just as the Latin Schools inherited their ideal of formal studies, like astronomy and arithmetic from the Quadrivium of the Middle Ages, so the mental disciplinarians of the nineteenth century inherited their ideal from the Latin school of the Renaissance.

It is true that the functions of school studies had not been so thoroughly differentiated then as now, the time for beginning the study of the classics had not been advanced to the period of secondary instruction, and therefore, arithmetic received a comparatively small part of the time given to school work. But the books inspired by the disciplinary idea had a distinctive content (pp. 174-176), operations extended over a large number field, lack of commercial problems, prominence of definitions and principles, and extreme classifications. These same features characterize the disciplinary arithmetics of to-day; and, in the light of history, should it not be so? It should, other things being equal, but they are not. We have a clearer and more correct idea of the disciplinary value of arithmetic now than schoolmen had then. We know that this value does not depend so much upon complex processes, definitions, principles, and minute classifications as upon the mathematical reasoning found in the applications of the subject. "Mathematics is the science which draws necessary conclusions." [1] "According to this view, there is a mathematical element involved in every inquiry in which exact reasoning is used, and one is not justified in calling reasoning mathematical unless it is exact." [2] An appreciation of the mathematical element in elementary arithmetic is chiefly gained by using the syllogism in solving concrete problems. In fact, the simple applications of arithmetic are the most available and sufficiently simple material for children to use as exercises in logic. For example, the second grade pupil who solves the problem, If one orange costs 2 cents what do five oranges cost?, traverses the steps of the syllogism. For the minor premise is, one orange costs 2 cents; the major premise is, 5 oranges cost 5 times as much as 1 orange; and the conclusion is 5 oranges cost 5 times 2 cents, or 10 cents. The complex problems of more advanced arithmetic are generally composed of

---

[1] Benjamin Peirce, Linear associative algebra (1870); also American Journal of Mathematics, Vol. 4.

[2] Maxime Bôcher, Bulletin of the American Mathematical Society, Vol. XI, Number 3 (1904), p. 117.

a series of steps, each of which is solved by the application of the syllogism, as in the simplest case.

For mind training the concrete side of arithmetic is more efficient than the abstract, because there is an unlimited amount and variety of the former, simple in point of logic, while there is little of the latter, whose logic is not beyond the elementary pupil's powers. Besides having variety the concrete side possesses interest gained through the correlation of arithmetic with other school subjects and through the interpretation of all environment in its quantitative aspect, whereas the abstract is usually uninteresting to children.

It has still another advantage over the abstract in that it deals with the same material which is used in other school subjects where the reasoning does not relate to quantity, although it is till mathematical. We are accustomed to say that arithmetic is the only subject from which the elementary school pupil can obtain practice in mathematical reasoning. But, "Mathematics does not necessarily concern itself with quantitative relations, any subject becomes capable of mathematical treatment as soon as it has secured data from which important consequences can be drawn by exact reasoning."[1] Thus, all of the following, though drawn from different subjects, are examples of mathematical reasoning:

1. Geography. a. There is cheap water power wherever there are rapidly flowing rivers.
   b. There are rapidly flowing rivers in New England.
   c. Therefore, there is cheap water power in New England.

2. Applied Arithmetic. a. The ratio of the circumference to the diameter of any circle is π.
   b. The diameter of a circle is 3 ft.
   c. Therefore, the circumference of the circle is $\pi \cdot 3$ ft.

3. Pure Arithmetic. a. A fraction whose numerator is greater than its denominator is an improper fraction.
   b. In $\frac{8}{3}$ the numerator is greater than the denominator.
   c. Therefore, $\frac{8}{3}$ is an improper fraction.

[1] M. Bôcher, Bulletin American Mathematical Society, Vol. XI, No. 3, p. 118.

4. History. a. Oppression of a people means revolution, and revolution means democratic institutions.
b. There is oppression in country A.
c. Therefore, there will be democratic institutions in country A.
5. Pure Mathematics. a. An A-object is a necessary and sufficient condition for a B-object, and a B-object is a necessary and sufficient condition for a C-object.
b. α is an A-object.
c. Therefore, there is a C-object.

It is sometimes claimed that arithmetic affords better discipline in reasoning than does history, because the data in history are subject to exceptions and lacking in generality. Thus, examples 2 and 3 above would be regarded as having greater educational value than example 4, because oppression has not always led to revolution, nor revolution to democratic institutions. But mathematical reasoning is not concerned with the validity of its data; therefore, as an exercise in mathematical logic, example 4 is in no way inferior to the others. If the soundness of the data be considered, the study of history would seem to be more disciplinary than that of arithmetic. For, in arithmetic no forethought can be exercised in selecting true data, since the data are determined *a priori*. From this point of view modern grammar school teaching, which encourages exact reasoning from cause to effect in regard to data drawn from history, from geography, and from industrial and domestic science is really securing the essence of mathematical discipline through varied symbols of expression.

Thus it appears in selecting the subject-matter of arithmetic for disciplinary purposes that the concrete side should have the preference, because it furnishes material suited to easy logical thinking; material which is varied, abundant, interesting, and related to other school subjects.

The conviction that arithmetic supplies a certain kind of information needed in non-technical daily life has never in a large way influenced writers in the selection of subject matter. The probable reason for this is that the average citizen, not engaged in a trade or business especially requiring a knowledge of arithmetic, uses very little of the subject.[1] Ancient peoples like the Chinese, Hindus, and Hebrews, who conceived of no special reason for teaching arithmetic used the merest elements; practically all of the arithmetics of the sixteenth century agreed in the material essential to the needs of the common people, and similarly, all arithmetics of to-day agree in the subject matter pertaining to this purpose. But, the broader idea of information giving, that of presenting the subject for its own sake, and the broader idea of knowledge getting, that of learning for the pleasure of knowing, have greatly influenced the selection of the subject matter of arithmetic. The Latin School books (pp. 174-176) of the sixteenth century show the effect of this influence. As a rule they contain a more complete list of topics than do the Reckoning School books (pp. 183-184). They often contain, in addition to a rounded treatment of the theory of the subject, various practical rules, much material of historical interest (pp. 129-131), and recognize the amenities of the subject (p. 159). It is the idea contained in the last two particulars which throws light on the selection of the materials of present day arithmetic.

Although it is customary to place the educational doctrine of interest at a very recent date, and correctly so in the sense of a formally stated theory, the essence of this idea has long been appreciated. It was this central thought of education that led the Latin School writers of the sixteenth century to humanize arithmetic by applying it to historical data, and by emphasizing the amenities of the subject. There is reason to believe that this idea was strong enough to have thoroughly vitalized the Latin School arithmetic had there been such subjects as Commercial Geography, Domestic Art, and Nature Study in the schools, available for correlation. Furthermore, that these authors, although necessarily unaware of the results of modern researches into child nature, grasped the importance

[1] David Eugene Smith, The Teaching of Elementary Mathematics, page 21, New York, 1900.

of the play or game element in education, appealed to curiosity through magic squares and other remarkable properties of number,[1] and recognized the sociological phase through problems touching social usages and conditions. One would seem justified in concluding that, since men while groping after educational doctrine selected a part of the subject-matter of arithmetic on the basis of interest, writers to-day under the present flood of educational light should consult the natural instincts of the individual in selecting such material.

There is evidence of a basis for number in the sense of rhythm and the tendency to repeated action early manifested in the child. The tendency to imitate the doings of others correlates the simple muscular activities into more complex movements and enables the child to participate in games and occupations which have a quantitative side. The occupations and industries of the neighborhood, facts about food, clothing, and shelter, besides furnishing an abundance of material, make a basis for instruction in larger interests. In passing beyond the simple facts of home life, as the pupil's experience grows, the whole range of production, transportation, communication, and consumption, both local and national, are available as interesting applications of arithmetic. After leaving the primary school the pupil enlarges his social interests. His tendency to hero worship influences his intellectual tastes, and the time is right for problems about fire and police protection,

---

[1] E. g., Unicorn, De L'Arithmetica vniversale (1598), mentions this curiosity as taken from Frate Luca (Paciuolo), the point of interest being the repetition of the same digit in the product.

| 777 | 777 |
2	143
1554	2331
143	3108
	777
4662	---
6216	111111
1554	

222222	

about the army, the navy, the life-saving service and similar things of local or national concern. Even the ethical phase of instruction is not unrelated to arithmetic, for acts of charity and self-sacrifice in the school, the neighborhood, and the state dignify the problems of economics.

Thus we have seen that the early printed arithmetics in their culture phase were prophetic of the important rôle which the subject is to play in education.

The selection of arithmetic according to its propædeutic value relates to the scholar's need of a basis for higher mathematical study. The sixteenth century possessed some of the greatest mathematicians of all time, some who did the world an inestimable service by advancing the science of mathematics. It is notable that such men as Tartaglia, Cardan, and Rudolff placed at the foundation of their works a well rounded treatment of theoretic arithmetic. It is probably true that mathematics for the sake of its presentation and advancement as a science requires a theoretic basis in arithmetic which should be considered in the selection of material for the purpose of its study.

Finally, there should be considered in the selection of the subject-matter of arithmetic the influence of tradition. The effect of this influence may not be always entirely separable from that of either the needs of the business man or from those of the scholar, for many business customs reach far back into history, and the scholar's interest pertains to all ages, but it has one characteristic, namely, the tendency to perpetuate things regardless of their usefulness or interest. Just as certain arithmetics of the sixteenth century contained material which was there simply because it had long been in arithmetics (pp. 32-34, 159), so some text-books of to-day contain matter whose presence has no other justification. If we adopt the theory that a sufficient amount of mental discipline can be obtained from utilitarian subject-matter, then the following items may well be omitted from twentieth century arithmetic.

Concerning Integers:

Greatest common divisor of large numbers and the Euclidean method.

The need for this process disappeared in the seventeenth century with the introduction of the notation of decimal fractions. Before that time it was necessary to find the greatest common divisor of the terms of a fraction in order to reduce it to its lowest terms (pp. 95-96).

Least common multiple of large numbers, or of those not readily factored.

The need for this process is confined to reducing fractions to a common denominator, but there is no actual demand for the treatment of fractions whose denominators are large numbers not readily factored.

Cube root, especially of large numbers not readily factored.

There is scarcely any excuse for teaching the general process of extracting cube root in the grammar school, or, in fact, square root, although the latter is sometimes met in practical measurement. The elementary school pupil seldom understands the reasoning involved in the process and therefore loses even the supposed mental training.

Progressions.

These subjects have no vital applications, and their theory belongs to algebraic analysis.

Concerning Fractions:

Complex fractions.

Drill work in fractions above thousandths.

All fractions not common in business practice, as 39ths, 47ths, 61sts, and the like. In such matters the question is not so much one of omission as of emphasis. The presence of such fractions in arithmetic may even be desirable, but continuous drill work with them is deadening.

Concerning Decimals:

Decimals beyond thousandths should not receive emphasis.

All practice in circulating decimals.
Reduction of decimals to common fractions should receive little emphasis.
Concerning Denominate Numbers:
Troy weight.
Apothecary's weight.
Surveyor's measure.
Duodecimals.
Not only should *all obsolete tables* be eliminated, but also those which are of use to specialists only.
Gill, perch, mill, and rod. The last is still spoken of in rural districts, but is seldom met in practical calculation. There is no defence for its great prominence in text-book exercises.
Tables of English Money should receive less attention than the exchange value of the pound sterling, the mark, and the franc.
Compound numbers of more than two or three denominations are not justifiable in operations.
Concerning the applications of arithmetic:
Profit and Loss as a separate subject. A few problems to illustrate percentage of gain and loss are sufficient.
True discount. Bank discount has taken its place entirely.
Partial payments in the form of state rules and irregular indorsements. Promissory notes which provide for payment before maturity are drawn with the privilege of paying stated amounts on interest days.
Annual interest, except in the form of bond coupons.
Equation of payments.
Partnership with time. Partnership without time may serve as an introduction to the explanation of the modern Stock Company.
Alligation.
Compound Proportion. Simple proportion is important, but the old form and the traditional processes of

EDUCATIONAL SIGNIFICANCE

inversion, alternation, composition, and so on, are being replaced by the simple equation.

Besides these whole topics there are many types of problems which have become obsolete. The chief ones are:

Problems in commission that represent the agent as receiving money from his principal after deducting his commission.

Problems in stocks that represent the purchase and sale of fractional shares of stock.

Problems in exchange that represent all rates of exchange at par and that do not conform to modern banking customs.

Problems in compound interest, apart from some bank or life insurance reckoning in which tables are employed.

Then there are the objectionable *inverse problems* found everywhere, as: Given the proceeds, rate, and time to find the face. Given the rate and amount to find the base. Given the rate, time, and interest to find the principal. Such problems may occasionally be permitted for the purpose of jogging the intellect, but seldom on the ground of utility.

Having discussed the bases of selection of subject-matter, the organization of materials may next be considered. Although any arrangement of subject-matter must have a bearing upon method, it may be made for logical rather than for educational reasons. In the making of sixteenth century arithmetics there were three plans of construction. The first and most common was the prevailing nineteenth century type. The whole realm of numbers was presented at the outset (pp. 36-77) and was represented under each operation. The four processes were repeated with fractions and often with denominate numbers. Another plan, best illustrated by Cardan,[1] was based upon the idea of teaching all the operations with each kind of number. The following outline of the first few chapters will illustrate:

[1] Cardan Practica Arithmetice (1539).

Chapter I	On the Subjects of Arithmetic.
	The subjects defined are: integral numbers, fractions, surds, and denominate numbers.
Chapter II	On Operations.
	There are seven operations: numeration, addition, subtraction, multiplication, progression, division, and the extraction of roots.
Chapter III	Numeration of Integers.
Chapter IV	Numeration of Fractions.
Chapter VI	Numeration of Denominate Numbers.
Chapter VII	Addition of Integers, including denominate numbers.
Chapter VIII	Addition of Fractions.
Chapter IX	Addition of Surds.
Chapter X	Addition of Powers.
Chapter XI	Subtraction of Integers and Denominate Numbers.

The third plan was a modification of these two in which a subject like denominate numbers occurred under two or three operations.

Although these schemes of arrangement were not based on avowed educational principles, they are none the less suggestive at the present time. Educators are generally agreed that the extreme topical plan of nineteenth century arithmetics is defective, and are seriously questioning the so called spiral plan, hence it may be useful to know by reference to sixteenth century arithmetic that there is no practical arrangement except a combination of the first and second plans described above. The scheme of grading the subject according to the size of the numbers and complexity of processes, instead of by kinds of numbers or kinds of processes seems to be an essential for primary teaching, but its value depends upon the size of the groups and upon the systematic treatment within each group. Some writers have chosen a group of topics, reproducing them every ten pages and adding slowly to the content presented. Some have chosen a group to represent a term's or a year's work, reproducing and extending the content in each succeeding period. Others have reduced the amount of repetition to a minimum by giving only two cycles, one for the primary school and one for the grammar school. The proper number of periods lies between these extremes and probably approaches the larger rather than the smaller cycle. The minimum cycle leads to confusion and scrappiness, while the larger cycle makes possible the systematic treatment of addition, subtraction, multiplication, and division separately under each kind of number within each group. It not only makes possible the appearance of these processes, but it insures to each an extent of application sufficient to leave an impression of its importance upon the pupil.

Method

Method as used in this article relates to an author's manner of treatment of subject-matter and not to the teacher's mode of presentation of it in the class room. It is by considering method in this aspect that one obtains most light from sixteenth century sources on the teaching of arithmetic, because the textbooks constitute the chief source of information concerning the mathematical instruction of that time. Even from this narrower point of view one cannot expect to gain information on all present questions of method, since the text-books of that time were written before much of modern educational doctrine saw the light. But there is enough of suggestion to justify a comparison of the methods of development of subject-matter at that time with those prevalent to-day, and for this purpose we may consider three plans, the synthetic, the analytic, and the psychologic.

The synthetic method is the form in which the mathematician casts the finished product of his reasoning. It rarely is the way by which he reaches the truth, but having reached it, the synthetic development of the steps in the process makes an elegant and direct exposition.

The analytic method is the process of experimentation and discovery. It is the pulling to pieces and comparison of parts which show on what principles the system may be built up.

The psychologic method seeks to develop the subject along the path of least resistance by taking into account all accepted educational principles. This method is not wholly separate from the other two any more than logic is separate from psychology. In general, it conforms now to one and now to the other; but its characteristic feature consists in this, that it follows psychological principles, whereas the other methods follow the canons of logic.

All of these types of development are represented among sixteenth century arithmetics. The synthetic type, however, was the common method, the others being exceptional. Although its use was not confined to one school of writers, it prevailed almost exclusively among those of the Latin School. It was the traditional method of the ancient mathematicians, and the great classical scholars of the sixteenth century, as Paciuolo, Cardan, Ramus, Tartaglia, and Unicorn, preferred its elegant form of expression. Of course, arithmetic does not furnish opportunities for demonstrations to the same extent that geometry does; there is more of definition and mechanical process; but the spirit of the synthetic method is basal in all dogmatic treatments and in all topical arithmetics in which abstract theory precedes the concrete matter. This is the type represented by the old style books in use to-day. It is a relic of the old education in which adult psychology stood in lieu of child psychology and information giving in place of self-realization.

The sixteenth century arithmetics which may be called analytic were cast in the catechetical form, a style somewhat prevalent for half a century. Among the first of these books was one by Willichius (1540), but it was not a very successful arithmetic. Perhaps the best extant example of this method is Recorde's Ground of Artes. The following is an illustration taken from his clear method of teaching the significance of place value in notation:

" M. (Master) Now then take heede, these certayne values every figure representeth, when it is alone written without other figures joyned to him. And also when it is in the first place though many others doo follow: as for example. This figure 9 is IX. standing now alone.

"Sc. (Scholar) How, is he alone and standeth in the mydle of so many letters?

"M. The letters are none of his felowes. And if you were in Fraunce in the middle of M. Frenchmen, if there were none Englysh man with you, you wolde recken your selfe to be alone.

"Sc. I perceaue that." fol. Bvii verso.

The catechetical method is one of those extreme forms of presenting arithmetic which has been tried and found wanting. But the lesson for present purposes is not that arithmetics should not be analytic in form, but that in making them analytic, there should be no attempt to usurp the function of the teacher. The ideal arithmetic must be inductive and must suggest ways of presenting subjects in the class-room, but all arithmetics which may be designed to serve both as text-book and teacher will prove unsuccessful as were the catechetical ones of the sixteenth century.

Among the sixteenth century writers who were less enslaved to the classical tradition, that is, the authors of the practical arithmetics of that period, are found those whose works represent the third or psychological method of development. For, although these writers were practically bound by prevailing conditions to dogmatic instruction, and, although they lived before the time of genetic pschology, they were not without educational sense.

A noted example is that of Riese (p. 181) who recognized the following principles:

1. From the concrete to the abstract—by placing reckoning with counters before reckoning with figures.

2. From the simple to the complex—by presenting the full form of processes before the abridged form.

3. Repetition, practice makes perfect—by working over the same material in different forms.

It is significant that the authors who possessed this psychological insight belonged to the practical school rather than to the disciplinary school, and that the most useful and popular books of that century were those conforming to their method. The man with the greatest educational grasp, Adam Riese, was the greatest reckoning master and wrote the greatest reckoning book of his time. This is exactly in accord with what promises to be true in the twentieth century, namely, that the ideal text-book will be the utilitarian arithmetic constructed according to the psychological method.

Besides the results of these general comparisons relating to the organization of subject-matter, sixteenth century arithmetic set various precedents and is suggestive in respect to many details. The educational significance of these particulars will best be expressed by grouping them in four classes: those pertaining to definitions, to symbolism, to processes, and to applications.

We have already noted that formal definitions, although not abandoned by any class of writers, were especially emphasized by the Latin School men. It was their text-book that set the practice, characteristic of all disciplinary arithmetics, of defining terms and processes at the outset. But the style of the definition is significant. Thus, addition was generally defined as *the collection of several numbers into one sum* (pp. 35-36) in place of *the process of finding the sum of two numbers.* Subtraction was generally defined as *taking a smaller number from a larger one,* which is more suggestive than the definition, *the process of finding the difference between two numbers.* Certain writers improved on this and even recognized subtraction to be the inverse of addition. Multiplication was generally defined as *repeating one number as an addend as many times as there are units in another,* a better definition than *the process of finding the product of two numbers,* although it is not generally applicable to fractions without modification. Division was generally defined as *finding how many times one number was contained in another,* the partitive phase often being included, a more definite form than *the process of finding the quotient.*

It is true that sixteenth century definitions were not general, nor can such definitions be used in elementary work. A statement which tells nothing and one which states an important truth unintelligibly are equally useless. It is this fact which has led modern teachers to the extreme of wholly neglecting definitions. But the power of expressing thought is too significant to be crippled. Descriptions of a process or of the characteristic property of a term leads to clearness and efficiency. Sixteenth century arithmetic points to the conclusion that all definitions used in teaching should be working definitions, that is, they should state how the process is performed. It is possible to formulate statements of this kind that are not beyond the experience of the elementary school pupil, and which are sufficiently general to admit of extension as new fields of mathematics are entered.

Any phase of the growth of mathematical notation is an interesting study, but the chief educational lesson to be derived is that notation always grows too slowly. Older and inferior forms possess remarkable longevity, and the newer and superior forms appear feeble and backward. We have noted the state of transition in the sixteenth century from the Roman to the Hindu system of characters (pp. 24-26), the introduction of the symbols of operation, +, —, (pp. 53-55) and the slow growth toward the decimal notation (pp. 72, 75). The moral which this points for twentieth century teachers is that they should not encourage history to repeat itself, but should assist in hastening new improvements. For example, the use of x for (?) in equations, singular abbreviations, as lb. for lbs.; and the use of ‰ for per thousand; ⅔ for $\tfrac{2}{3}$; $ for $; and a convenient abbreviation of denominations of the metric system.

No mention of Roman notation can pass without reference to the question, Why are we teaching it to-day? Less than a decade ago, it appeared that the traditional clock-face and the numbering of introductory pages and chapters with Roman numerals were doomed. But the recent craving for antiques and its influence on certain crafts are making a knowledge of Roman notation to thousands still desirable.

The practice in sixteenth century arithmetics of treating very large numbers under the notation of integers was a prominent feature (pp. 34-40). Tonstall, for example, taught the reading of integers to five periods and remarked that scarcely ever in human experience do larger numbers occur. The treatment of large numbers so early was chiefly due to the topical system which required the explanation of reading and writing numbers, as large as the wisest might ever encounter, to be placed in the first chapter. Then too, for the purpose of exhibiting the idea of periods, a number less than one million was scarcely effective. Pestalozzi and his precursors changed all this by grading arithmetic, and we might say that large numbers have properly disappeared were it not for the gigantic enterprises of our century. Let no one endeavor to confine arithmetic to thousands when the daily press, in describing the improvements in our own metropolis, deals with numbers like the following: " Plans accepted and plans that are certain of acceptance provide for an expenditure of *five hundred million dollars* within the next few years." " Two separate plans for the extension of the subway system of New York City representing a cost of *two hundred thirty million dollars* are now under consideration by the rapid-transit commission." " In improving the Grand Central Station *one million five hundred thousand* cubic yards of earth will be removed, and thirty thousand tons of structural steel be used." "' In all *two million* cubic yards of earth and rock will be carted away before the work of building the Pennsylvania Station can be begun." Let no one attempt to limit arithmetic to millions when our statistical reports contain data like these: " The annual number of letters transmitted through our post-offices is 20,000,-000,000 and of newspapers 12,000,000,000." " The amount of deposits in the savings banks of the United States in one year was $2,769,839,546." " The total amount of life insurance policies in force is $9,593,846,155, and the value of our railroads and equipment is $10,717,752,155."

We cannot deny the necessity for these numbers, but we can defer them to the higher grades of the grammar school.

It is only in connection with the larger interests that these numbers are met, hence they should be reserved for those pupils who are able to appreciate their uses.

Another feature of the arithmetic of the Renaissance was the variety of ways used to perform the processes. E. g., there were three methods of subtraction (p. 51), eight methods of multiplication (p. 62), and seven methods of division (pp. 69-72). This excess of variety was characteristic of the encyclopedic and Latin School writers, and probably was due to the tendency to follow Boethius and Hindu-Arabian classics. It is quite impossible by reference to sixteenth century arithmetic to prove any method to be the preferred one. There is precedent for almost every form. Some writers added upward, and others added downward, (pp. 45-46); some added, subtracted, and multiplied from left to right and others from right to left (pp. 51, 66); some placed the difference above the minuend and others below the subtrahend (p. 52). But the practical and commercial arithmetics generally presented one or two methods, although not always the same ones. The latter custom is followed to-day in most cases; but there are exceptions, as in the case of subtraction and division. Teachers are asking: " Shall we teach the plan of taking a unit from the next higher order of the subtrahend, or increase the minuend by ten and add one to the next order of the subtrahend?" The following from a New York educational journal shows the importance attached to this subject by a superintendent of schools:[1] "Letters received by the committee appointed at the Teachers' Institute show that the educators do not agree upon any best method, and I feel that it is criminal thus to lead the millions of school children into ways that are not the best and most practical at an annual expense of millions of dollars to the taxpayers." After investigating the subject by soliciting opinions from school men and business men his conclusion was: "What shall be done when doctors disagree?" It is safe to say that it is not the author's business to determine the only method, but to explain the advantages

[1] Educational Gazette, Vol. 22, No. 5, p. 186.

of the leading ones and to present one thoroughly, preferably the one personally believed in. This conclusion applies to division in the matter of making the divisor a whole number, or of writing the quotient above the dividend or at the right or under the divisor.

Something of educational significance attaches itself to the old galley method of division (p. 70), for the Italian, or downward method, to-day recognized to be by far the best of the half-dozen ways then in use, scarcely gained a foothold in the sixteenth century, although it was known at that time. The significance lies in the reason for the persistence of the galley method. It possessed the pictorial feature, it aroused curiosity, and it held interest by association with the fascinating concept of the ship.[1] There is now a tendency to abandon artificial means such as numbers arranged in squares, triangles, and fanciful forms for the purposes of drill on their combinations. But history tells us that the mind clings to such devices, and that they are a valuable element in teaching number when properly chosen and not used to excess.

Much is said in discussions of the details of grade work about the proper use of language, especially about such words as "borrow" and "carry." It would be difficult to establish general usage for these in sixteenth century arithmetic, because a translation of a foreign word is seldom unique. But there is no mistaking such a statement as Recorde's "keepe in mind" (p. 47, n. 1) for carry.

Probably no teacher of arithmetic would advocate the total neglect of short processes, but some prefer to regard them as a high polish to be added to the basal attainments of the elementary school, while others believe that the shorter forms of calculation should be taught in immediate sequence to the corresponding unabridged forms. Sixteenth century custom was in accord with the latter plan (p. 75).

The origin of proofs, or tests of the work of calculation,

---

[1] The old copy-books contain examples solved by pupils in order to shape an attractive form of galley. The same tendency is seen in the old crocetta and gelosia methods of multiplication (p. 63).

has been explained (pp. 44, 66, 75). It was seen that the original reason for their use vanished with the transition from the abacus reckoning to figure reckoning and that their use in the latter practice decreased through the century. This neglect increased with the spread of the Hindu system until, with the exception of the schools in certain European states, proofs of operations practically disappeared from arithmetic. In the latter half of the nineteenth century it is safe to say that in general the rank and file of the teaching body in America had no knowledge of the existence of such proofs. The answer book, or the teacher's results, or the answer found by the majority of the class under instruction constituted the only court of appeal in determining the correctness of a solution. But the methods of testing operations in the form of casting out nines or by reverse processes or by substitution begin to appear in recent arithmetics, not because they are an inheritance, but because they supply an educational need. For it is now generally held that convenient tests are a valuable means of developing the self-confidence and independence of the pupil in the matter of calculation. Thus, we may not derive our present reasons for teaching proofs from sixteenth century arithmetic but rather the methods themselves.

Faith in the Grube plan for teaching the elementary number facts is rapidly waning,[1] and sixteenth century arithmetic throws some light on this movement. The chief claim for the Grube method is the thoroughness secured by successively treating each integer in relation to all the integers preceding it. But this does not take into account that some combinations of integers are less useful than others and, therefore, should receive less emphasis. This is now recognized as a vital defect and one which is not inherited from the masters, for, although the early printed arithmetics often contained multiplication tables to 36 x 36 (p. 58), their authors took pains to designate the most useful ones. E. g., Tartaglia called the

[1] David Eugene Smith, The Teaching of Elementary Mathematics, p. 110. McLellan and Dewey, Psychology of Number, pp. 85-92. McMurry, Special Method in Arithmetic, p. 46 *et seq.*

tables of 12s, 15s, 20s, 24s,—Venetian, because they were of special use in computing with Venetian denominations (p. 61). Then the Reckoning Books or practical arithmetics of that time devoted little attention to drill on all combinations of numbers in a given field; the products of 10 x 10 were usually recommended (p. 60, n. 1), but formal lists of all these facts were often omitted (pp. 65, n. 3, 66, Sluggard's Rule).

We are now passing through a period of neglect of detailed explanation of processes with abstract numbers. Writers have reached the extreme in this particular, and fuller treatments are again appearing in recent books. No doubt this feature of arithmetic was exaggerated in the old style books of the nineteenth century, but even in them the practice was not comparable with that of the sixteenth century. The early textbooks cannot be taken as a guide in this matter, because the prominence given to processes by them was largely due to the novelty of the Hindu algorism.

Teachers sometimes fail to distinguish practices which are merely conventional from those which should be followed for the sake of logic or for educational reasons. This failure is sufficiently prevalent to command attention at state institutes for teachers. Among these practices is the one relating to the performing of processes in a series. E. g., $2 + 3 \times 5 - 6 \div 2$. This has the value 14 and not $9\frac{1}{2}$ or some other value, because mathematicians have established this convention for a series of operations: the processes of multiplication and division take precedence of addition and subtraction. The convention might have been to perform the operations in order from left to right, and some teachers proceed as if that were the case. The trouble with these teachers is that they are not aware that it is a matter of convention, consequently they do not seek to know what the custom is. There is precedent in sixteenth century for the present order (p. 99, n. 4), and when such expressions occur in text-books the customary method of simplification should be given. Another question which receives some attention in discussions on the teaching of arithmetic is:

Which shall be taught first, long division or short division? This is not an arbitrary matter, like the one above referred to, but depends upon the educational axiom: Proceed from the simple to the complex. In the early printed arithmetics the unabridged processes usually preceded the abridged (p. 74).

The first printed arithmetics also throw some light on the teaching of fractions. The fraction from the earliest times has been much more difficult to master than the integer. The Egyptian tables of unit fractions found in the papyrus of Ahmes [1] exhibit the meagre knowledge of fractions which the early civilizations possessed. The Greeks and Romans made little progress; e. g., the Greeks [2] wrote $\iota\delta'\ \lambda\epsilon''\ \lambda\epsilon''$ for $\tfrac{14}{35}$, and the Romans used a still more clumsy notation. Even the introduction of the Hindu numerals did not sufficiently simplify the work with fractions. The decimal form is the only one in which the operations are practically as simple as those with integers, but we still have large use for the common fractions, and their teaching gives rise to several educational questions.

Since the spread of Pestalozzian ideas, the method of presenting fractions has been through sectioned objects and diagrams. In this plan the unit is made prominent. A plan recently recommended is that of representing the fraction as a ratio, which, in the concrete aspect, depends upon the act of measuring, and which emphasizes the collection or group of units in place of the absolute [3] unit. A third plan suggested by the evolution of our number system is to define the fraction as an indicated quotient as soon as inexact division is encountered, for the disposition of the remainder gives the logical opportunity for introducing the fractional notation. Of course, if this were done in primary teaching, concrete illustrations for the purpose of giving content to the fractional symbol would not be excluded. It is quite probable that no one of

[1] Eisenlohr, Ein mathematisches Handbuch der alten Ægypter (Leipzig, 1877).

[2] Gow, History of Greek Mathematics, pp. 42, 48.

[3] McLellan and Dewey, Psychology of Number, pp. 157-162.

these methods is best, and that all three should find place in the teaching of fractions. The partition of the single thing, the partition of the group, or measured unit, and the quotient of two integers all appear to be essential to a general concept of the fraction. Furthermore, this is in accord with the treatments in sixteenth century arithmetics, for Köbel used the first plan [1] and called into service the now illustrious apple (p. 85). Writers who combined fractions and denominate numbers used the second plan, and others, as Ramus and Raets, used the third plan (p. 87). Tonstall suggested an exercise which, if used in connection with the last form would assist in clarifying the pupil's notion of the fraction, namely, the consideration of the effect upon the value of the fraction produced by varying its terms (p. 89).

No one seriously questions the logical order of addition, subtraction, multiplication, and division in the field of integers (the Grube simultaneous plan being a misnomer), but in the case of fractions this order may well be violated, even to a greater degree than at present.

The teaching of fractions by sectioning objects leads early to such products as $2 \times \frac{2}{5} = \frac{4}{5}$ and $\frac{1}{2}$ of $\frac{4}{5} = \frac{2}{5}$, not necessarily before the presentation of sums like $\frac{1}{5} + \frac{2}{5} = \frac{3}{5}$, but generally before those like $\frac{1}{3} + \frac{1}{5} = \frac{8}{15}$. In other words, teachers of primary arithmetic recognize that certain products in the field of fractions are more easily found than the sums of fractions having different denominators. But writers of text-books, especially in their formal treatments, have given little heed to this fact, although much was made of this feature during the first century of printed books. The Bamberg Arithmetic (1483) (p. 181) placed the processes with fractions in the following order: multiplication, addition, subtraction, and division. Calandri (p. 94) and Paciuolo adopted the same order, and the latter explained his position on educational grounds (p. 94).

The multiplication of a fraction by a fraction gives rise to a special difficulty, namely, the explanation of " times " in cases

---

[1] See also Champenois, p. 81 of this monograph.

EDUCATIONAL SIGNIFICANCE

like $\frac{1}{5} \times \frac{1}{5} = \frac{1}{25}$. For lack of effective means of illustration most writers banish the usual symbol, ×, and substitute the word "of." It would seem to be a dangerous practice to set aside the general notation whenever a difficulty is encountered; and one may reasonably claim Trenchant's plan (1571) to be preferable, for he showed that, since the area of the whole square here shown is 1 × 1, or 1, the area of the small square should be $\frac{1}{5} \times \frac{1}{5}$, or $\frac{1}{25}$ (p. 106).

There are two methods in common use for dividing one fraction by another. First, reduce the fractions to a common denominator and divide the numerators. Second, invert the divisor and multiply the fractions. The first method is commonly taught to beginners, because it is more easily explained; but, since the second method is simpler in practice, a transition from the first to the second is necessary. It is not the custom of modern arithmetics to show the connection between these two plans, but sixteenth century arithmetic suggests that we might well make the connection in the following way: Divide $\frac{3}{4}$ by $\frac{2}{3}$.

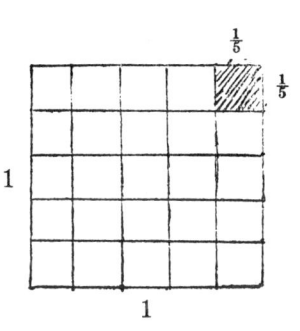

By the first plan

$$\frac{3}{4} \div \frac{2}{3} = \frac{3 \times 3}{3 \times 4} \div \frac{4 \times 2}{4 \times 3} = \frac{3 \times 3}{4 \times 2} = \frac{9}{8}$$

By the second plan

$$\frac{3}{4} \div \frac{2}{3} = \frac{3}{4} \times \frac{3}{2} = \frac{3 \times 3}{4 \times 2} = \frac{9}{8}$$

The second plan is the same as the first only the fractions with the common denominators are not written. Before writers began to invert the divisor they multiplied crosswise (p. 108) which is the very thing done in finding the fractions with a common denominator, and thus the connection between the two methods is made apparent.

In the problems arising from actual experience, fractions

usually occur in connection with denominate numbers, and in business problems the aliquot parts of one hundred furnish the fractions commonly met. This suggests that writers of text-books should place emphasis mainly on fractions whose denominators are not greater than one hundred and that little attention be paid to fractions whose denominators are prime numbers greater than five. This would be in accord with the custom of early arithmeticians, for, although they often indulged in large fractions, the decimal form not having been invented, they correlated denominate numbers with fractions (p. 102) and emphasized the aliquot parts of one hundred (p. 81).

We have already mentioned the importance of denominate numbers and the prominent place given to them in the first practical arithmetics, but there remain a few points of interest in relation to the method of presenting them for teaching purposes.

The money system of a nation enters so largely into the data of its arithmetic that this system becomes a controlling factor both in the matter of material and of method. The money systems of Europe in the sixteenth century were not decimal systems, consequently operations involving them were comparatively complex. This circumstance coupled with the fact that the variety of weights and measures was great (p. 83) necessarily led to much adding, subtracting, multiplying, and dividing with compound numbers having several denominations (p. 84). This practice encouraged by the survival of many awkward systems has tended to perpetuate the processes with compound numbers to the present time. But the increasing popularity of the decimal system and the practice of expressing compound numbers in terms of the larger units or fractions of the same are sufficient reasons for limiting the operations with compound numbers to those having only two or three denominations.

Another form of exercise that has not wholly disappeared from arithmetic is the reduction from one table of denominate numbers to another. E. g., find how many pounds Troy there

EDUCATIONAL SIGNIFICANCE

are in 17½ lb. avoirdupois. This unquestionably is a type derived from sixteenth century problems of reduction made necessary at that time by the lack of uniformity in the value of current units. An example of this diversity may be seen in the following from Riese:[1]

10 pounds at Venice	=	6 pounds at Nuremberg
3 centner at Eger	=	4 centner at Nuremberg
10 pounds at Nuremberg	=	11 pounds at Leipzig
100 pounds at Nuremberg	=	128 pounds at Breslau
7 pounds at Padua	=	5 pounds at Venice
10 pounds at Venice	=	6 pounds at Nuremberg
100 pounds at Nuremberg	=	73 pounds at Cologne

But the day of diversities of this kind having passed so far as practical calculation is concerned, it is difficult to find a reason for continuing the practice in our arithmetic of reduction from one table of denominate numbers to another.

Another matter in connection with the presentation of denominate numbers is worthy of notice. The careful grading of primary arithmetic and especially the spiral plan (p. 200) have tended to distribute the subject-matter of weights and measures throughout the whole course in arithmetic. Some educators scent danger here, fearing that the subordination of so important a subject as denominate numbers may lead to a scrappy presentation and unsystematic knowledge. A recent remedy is found in the plan of placing a thoroughly organized review chapter in grammar school arithmetic. Sixteenth century arithmetic suggests another solution, which consists of placing a section on denominate numbers under each process with integers and fractions and a final treatment under applications. For example, under addition of integers would be placed the addition of compound numbers, only such numbers and reductions being chosen as could be manipulated by pupils at that stage; and similarly for other processes. This plan is imperfectly shown in the Bamberg Arithmetic which presents the topics thus: Addition, Subtraction of Integers; Addition and Subtraction of Denominate Numbers. Mention has been made of more detailed examples (p. 94).

[1] Riese, Rechnung auff der Linien und Federn/ (1571 ed.).

Besides the questions concerning the proper selection of applications of arithmetic (pp. 187-199), there are several important considerations that relate to their form of presentation. The greatest question of method in this connection is: Shall the applications precede or follow the process to be applied? This query seems to imply the absurdity that the effect may precede the cause, until one determines which is the cause and which the effect. Since every unit of instruction should have its aim, and since the consciousness of this aim on the part of the pupil is a factor in his interest in the subject, a knowledge of the end for which he studies may well be outlined before he is set to acquire the means. In this sense the application may precede the arithmetical process. That is, the use to which the process is to be put may be proposed as an incentive for learning the process. For example, formal multiplication may be introduced in this way. A bushel of oats weighs 32 lb. Find the weight of 5 bu. by a shorter process than addition. The pupil who knows only formal addition uses the first process. But when his attention is called to the fact that his knowledge of the multiplication tables furnishes the sums of the columns he is ready to appreciate the second, or shorter form. This is not a new theory for it had a large number of adherents in the sixteenth century (pp. 48, 56, 76). Although arithmetical writers of that time were not concerned with primary instruction or method in the modern sense, nevertheless they often proposed concrete problems before explaining the processes which entered into their solution. For example, Champenois introduced the subjects of addition and subtraction by proposing military problems (p. 128), Baker took commercial problems for his method of approach, and Suevus employed facts of ancient history and fancies quite his own for his center of interest [1] (pp.

(1)	(2)
32 lb.	
32	
32	32 lb.
32	5
32	
10	10
15	15
160 lb.	160 lb.

---

[1] That the attempt to stimulate interest through concrete situations may

129-130. There was one writer, Robert Recorde, who employed the motive of utility in a masterly way. His plan was the precursor of the modern principle of appealing to the pupil's vital interests. It would be difficult to find a better type of instruction than his method of approach to the subject of addition by reference to his Oxford pupil's expense account:

" S. (Scholar) Then wyll I caste the whole charge of one monethes comons at Oxford with battelyng also.

" Master. Go to, let me see how you can doo.

" S. One wekes comons was 11 d. ob, q. and my battelyng that weke was 2 d. q. q. The seconde weekes cõmens was 12 d. and my batlyng 3d. The third wekes cõmõs 10 d. ob. & my batling 1 d. ob, c. The fourth wekes comos 11 d, q, & my batling 1 d, ob, c. These 8 sumes wold I adde into one whole summe."

But this method has fallen into complete neglect with the passing of the centuries between that time and the present. The customary practice is not sufficiently inductive. It presents the processes in the fields of integers, of fractions, and of denominate numbers as ends in themselves, and treats the ap-

also lead to artificial means is illustrated by the ingenuity of Suevus, who introduced Roman notation by the story of a famine.

ON THE GREAT FAMINE IN POLAND AND SILESIA.

"That the time of the famine may not be concealed, behold CVCVLLVM. That is, in order that the time of the famine and distress, which long ago took place in Poland and Silesia, shall remain concealed from no one, but shall be known by all, the year is to be reckoned from the little word CVCVLLVM, which here means a cap of sorrow."

$$\begin{array}{rcl} M &=& 1000 \\ LL &=& 100 \\ CC &=& 200 \\ VVV &=& 15 \end{array}$$

CVCLLVM = 1315

Sigismund Sueuus, Arithmetica Historica. Die Löbliche Rechenkunst (page 64). "Vt lateat nullum tempus famis Ecce CVCVLLVM. Das ist: Auff das die grosse Thewrung vnd Hungersnot/ die vor zeiten in Polen vnd Schlesien gewesen ist/ niemande verborgen bleibe/ sondern von menniglichen wol in acht genommen werde/ so sol man durch das Wörtlein CVCVLLVM, welches hier eine Trawerkappe heist/ die Jahrrechnung machen."

[3] Page 64.

plications as convenient drill work for fixing the methods of calculation. Applications, when valued for their own sake, are set apart from the processes so as to form an independent center of interest.[1] The true course doubtless lies between the usage of the present and that of the past. The present custom of process worship has led to poverty of ideas, and to approach every variety of calculation through a problem involving its use might lead to a confusion of ideas.

Another question of method is this: Is the great prominence now given to commercial arithmetic in all grades justifiable on educational grounds? The present place of the subject in instruction is indirectly due to sixteenth century teaching; for, when Pestalozzi founded primary arithmetic, he naturally drew his material from the books of the Reckoning Schools which had up to that time monopolized instruction in arithmetic. These schools had little to offer except commercial arithmetic plus some mensuration, the two phases of applied arithmetic united by Köbel (p. 164). Thus, the arithmetics of the nineteenth century became saturated with commercial arithmetic in a narrow sense. Money value was emphasized everywhere, " bought at " and " sold at " being the usual data. Subjects like partnership were introduced before the pupil had any feeling of interest in them, but modern educational research is finding more appropriate material for the applications of arithmetic in the lower grades,—things which come within the pupil's experience and for which he is willing to study the subject. For example, his games, purchases, and possessions. There is a quantitative side also to manual training, domestic art, geography, nature study, and drawing. If a boy is making a box, a model, or an iron ornament in his manual training work, there are related problems about size, amount, and cost of materials. If a girl is making an apron, or a book-bag, or cooking in domestic art, there are related problems about amount and cost of materials. Likewise, the geography reci-

[1] McMurry, Special Method in Arithmetic, p. 113 (New York, 1905).

tation suggests problems about distances, areas, population, and production. Nature study suggests problems about weight, time, and motion, and drawing is full of scale measurements and proportion. If the concrete material of the arithmetic hour is drawn in part from recitations in other subjects, not only is time saved and review secured, but the ideas of arithmetic are enriched by association with varied and vital interests.

Consequently, although sixteenth century arithmetic may have led writers to put too much commercial arithmetic into the primary course, it set a step in the direction of making arithmetic concrete and paved the way for a better and more teachable system of subject matter.

In the early arithmetics mensuration was presented in a separate chapter usually placed at the end of the book, which place it has since occupied. But we are now coming to a more efficient use of this subject in the teaching of arithmetic. Fractions are given concreteness by the handling of graduated rulers, scale relations are learned by drawing lines and figures, decimal fractions are illustrated and made familiar to the student by the use of the meter stick, and so on.[1] That is, the facts of measurement and related properties of geometric figures are being graded and correlated with number work from the fourth year to the eighth. This plan has the further advantage of preparing for the geometry of the high school, and of offering the opportunity for practical field mathematics, through determining heights, distances, and areas.

There is a class of problems that may be called factitious or artificial. For example, 100 potatoes are placed in a row at intervals of 10 yd. A basket is placed at one end of the row, how long will it take a person, who can walk 20 yd. a minute, to bring all the potatoes to the basket? In the sixteenth century such problems served as applications to the progressions (p. 110), and similar ones to proportion and evolution. The

[1] F. T. Jones, in School Science and Mathematics (Chicago), Vol. 5, No. 6, p. 408 (1905).
[2] W. T. Campbell, Observational Geometry, Boston (1901).

early writers understood the function of these exercises to be drill in processes which had no real applications, but which were valuable because of their importance in other branches of mathematics. But now, since the processes themselves have been promoted to more advanced mathematics, there is no good reason for retaining these artificial problems in elementary arithmetic.

Although there is no single rule that will solve all of the problems of arithmetic, there are two general methods which have wide application, unitary analysis and the equation. All grades of problems from " If one orange costs 3 cents what would 5 oranges cost?" to " If 5 men working 8 hours a day can dig a trench 3 ft. wide, 12 ft. deep and 300 ft. long in 10 days, how many men will it take working 10 hours a day to dig a trench $3\frac{1}{2}$ ft. wide, 18 ft. deep, and 450 ft. long?" may be solved by either method. Unitary analysis, although known in the sixteenth century (p. 137) was commonly modified into the Rule of Three (p. 132). This rule, a great favorite for centuries, is still preserved in the subject of Proportion (p. 134), a method now yielding to the equation. The last method, too, should not be thought of as a modern invention, but rather as a modern form of the sixteenth century Rule of Three. The solution of the following example from Thierfeldern by the Rule of Three shows a marked similarity to the present method by the simple equation: " If 18 florins minus 85 groschens are equal to 25 florins minus 232 groschens, how many groschens are there in 1 florin?"[1]

[1] Caspar Thierfeldern, Arithmetica Oder Rechenbuch Auff den Linien vnd Ziffern/ (1587).

"Item/ 18 *fl*. weniger 85 *gr*. machen gleich so vil *gr*. als 25 *fl*. ÷ 232 *gr*. wie vil hat 1 *fl*. groschen? Facit 21 *gr*."

"In disem beyden Exempeln/ addir das Minus/ und subtrahir das Plus/ wie hie." Page 110.

I. 18 *fl*. ÷ 85 *gr*. gleich 25 *fl*. ÷ 232 *gr*.
85 *gr*.

18 *fl*.   gleich 25 *fl*. ÷ 147 *gr*.

18 *fl*. ÷ 147 *gr*. gleich 25 *fl*.
18

147 *gr*. gleich 7 *fl*.

EDUCATIONAL SIGNIFICANCE

These solutions I and II depend upon the laws of transposition and are the same except that the unknown quantity, x, is missing from the first. But the ease with which the second form can be followed shows the advantage of the modern plan with x. Thus, although changed to a more convenient form by improved symbollism, the great method of the sixteenth century will become the favorite one of the twentieth.

Undoubtedly, one of the chief reasons why the equation did not take its place in arithmetic much earlier is the prominence given to the Rule of False Position (p. 153). The use of this method of approximation having been introduced from algebra delayed the more definite process of the equation.

In considering the form of presentation best suited to the more advanced applications of arithmetic one must take into account that arithmetic is an important factor in interpreting the world about us. "It is a standpoint from which the better to see through and around a great many important topics. Without the illumination from mathematics a great many important facts and bodies of knowledge in geography, history, natural science, and practical life remain hazy and not clearly intelligible."[1] Thus, the concrete material from which the processes of arithmetic may be taught should do more than furnish the center of interest. It should furnish types of quantitative experience of use in appreciating the larger interests of life. "It is now thought proper to take a class to a saw-mill, a stone quarry, a cotton factory, or a foundry as to a laboratory or a recitation room. The industries of the

```
7 fl. ——————— 147 gr. ——————— 1 fl.
                    facit 21
```

II. 1. Let x = the number of groschens in 1 florin
     2. Then 18x − 85 = 25x − 232
     3. Therefore, 18x = 25x − 147
     4.   "   18x + 147 = 25x
     5.   "   147 = 7x
     6.   "   7x = 147, and x = 21.

[1] McMurry, Special Method in Arithmetic (New York, 1905), pp. 113-114.

neighborhood become standards by which the world's work of various sorts is estimated and judged."[1]

Arithmeticians have been very slow to grasp this interpretative function of arithmetic while writers of text-books in other subjects have made marked progress in this direction. Geography, for example, no longer consists merely of unrelated facts about the political divisions and physical features of the earth, but treats of the influence of heat, moisture, soil, climate, and other factors on resources and industries together with the significance of the latter in determining national conditions and peculiarities. One cause which has helped to keep arithmetic in this backward condition is the disciplinary ideal inherited from the Latin Schools of the sixteenth century (pp. 174-178). This ideal has led writers and teachers to look upon the applications of arithmetic as an instrument of discipline to the exclusion of its larger function of information giving. For example, the chapter on percentage was given over by some to the consideration of the mechanics of its nine cases:

Base × rate	= percentage	Percentage ÷ rate	= base
Base × (1 + rate)	= amount	Amount ÷ (1 + rate)	= base
Base × (1 − rate)	= difference	Difference ÷ (1 − rate)	= base
Percentage ÷ base	= rate	Amount ÷ base	= 1 + rate
	Difference ÷ base	= 1 − rate	

instead of to its use in answering the quantitative questions of commerce and of the crafts and sciences. Another cause is the recent reaction against the topical plan. Sixteenth century arithmetic presented all its subject-matter both theoretic and applied arranged by topics (pp. 29-170), which remained the standard form until the closing decade of the nineteenth century when a school of writers favoring extreme gradation reduced the applications of arithmetic to a mass of unrelated questions. It is now necessary to reorganize the problems of arithmetic into groups and vitalize them so that they may shed light upon the various topics which school subjects should illuminate.[2]

[1] Dutton, School Supervision, p. 208 (New York, 1905).

[2] Smith and McMurry, Mathematics in the Elementary School (New York, 1903), pp. 58, 59.

teenth century arithmetic was taught in the universities. In fact, several authors, as Ramus, Widman, and Apianus were university professors. It is undoubtedly true that arithmetic, like other university subjects, was often taught by lecture, but there is nothing in the early teaching of arithmetic that suggests the advisability of using the lecture mode in the modern elementary school.

Among the ways most discussed at present for presenting subject matter in the class room is one known as the laboratory mode. The characteristic feature of this mode consists in the teacher directing the pupil in discovering and verifying important truths by the aid of some form of laboratory equipment. In mathematics the equipment consists of books, maps, charts, blanks, legal forms, drawing materials, physical apparatus, and other materials suited to the subject in hand. So far, the experiments in the use of this plan have practically been confined to secondary schools, but there is room for at least an adaptation of it in the elementary school. The history of the formative period of commercial arithmetic shows that its teaching began with this mode (p. 178 *et seq.*). The precursor of the Reckoning School was a system of apprenticeship. A knowledge of arithmetic was obtained by working in the ledgers of the counting-house, by keeping the public records of the municipality, by listing, weighing, and measuring in the warehouse and by serving the surveyor in the field. The modern business college mathematics in which nominal sales, shipping, and banking departments lend a semblance of reality to the work are in harmony with the historical development of business arithmetic. And one may reasonably ask, in view of the present movement toward the vitalization of arithmetic, toward its application to manual and domestic arts, and toward the recognition of its interpretative function in the economic questions of our people, if the spirit of the laboratory mode may not be a needed element in teaching elementary arithmetic in our public schools?

SUMMARY

From the foregoing we may conclude that the teaching of arithmetic in the sixteenth century supports the following general theses:

Concerning Subject-Matter

1. Rapid commercial and industrial development has a vitalizing effect upon the subject-matter of arithmetic. It tends to enrich its problems; it encourages improved methods of calculation and conditions the selection of denominate numbers. Commercial development had this controlling tendency in the sixteenth century, and it is exerting the same influence in the twentieth century.

2. The disciplinary function of arithmetic reaches its greatest efficiency through the uses of number rather than through the properties of numbers, a principle not generally recognized in the Latin School books. The culture ideal has always led to the selection of subject-matter having a many-sided interest, and the propaedeutics of arithmetic at present, as in the past, require the retention of certain theoretic matter.

3. Traditional custom is not a safe guide in the selection of subject-matter, since it tends to perpetuate obsolete material. Present commercial, industrial, and educational needs are the true basis of such selection.

4. The two sixteenth century schemes of arranging subject-matter, namely, by kinds of numbers and by kinds of processes have proved failures in modern graded curricula. Present needs can be met only by a combination of the two plans.

Concerning Method

1. The psychologic method produces ideal modern books. The arithmetic of the Renaissance furnishes excellent specimens of the synthetic and analytic methods, and marks the birth of the psychologic. The last method is eclectic, taking the best features from the other two, and, besides, pursues the path of least resistance in accord with modern educational principles.

this country, mass instruction will be inevitable for a long time to come, much is said about the advantages of individual instruction, and many devices are being employed to obviate the defects of the class system. Among these is the laboratory mode discussed on page 225. The common plan of teaching in the sixteenth century was the individual one (p. 180), and many arithmetics were written in conformity with this practice. It was often stated in the prefaces of these books that they were also adapted to self-instruction. This was true, for example, of the Bamberg Arithmetic, of Köbel's Zwey Rechenbuchlin, and of Recorde's The Ground of Artes. The characteristic feature of these books, excluding an occasional work like Recorde's, was the direct presentation of processes. The formal rule, the "Thue ihm also" of Riese, was the signboard over every new path. Thus, history suggests that the present danger to arithmetic in individual instruction may consist in this, that the teacher who attempts to instruct even a small class on this plan is liable to fall into the error of dictating method instead of directing it.

The practice of merely assigning lessons to be learned outside of school hours and recited at the next meeting of the class, commonly called the recitation mode, is an outgrowth of modern machine teaching. There is no evidence that arithmetic was taught in this fashion in the sixteenth century; on the contrary, the contents of the text-books and the use of the separate problem book [1] indicate that the time spent in school was given to instruction, and that the work assigned was in the form of applications. It is safe to say that sixteenth century teaching of arithmetic with all its faults was better than the so-called recitation mode.

There is still an occasional educator who believes in the lecture mode of instruction, who holds that text-books have disadavantages which outweigh their usefulness; but, since there is no likelihood of this mode's becoming common in our elementary schools, it may be passed over briefly. In the six-

---

[1] As Rudolff's Exempel Buchlin (p. 182, this monograph).

Mode

In addition to the questions which relate to the selection of subject-matter and to its organization for teaching purposes, there are questions concerning the mode of class-room instruction. By mode is here meant the form of class exercise.

Although, directly, sixteenth century arithmetic throws little light upon this department of teaching, indirectly it has important bearings. For, among the modes in use to a greater or less extent at the present time, the early printed arithmetics touch in a significant way the heuristic, the individual, the lecture, the recitation, and the laboratory modes. The bearing is an indirect one, because it is largely through the method of the subject-matter that one must determine the mode of teaching at that time. This plan of investigation, which would, in general, be misleading, is quite safe in the present instance, because the authors of many of the most significant arithmetics were prominent teachers; and besides formulating the subject-matter in harmony with their favorite mode, they often named in the prefaces or introductions to the works the kind of teaching for which their arithmetics were adapted (pp. 178, 186).

The heuristic mode finds its prototype in the catechetical books (p. 202). There can be no mistaking the form which teaching assumed that drew its material from these books. The purely catechetical mode, of course, was not heuristic, but such a treatment as Recorde's (p. 202) contains the developing process, the real unfolding of new ideas by means of suggestion and skillful questioning. Perhaps the most important lesson to be drawn from this is that the heuristic mode of teaching should not be carried to an extreme, that is, should not reduce all instruction to a system of interrogations lest it suffer the fate of the purely catechetical form (p. 203). A lesson of secondary importance concerns the function of oral arithmetic. If the historical precedent be followed, we may infer from Fischer, Suevus, and Recorde that the oral work of the recitation should be given more to the development of new ideas than to drill upon those already taught.

Although on account of the vastness of public education in

The following details of method find support in the first century of printed arithmetics:

1. Artificial means for making number work interesting should not be abandoned.

2. Number combinations are not equally important.

3. Unabridged processes should precede abridged ones.

4. Methods of testing the work of calculation should be given.

5. Definitions are desirable in arithmetic. In cases of processes they should tell how the operations are performed. They should also admit of easy extension to cover the processes when new fields of numbers are entered. Sixteenth century definitions are superior to most modern ones in this respect.

6. In regard to notation we may learn from the results of conservatism in the past how necessary it is to welcome improved symbolism.

7. Our books should explain the processes by the generally preferred methods. The best text-books among the early arithmetics did this. Encyclopedic works, now as well as then, are valuable only for reference.

8. The partitive idea, the measuring idea, and the ratio idea are necessary to the concept of the fraction. All of these ideas were recognized in sixteenth century arithmetic.

9. In the formal treatment of fractions the logical order, addition, subtraction, multiplication, and division should be replaced by the psychological order, multiplication, addition, subtraction, and division.

10. Fractions should be correlated with denominate numbers.

11. The presentation of denominate numbers should be distributed under the processes with integers and fractions. In compound numbers only those of two or three denominations require emphasis, and reductions from one table to another are no longer necessary.

12. The applications of arithmetic may be proposed as incentives for learning the processes. They should be classified in accordance with the aims and motives of the different

periods of school instruction and should perform an interpretative function.

13. The simple equation is an improved form of sixteenth century analysis and promises to become the favorite method for solving the problems of arithmetic.

Concerning Mode

1. The heuristic mode as used in the sixteenth century suggests that oral work should be used chiefly to develop new ideas.

2. The individual mode is apt to result in dogmatic instruction.

3. The recitation mode finds no precedent in early teaching.

4. The lecture mode has no place in elementary arithmetic.

5. Renaissance arithmetic suggests the use of the laboratory mode.

Thus, we conclude that the history of the formative period of arithmetic supplements in many ways the conclusions of educational theory in regard to the subject-matter, method, and mode of modern arithmetic.

INDEX

Abacist, 53
Abacus, 25, 46, 74, 209
Abstract Problems, 56, 192
Addends, 51
Addition, 26, 35, 201
  of integers, 41, 61, 175
  of fractions, 98
Ahmes, 211
Alcuin, 160
Algorism, 27, 61, 168
Al Khowarazmi, 36
Aliquot parts, 81, 82
Alligation, 132, 151, 157, 198
Amenities, 194
Andres, 28
Apianus (Bienewitz), 27, 28, 150, 181, 182, 225
Applications, 216, 218, 220, 222, 227
Applied Arithmetic, 97, 127, 129, 131, 169, 176, 198
Approximations, 66
Arabs, 36
Archimedes, 177
Area, 79
Aristotle, 29
Arithmetic, 35
Articles, 38
Aryabhatta, 132
Ascham, 171
Assize of Bread, 132, 157
Associative Law, 47, 100
Aventinus, 28
Bachet de Mézeriac, 159
Baker, 23, 30, 48, 53, 69, 74, 75, 81, 97, 99, 103, 108, 109, 113, 121, 138, 142, 151, 183, 186, 188, 216
Bamberg Arithmetic, 27, 76, 212, 215, 224
Banking, 146
Barter, 132, 150
Bhaskara, 36
Binomial Coefficients, 113
Biórdi, 158
Bôcher, 191, 192
Boethius, 30, 35, 187, 207
Bookkeeping, 183
Borgi, 37, 39, 52, 57, 61, 67, 94, 110, 133
Borgo. See Paciuolo.
Bosanquet, 90

Brahmagupta, 149
Brooks, 27, 53
Business Applications, 186
Buteo, 31, 119, 134
Calandri, 67, 69, 71, 75, 94, 104, 131, 137, 160, 169, 183, 187, 212
Calculation, 66, 78, 85, 86
Campbell, 219
Cantor, 27, 29, 36, 65, 76, 123, 148
Cardanus, 37, 42, 84, 100, 154, 173, 186, 196, 199, 202
Casting Accounts, 23
Casting out Nines, 45, 52, 74
Casting out Sevens, 66, 74
Cataldi, 39
Cataneo, Girolamo, 78, 79
Cataneo, Pietro, 60, 150, 164
Catechetical Arithmetic, 202
Chain Rule, 132, 148
Champenois, 30, 45, 48, 49, 56, 69, 73, 75, 86, 104, 105, 106, 114, 116, 121, 128, 216
Chiarini, 80, 158
Chuquet, 39
Ciacchi, 101, 150
Cicero, 129, 172
Circular Numbers, 33
Cirvelo, 39, 47, 58, 65, 84, 90, 91, 126
Classification, 32-34, 187
Clavius, 47, 173
Clichtoveus, 35
Commercial Arithmetic, 35, 83, 179, 187, 207, 219
Commercial Problems, 57, 169, 178, 184, 191
Commission, 199
Common Denominator, 97, 98, 101, 108
Compayré, 171
Complementary Multiplication, 65
Complex Fractions, 197
Composite Numbers, 32
Conant, 146
Concrete Problems, 46, 48, 56, 68, 76, 216
Correlation, 194
Counters, 24, 46
Courses of Study.
  in Latin Schools, 172
  in Reckoning Schools, 180

229

INDEX

Cube Root, 125, 197
Cubic Numbers, 33
Culture Value, 178
Cunningham, 141, 150, 157
Custom House, 83
Decimals, 66, 95, 197, 198, 214
Dedekind, 32
Defective Numbers, 33
Definitions, 191, 204, 227
    of numbers, 29
    of processes, 35
    of fractions, 85
De Morgan, 23, 34, 36
De Moya, 183
De Muris, 127
Denominate Numbers, 49, 56, 60, 77-85, 97, 135, 184, 186, 190, 198, 214, 215, 217, 226
Dewey, 211
Diagrams, 106, 124
Digits, 38
Diophantus, 177
Di Pasi, 83, 148
Discount, 169, 198
Division, 27, 36, 201
    of integers, 69-76
    downward method, 70, 71
    twelve cases, 73
    of fractions, 107
Doubling, 36, 47, 76, 109
Duplatio. See Doubling.
Duties, 169
Dutton, 222
Eisenlohr, 211
El Hassar, 36
Equation of Payments, 132, 145
Equations, 55
Euclidean Method of G. C. D., 96
Evolution, 121-127
Exchange, 24, 132, 146, 158, 199
    Bills of, 146
Factor Reckoning, 132, 142
Finæus, 75, 119, 157, 165
Finger Reckoning, 28
Fischer, 172, 174, 180, 223
Fractions, 85-110, 227
    Classes of, 90-92
    Definitions of, 85-90
    Order of processes in, 93-95
    Reduction of, 95-98
    Teaching of, 212-214
Freidlein, 24
Galley Method, 69, 70, 208
Gauge, 145, 165, 184
Gemma Frisius, 30, 36, 37, 59, 69, 76, 77, 86, 94, 103, 132, 138, 153, 173, 176, 177
Gerhardt, 51
Ghaligai, 94, 122, 150, 159
Gio, 88

Girard, 174
Golden Rule, 132
Gow, 34, 211
Grammateus. See Schreiber.
Graphical Methods, 106, 213
Greatest Common Divisor, 95, 96, 197
Grube, 209, 212
Halving, 36, 76
Hanseatic League, 178, 179
Heer, 133, 150, 180
Henry, 24
Herbartian Preparation, 139
Hindu Numerals, Symbols, 24-26, 37, 41, 186, 209
Hispalensis, 90
Incommensurables, 35
Integers, 197
Interest, 132
    Annual, 198
    Compound, 145, 199
    Simple, 143
    Tables of, 144
International System, 80
Inverse Operations, 74, 199
Inverse Rule of Three, 132, 138
Involution, 121-127
Jacob, 45, 132, 152, 158, 181, 183
Jacoba, 36
Jean, 82, 83, 144, 168
Jewish Profit, 145
Jones, 219
Jordanus, 35, 76, 119
Kästner, 26
Kettensatz. See Chain Rule.
Knott, 26, 27
Köbel, 37, 46, 48, 53, 60, 74, 76, 81, 85, 91, 107, 121, 164, 181, 184, 186, 212, 218, 224
Kuckuck, 23, 24, 27
Lamy, 171
La Roche, 39
Latin Schools, 170, 178, 179, 190, 204, 222
Least Common Multiple, 197
Legendre, 34
Leonardo, 76, 149, 150
Leslie, 27, 29
Licht, 26
Lilivati, 36, 51
Linear Numbers, 32
Logarithms, 168
Luther, 171, 173
Magic Squares, 195
Masudi, 159
Maurolycus, 30, 35, 177
McLellan, 211
McMurry, C., 218, 221
McMurry, F., 222
Mediatio. See Halving.
Melancthon, 171

INDEX

Mensuration, 163, 184, 218
Method, 185, 201
   Analytic, 226
   Psychologic, 226
   Synthetic, 226
Million, 38, 39
Mint and Mintage, 132, 147, 151
Mixed Numbers, 101, 103, 105
Mode, 185, 223, 228
   Heuristic, 223, 228
   Individual, 224, 228
   Laboratory, 225, 228
   Lecture, 224, 228
   Recitation, 224, 228
Monroe, 30
Moya, 29
Müller, 54
Multiplication, 27, 35, 201
   of integers, 57–59
   Eight methods of, 62–65
   of fractions, 104
Nasmith, 157
Neander, 171
Nicomachus, 30, 35, 187
Notation, 37, 205, 206
Noviomagus, 28, 29, 42, 98, 111
Numeration, 37, 129
One-to-one Correspondence, 32
Onofrio, 154
Operations, 76, 77, 191
Order of Processes, 212
Orders, 38
Ortega, 141, 183
Overland Reckoning, 132, 157
Paciuolo, 28, 29, 32, 39, 45, 61, 64, 71, 72, 94, 126, 146, 169, 186, 187, 195, 202
Partial Payments, 198
Partnership, 132, 139, 140, 198
Peacock, 23
Peirce, 191
Percentage, 158, 212
Per cent Sign, 158
Perfect Numbers, 33
Pestalozzi, 206, 218
Piscator. See Fischer.
Place Value, 38
Planudes, 69, 90
Plato, 30, 178
Polygonal Numbers, 30
Powers, 121
Practical Arithmetic, 24, 80, 117, 128
Primary Arithmetic, 218
Processes, 27, 73, 175, 184, 207, 226, 227
   with fractions, 93
   with integers, 36, 83
Profit and Loss, 132, 198
Progressions, 110–116, 186, 219
Proofs, or Tests, 44–46, 52, 66, 74, 109, 111, 208

Proportion, 117–120, 132, 134-135, 186, 220
Ptolemy, 177
Puzzles, 159–163, 186
Quadrans, or Quadrant, 165
Quadrivium, 190
Rabelais, 171
Raets, 38, 44, 80, 87, 97, 100, 143, 183, 187, 212
Ramsey, 141
Ramus, 36, 48, 50, 52, 59, 89, 95, 98, 120, 134, 172, 173, 174, 176, 186, 202, 225
Rashtrakúta, 31
Ratio, 117–120
Reckoning. See Abacus, Finger, Hindu, Counters.
Reckoning Book, 164, 174, 181, 187-9, 210
Reckoning Master, 178, 179, 180, 184
Reckoning Schools, 178, 179, 180, 218, 225
Recorde, 22, 28, 38, 39–41, 47, 49, 183, 188, 202, 208, 217, 223, 224
Regula del chatain, 150
Regula Fusti, 132, 152
Reichelstain, 184
Renaissance, 23, 30, 170, 190, 207, 226
Rents, 132, 157
Riccardi, 23
Riese, 23, 60, 65, 67, 77, 84, 97, 99, 110, 112, 136, 140, 142, 145, 146, 149, 153, 169, 173, 181, 182, 187, 203, 204, 215, 224
Rodet, 132
Roman Symbols, 24, 27, 28, 37, 91, 205
Roots, 37, 111, 113, 121–127, 186
Rouse, 172
Rudolff, 26, 57, 60, 84, 94, 96, 99, 101, 108, 143, 148, 150, 151, 169, 181, 182, 184, 187, 196, 224
Rule of Drinks. See Virgin's Rule.
   of False Position, 132, 153, 221
   of Three, 109, 131, 132, 137–139, 142, 149, 220
Rule of Two, 138
Rules, Minor, 156
   in verse, 184
Salaries of Servants, 132, 157
Sayce, 90
Savonne, 183
Schools of Teaching Orders, 170
Schreiber (Grammateus), 183
Scratch Method, 69, 122
Seeley, 171
Series, 110, 111
   Arithmetic, 110
   Geometric, 110
   Harmonic, 110
Sfortunati, 142

INDEX

Short Division, 72, 74
Short Methods, 46, 47, 67, 75
Sluggard's Rule, 65, 66
Smith, D. E., 23, 158, 194, 209
Solid Numbers, 33
Species, 36, 77, 110
Square Numbers, 33
Steinschneider, 153
Sterner, 26, 29
Stevinus (Stevin), 30, 96, 120, 172
Stifel, 23, 150, 172, 173, 174
Stocks, 199
Stoy, 29
Sturm, 171, 184
Subject-Matter, 185, 186–201, 226
Subtraction, 26, 35, 45
 of fractions, 102
 of integers, 49, 53, 55, 61
Suevus, 37, 129, 130, 131, 139, 217, 223
Superficial Numbers, 33
Superfluous Numbers, 33
Suter, 36, 51
Syllogism, 191
Symbolism, 53–55
Tables, 41, 44, 50, 56, 57, 59, 82, 92, 144
Tagliente, 28, 75
Tare, 169
Tartaglia, 35. 41, 44, 45, 50, 53, 58, 61, 65, 66, 70, 72, 73, 75, 87, 88, 93, 99, 119, 121, 146, 147, 154, 168, 169, 186, 187, 196, 202, 209
Taxes, 169
Terence, 172
Theoretic Arithmetic, 24, 128, 196
Thierfeldern, 55, 107, 108, 113, 121, 151, 153, 170, 220

Tollet Reckoning, 27
Tonstall, 35, 39, 42, 49, 50, 58, 65, 73, 89, 100, 103, 111, 117, 118, 124. 125. 141, 143, 154, 175, 206, 212
Trenchant, 35, 36, 46, 49, 53, 56, 67, 74, 87, 98, 102, 106, 122, 123, 124, 128, 142, 146, 158, 183, 213
Treutlein, 23, 27, 69, 90
Treviso Arithmetic, 24, 39, 138, 183, 187
Triangular Numbers, 33
Trotzendorf, 170
Unger, 37, 39, 53, 146, 149, 170, 171, 172, 179, 180
Unicorn, 31, 45, 53, 65, 72, 88, 117, 121, 186, 195, 202
Unitary Analysis, 137, 138, 169, 220
Unity, 29, 30
Usury, 141
Van Ceulen, 120, 183
Van der Scheure, 55, 92, 105, 109, 110, 111. 143, 145, 156, 186, 187
Villicus, 27, 29, 150
Vincentino, 119
Virgin's Rule, Regula Cecis, 132, 153
Visirbüch, 164
Voyage, 132
Wagner, 181, 187
Weights and Measures, 80, 85, 120
Weissenborn, 30, 65
Welsch Practice, 132, 135–137
Wencelaus, 54, 72, 104, 158, 183
Widman, 27, 28, 38, 54, 77, 126, 127, 149, 150, 154, 162, 181, 225
Willichius, 202
Woepcke, 24
Wolf, 184
Zero, 29, 31, 42